DATE			

IMAGINATIVE REASON

The Poetry of Matthew Arnold

IMAGINATIVE REASON
The Poetry of Matthew Arnold

A. DWIGHT CULLER

GREENWOOD PRESS, PUBLISHERS
WESTPORT, CONNECTICUT

Library of Congress Cataloging in Publication Data

Culler, Arthur Dwight.
    Imaginative reason.

    Reprint of the 1966 ed. published by Yale University
Press, New Haven.
    Bibliography: p.
    Includes index.
    1. Arnold, Matthew, 1822-1888--Criticism and inter-
pretation. I. Title.
[PR4024.C8 1976]   821'.8   76-42264
ISBN 0-8371-8979-9

REF
PR
4024
.C8
1976
Cop. 1

Published with assistance from the foundation

established in memory of Philip Hamilton McMillan

of the Class of 1894, Yale College.

Originally published in 1966 by Yale University Press, New Haven

Reprinted with the permission of Yale University Press

Reprinted in 1976 by Greenwood Press, Inc.

Library of Congress Catalog Card Number   76-42264

ISBN 0-8371-8979-9

Printed in the United States of America

To my mother
and
the memory of my father

The poetry of later paganism lived by the senses and understanding; the poetry of mediæval Christianity lived by the heart and imagination. But the main element of the modern spirit's life is neither the senses and understanding, nor the heart and imagination; it is the imaginative reason.

—*Arnold*, Pagan and Mediæval Religious Sentiment

ACKNOWLEDGMENTS

It is a pleasure to acknowledge my indebtedness to Mr. Arnold Whitridge, grandson of the poet, for allowing me to quote from unpublished manuscripts and also for giving me access to his magnificent collection. For allowing me to see materials in their possession I am indebted to the following: the late Miss Dorothy Ward, Mr. and Mrs. Anson Arnold-Forster, the Marquis of Lansdowne, Professor Arthur Kyle Davis, Jr., and Professor James H. Broderick. Professor Broderick has also read my manuscript in its entirety and made many useful suggestions. I am indebted to the John Simon Guggenheim Memorial Foundation for a research grant and to Yale University for a Senior Research Fellowship. The staffs of the Yale University Library and the Library of the British Museum have been most helpful. My wife has assisted me at every turn, and I am obliged to Mr. Richard C. Clay for typing much of the manuscript.

Part of the last chapter was originally given as a lecture at the University of Notre Dame. I have not attempted to remove all the marks of so pleasant an occasion.

Like everyone else who writes on this subject, I am in great debt to previous Arnold scholars, but I should like to single out for special mention the work of C. B. Tinker and H. F. Lowry. I have listed Kenneth Allott's edition of Arnold's poems in the bibliography, but it unfortunately appeared too late for me to make much use of it.

A.D.C.

CONTENTS

INTRODUCTION: THE WORLD OF THE POEMS

They will not . . . understand that they
must begin with an Idea of the world . . .
—Arnold to Clough

The first two poems which we have from the pen of Matthew Arnold almost epitomize the entire course of his poetic development. Both were written when he was thirteen, the one while he was on holiday on the Isle of Wight and the other a few months later when he was preparing to leave home for the first time to attend a public school. In the former, *Lines written on the sea shore at Eaglehurst, July 12th, 1836,*[1] we are told that in olden time Naiads lived in halls of coral beneath the sea, remote from angry winds and waves, and there, in their sportive mirth, presided over favored glens on the shore. What Naiad or Nymph presides over thy quiet and wooded shores, O Eaglehurst? Thou art worthy of the love of Thetis herself. The last lines of the poem are obscure, but they turn on the thought that the wave seems to be struggling to lave the foot of yonder castled cliff, and though the cliff frowns down upon it as a firm "barrier" denying it entrance to the land, other scenes, of flowery fields

1. MS in the possession of Arnold Whitridge. The text has been published in Iris Esther Sells, *Matthew Arnold and France: The Poet* (Cambridge, 1935), pp. 257–58.

and woods and bowers, appeal to its Fancy and invite it on to a kind of marriage with the land. In personal terms, one sees in the frowning castled height the figure of Dr. Arnold, and indeed this poem was written in a moment of truancy. The family was planning some excursion, and when the moment came to depart, Matthew was missing. He was found down by the shore with this poem as his only excuse.

In the other poem, *Lines written on first leaving home for a public school*,[2] he tried to do better. We are told that Dr. Arnold prayed over his young son on the eve of his departure, and in all likelihood the poem echoes this prayer. Certainly, it expresses very solemn thoughts about the dangers that beset us "as we labour up life's toilsome hill, / Or with a slower step descend," and it takes comfort in the fact that when we seem most forsaken, "yet there gleams one ray of light / To guide us through our Trials here." This ray of light turns out, unfortunately for the metaphor, to be "the sound of Home," Dr. Arnold's voice having apparently prevailed over the original figure of illumination. Nonetheless, the ray, or sound, is then invoked, "Oh! Stand a Barrier 'gainst all Ill . . . . / Where e'er our fancy Stray be with us still," for in this poem, unlike the Eaglehurst poem, the barrier which opposes Fancy is a good, and we are not stealing up inlets into secret dells but are mounting the toilsome hill of Truth which we find again in *Thyrsis* and *Rugby Chapel*. The dells and secret inlets, on the other hand, we find again in *The Forsaken Merman* and *The Scholar-Gipsy*.

Indeed, in these two childhood poems we see already developed not merely diverse themes which Arnold will later pursue but also the beginnings of what we may call his poetic or imaginative world.[3] This world consists of a symbolic landscape, a group

2. MS in the possession of Arnold Whitridge.

3. The idea of such a world has been developed by a number of critics, most recently by Alan H. Roper, "The Moral Landscape of Arnold's Poetry," *PMLA*, 77 (1962), 289–96. My own earlier version is in the introduction to my edition, *Poetry and Criticism of Matthew Arnold*, Riverside Editions (Boston, 1961), from which I have taken a few sentences.

of related figures, and the myth or history of their lives. It is of great importance in the study of Arnold's poetry not merely because it is the symbolic language which Arnold's poems speak but also because it is the ultimate source of their unity. Lionel Trilling has said, "Arnold never set great store by philosophic consistency in his poetry; conflicting views of Nature appear in each of the two early volumes and seem to have been held simultaneously." Yet Arnold himself wrote to Clough, "For me you may often hear my sinews cracking under the effort to unite matter." True, he also said, "Fret not yourself to make my poems square in all their parts . . . my poems are fragments [because] I am fragments." Yet his poems are not fragments if one regards them, not as a closed philosophic system, but as an imaginative world which provides for several different systems and moves us dynamically from one to another. Arnold is rather like the three blind men who said the elephant was very like a rope, very like a tree, very like a wall. All are right if you know at what part of the elephant they are standing. Similarly, if you know at what point in his imaginative world Arnold is standing and in which direction he is looking, his poems will cohere perfectly with one another. For this reason, before examining the individual poems, we need to mount up into a tower and gain a general view of Arnold's imaginative world. We may apply to ourselves what Arnold said of Keats and Browning: "They must begin with an Idea of the world in order not to be prevailed over by the world's multitudinousness."[4]

The central feature of Arnold's world is a river which the poet unabashedly calls the River of Life or of Time. Characteristically, this river takes its rise in some cool glade on a high mountain, flows down through a gorge onto a hot and dusty plain, and then, after almost losing itself in the sands of the desert, empties at last

4. Lionel Trilling, *Matthew Arnold* (New York, 1949), p. 94; *The Letters of Matthew Arnold to Arthur Hugh Clough*, ed. H. F. Lowry (Oxford, 1932), pp. 65, 97; *Unpublished Letters of Matthew Arnold*, ed. Arnold Whitridge (New Haven, 1923), p. 18.

into the full and glimmering sea. Needless to say, there are many variations upon this scene, and the one essential thing is that there should be three distinct regions which are separated from one another by some kind of "gorge." Borrowing phrases which Arnold himself employs, we may call these regions the Forest Glade, the Burning or Darkling Plain, and the Wide-Glimmering Sea. In the poem *The Future*, which is Arnold's most straightforward exposition of the River, these regions are identified with the past, the present, and the future, and that is generally the case when the River denotes historic time. More frequently, however, it denotes the life of the individual, and then the three regions are childhood, maturity, and old age or death. Whichever they be, they invariably have the same character: the first is a period of joyous innocence when one lives in harmony with nature, the second a period of suffering when one is alone in a hostile world, and the third a period of peace in which suffering subsides into calm and then grows up into a new joy, the joy of active service in the world.

The basis for this view is found in a conception of history which was widespread in Arnold's day.[5] It was put forward by Herder, Goethe, and Novalis in Germany, by the Saint-Simonians in France, and by Carlyle in England. Carlyle's *French Revolution* presupposes it, and his *Sartor Resartus* sets it forth in personal terms. Diogenes Teufelsdröckh moves from childhood faith and joy, through the interregnum of the Everlasting No and Center of Indifference, to the mature faith of the Everlasting Yea. Similarly, Arnold, in *Stanzas from the Grande Chartreuse*, represents himself as

> Wandering between two worlds, one dead,
> The other powerless to be born.[6]

5. Cf. René Wellek, "Carlyle and the Philosophy of History," *Philological Quarterly, 23* (1944), 55–76.

6. Arnold's poetry is quoted from *The Poetical Works of Matthew Arnold*, ed. C. B. Tinker and H. F. Lowry (Oxford, 1950). References are given only when it is not clear from the context what poem is being cited.

According to all these writers, this threefold pattern of history arose from the alternation of vital or organic periods, which are periods of faith and imagination, with mechanical or critical periods, which are periods of skepticism dominated by the understanding. (Arnold in "The Function of Criticism at the Present Time" calls them "epochs of expansion" and "epochs of concentration.") Actually, however, a later vital period never simply repeated an earlier one but rather incorporated into itself the lesson of the intervening critical period. Thus the total pattern was always a threefold cycle of thesis, antithesis, and synthesis, repeating itself over and over again. In *Westminster Abbey* Arnold presupposes that the cycles will go on ascending forever, and in *Obermann Once More* he sees a series of them in the past. But in general, the poem *The Future* is right in assuming that a particular individual never takes in more than a single cycle of three, and that for him these are the past, the present, and the future. The present is always mechanical because this is the kind of theory of history that arises in mechanical periods. It declares that things were better in the past and that they will be better again in the future. In other words, it is the historical equivalent of the tragic view of life. As such, it is related to the great tragic patterns of the past—the cycle of birth, death, and rebirth which was the basis of Greek tragedy, and the cycle of Paradise, the expulsion from Paradise, and the "Paradise within thee, happier far," which is the substance of Christian myth. In Arnold's day the particular movements involved were the thesis of Romanticism, the antithesis of Utilitarianism, and the synthesis of Christian humanism.

Though we have called the three regions of Arnold's world the Forest Glade, the Burning or Darkling Plain, and the Wide-Glimmering Sea, it should be understood that Arnold's symbols sometimes take forms not actually denoted by these names. He has, for example, a minor but pervasive ship-and-sea symbolism which is quite distinct from his symbolism of river and land. Nonetheless, it has the same structure and conveys a similar meaning. For his image of the Sea of Life (not to be confused with the sea into which the River of Life flows, which is more nearly a Sea of Death) is precisely comparable to the darkling plain. In one poem he even calls it the "watery plain." Further, there is an undersea world, consisting of "kind sea-caves" and coral halls, which has the same remote, pastoral character as the forest glade. The fullest development of this is in *The Forsaken Merman*, but there are also suggestions of it in the Eaglehurst poem, the sonnet *Written in Butler's Sermons*, and *To Marguerite —Continued*. And finally, parallel to the wide-glimmering sea is an alternative symbol for the third phase of life which we may call the City of God or Throne of Truth. This region, which is placed on high and is reached by strenuous effort, not by drifting down a stream, is very different in its implications from the wide-glimmering sea. Indeed, the alternatives are probably related to those of mountain glen and coral hall in the first phase of the myth, and whether one proceeds out of the deep unto the deep or out of the heavens unto the heavens are alternatives that Arnold kept open in his mind. In the early poem *In Utrumque Paratus* he speculates that life may have originated in the depths, in the fecund body of Nature, or on the heights, in the pure mind of God, and he is "ready for either alternative"—*in utrumque paratus*.

The first region of Arnold's world is usually presented as a place of deep or variegated shadow, cool and well-watered, with clear-running streams or bubbling fountains. Usually it is set on the shoulder of a mountain, but it may be in the corner of an upland field or in some sun-dappled meadow deep in the woods. It may even be on an open heath so that it is screened by trees or protected by some depression in the land. For its main characteristic, apart from the springlike and virginal quality of its vegetation, is that it is secluded from the world, withdrawn and remote, and that the persons who inhabit it, who are mostly youths and children, live there in pristine innocence, untroubled by the problems which will later shake them in the world.

The principal examples of this glade in Arnold's poetry are the "queen's secluded garden" in which Sohrab was raised as a child, the "green circular hollow in the heath" in which the children of Tristram and Iseult listen to their mother's story, and "the last / Of all the woody, high, well-water'd dells / On Etna," of which Callicles sings to Empedocles. Standing for them all might be that in *Stanzas from the Grande Chartreuse* in which the poet, taunted with his unfitness for the world, replies,

> We are like children rear'd in shade
> Beneath some old-world abbey wall,
> Forgotten in a forest-glade,
> And secret from the eyes of all,
> Deep, deep the greenwood round them waves,
> Their abbey, and its close of graves!

Even Oxford, as described in the *Essays in Criticism*, "steeped in sentiment as she lies, spreading her gardens to the moonlight, and whispering from her towers the last enchantments of the Middle Age,"[7] is essentially a forest glade.

In its early stages the glade is intensely feminine and maternal. Indeed, the undersea world of *The Forsaken Merman* is distinctly a womblike place in which children and other fishlike creatures float about in a brine until at last, rejected by their mother, they come to the surface, crying and "wild with pain." Not so deeply primitive are the other uses of the symbol, but, in their use of geological images and a subtle incest theme, they still suggest a Freudian unconscious or a time prior to individuation. In the sonnet *Written in Butler's Sermons* it is said,

> Deep and broad, where none may see,
> Spring the foundations of that shadowy throne

7. *Essays in Criticism: First Series* (New York, 1902), pp. x–xi; Super, *3*, 290. For Arnold's prose works reference will be made to the Eversley editions published by Macmillan and Co. and also, when the volume in question has appeared, to *The Complete Prose Works of Matthew Arnold*, ed. R. H. Super (Ann Arbor, 1960–).

> Where man's one nature, queen-like, sits alone,
> Centred in a majestic unity;
> And rays her powers, like sister-islands seen
> Linking their coral arms under the sea.

Similarly, in *To Marguerite—Continued* it is asserted that although on the surface we are islands, "Surely once . . . we were / Parts of a single continent!" and this is further evidenced by the fact that underneath the sea the islands are connected with one another by a deep volcanic fire. So, too, in *Empedocles on Etna* the Liparëan islands are connected with each other, and with Etna, by "sister-fires," although on the surface they are connected only by "a road of moonbeams."

Putting behind us the undersea version of Arnold's world and coming up into its more normal pastoral form, we find that it is still presided over by queens and mothers, ultimately by the Great or Mighty Mother, Nature.[8] Gradually, however, as the children grow up, sisters and mothers are forgotten, and then it becomes a young man's world in which youth ranges freely with his male companions. His activities are three: the hunt, love, and poetry or song. Love, however, quickly turns to sexual passion, which is a subject for the burning plain, and so the prime activities are the hunt and poetry or song.

The hunt is Arnold's main symbol for the active life in the world of nature. It is true that in *Stanzas from the Grande Chartreuse* the children of the abbey were unable to follow the hunters, who symbolized to them the life of pleasure, and to the pure contemplatives of *Thyrsis* and *The Scholar-Gipsy* the troops of Oxford hunters somewhat disturbed the landscape with their clatter. But Rustum remembered with pleasure the life he led

> in that long-distant summer-time—
> The castle, and the dewy woods, and hunt

8. *The Youth of Nature*, 77; *Thyrsis*, 177, 179; *Westminster Abbey*, 86, 115.

And hound, and morn on those delightful hills
In Ader-baijan.

Tristram was a "peerless hunter" before his life was poisoned by
Iseult of Ireland, and the young huntsman who stares down upon
him from the arras is inclined to cheer his dogs into the brake
(though "the wild boar rustles in his lair") rather than linger in
that world of heated passion. Both Æpytus in *Merope* and the
Duke of Savoy in *The Church of Brou* die in hunting accidents,
the one pursuing the stag in Arcadian dales and the other pursu-
ing the boar in the crisp woods of France. In both cases this is the
crucial event which moves the action of the poem from one phase
of life to another.

Tristram was both hunter and poet, as his gold harp and dark
green forest-dress suggest, but generally in Arnold the poet
roams the woodlands without hunting. In *The Strayed Reveller*
Ulysses hunted with Circe, but he is clearly to be contrasted
with the more dreamy youth who, having descended from his
hut up at the valley-head, merely sits on the steps and lets the
forms of things pass through his mind rather than he through
the forms. The youths who descend from the upland valleys
to the palace of the New Sirens are poets, and so too are various
figures in *The Scholar-Gipsy*, *Thyrsis*, and the lyrics of Callicles.
Callicles himself is the best example, unless one except Words-
worth, who, in *Memorial Verses*, is primarily for Arnold a poet
of the forest glade.

> He laid us as we lay at birth
> On the cool flowery lap of earth,
> Smiles broke from us and we had ease;
> The hills were round us, and the breeze
> Went o'er the sun-lit fields again;
> Our foreheads felt the wind and rain.
> Our youth return'd; for there was shed
> On spirits that had long been dead,

> Spirits dried up and closely furl'd,
> The freshness of the early world.

If one wanted a single line to express the character of the forest glade, it would be, "The freshness of the early world." If one wanted a single word, it would be that word, so important both to Romantic poetry and the poetry of Arnold—"Joy." Joy is what the forest glade possessed and what the burning plain has lost.

The moment of transition between the forest glade and the burning plain—as also between the burning plain and the wide-glimmering sea—is what Arnold calls the Gorge. When he is using his ship-and-sea imagery, the gorge takes the form of a strait or narrows which the ship must negotiate to get from one body of water into another. We have examples in *Stanzas from Carnac* and *The Scholar-Gipsy*. When he is using the alternative image of the pilgrim and the City of God, it takes the form of a mountain pass or narrow defile. There are examples in *Sohrab and Rustum*, *Balder Dead*, and *Rugby Chapel*. In *Balder Dead* it also takes the form of the bridge and grate which have to be negotiated by the messenger Hermod in going from the world of the gods to the world of the dead. In poems which make use of the undersea world, it is the turbulent surf at the junction of sea and land. In *The Forsaken Merman* the children have to go through this surf in passing from their coral halls to the windy shore, and in *Dover Beach* it is "the long line of spray / Where the sea meets the moon-blanch'd land," which separates the Sea of Faith from the darkling plain. In *Stanzas in Memory of the Author of 'Obermann'* we are told that the modern generation was reared in hours

> Of change, alarm, surprise—
> What shelter to grow ripe is ours?
> What leisure to grow wise?
>
> Like children bathing on the shore,
> Buried a wave beneath,

> The second wave succeeds, before
> We have had time to breathe.

Finally, in Arnold's more usual symbolism the Gorge is an actual gorge in which the River of Life, foaming between black, threatening cliffs, plunges in torrents down to the burning plain. There is something of the same feeling that we get in Wordsworth's Simplon Pass passage, of sick fear and giddy tumult, of noise and dark confusion, but for Arnold it is a traumatic experience. In *The Future* it is explicitly made the end of the first phase of life:

> Where the snowy mountainous pass,
> Echoing the screams of the eagles,
> Hems in its gorges the bed
> Of the new-born clear-flowing stream.

In *A Dream* we have an almost archetypal presentation of this moment. "We sail'd, I thought we sail'd / . . . down a green Alpine stream." The banks of the stream have all the sun-drenched beauty of the forest glade, and on a balcony overlooking the stream are two girls, of whom the poet says that "more than mortal impulse fill'd their eyes." The youths, responding to this impulse, rose, then gazed:

> One moment, on the rapid's top, our boat
> Hung poised—and then the darting river of Life
> (Such now, methought, it was), the river of Life,
> Loud thundering, bore us by; swift, swift it foam'd,
> Black under cliffs it raced, round headlands shone.
> Soon the plank'd cottage by the sun-warm'd pines
> Faded—the moss—the rocks; us burning plains,
> Bristled with cities, us the sea received.

The burning plain, the second region of Arnold's world, is the very antithesis of the forest glade. Far from being a place where one is united with his mother, it is likely to be a place where, out of ignorance, he fights with his father. For this reason it is often shrouded in darkness, in fog or swirling sand. But whether it be represented as a bleak and wintry upland or a hot and arid desert, it is always barren of vegetation. Moreover, where the glade was an enclosed, protected place, the plain is precariously open and exposed. It is the Victorian equivalent of the Wasteland. As such, it is at once empty and terrifyingly full: the one thing that it is not is harmoniously unified. For whereas in the forest glade man was in union with God, nature, and his fellow man, here he is abandoned by God, divorced from nature, and alienated from his fellow man. What is more, he is alienated even from himself, as the symbol of the river makes clear.

For when the River of Life flows down onto the burning plain, it is immediately split into several channels. As Arnold says of the Oxus,

> then sands begin
> To hem his watery march, and dam his streams,
> And split his currents; that for many a league
> The shorn and parcell'd Oxus strains along
> Through beds of sand and matted rushy isles—
> Oxus, forgetting the bright speed he had
> In his high mountain-cradle in Pamere,
> A foil'd circuitous wanderer—

These channels, one flowing out into the desert, another by a great city, and another toward a grove of palms, are symbols of the partial and fragmented lives which we lead as creatures of the plain. *Terrae filii* is the name which Arnold gives them in his essays, and it is a name which would well denote them here. Basically, they are three or four in number, and since they are not really distinct persons, but rather roles which the Youth is likely to take up in order, we may present them in a kind of narrative of what happens to the Youth when he descends to the burning plain.

His first reaction is one of anger. Looking around on the waste and desolate scene, he is bitterly indignant that the world should be such a place and that all his childhood dreams have been destroyed. And so, railing harshly against the gods, he flings himself out into the desert and races madly over the sands in the insane hope that there is some escape. We see him in the daemonic questers in *Resignation* and in the frail figure clinging to the bark in *A Summer Night*. Ultimately, of course, he is shipwrecked, or sinks down exhausted, or loses his way, and at this point he decides that he had better do as others have done before him, knuckle under and submit to the powers that be. And so he enters one of the great cities which line the banks of the now sluggish river and there gives himself to a life of "quiet desperation." In his first state Arnold calls him a Madman, in his second he calls him a Slave. Ostensibly, the two states are the very antithesis of one another, but ultimately they are seen to be much the same. For the Madman is as much a slave to his own passions as the Slave is to the world, and the world is as arid and lonely a desert as the desert is itself. Therefore, the poet cries,

> Is there no life, but these alone?
> Madman or slave, must man be one?[9]

Yes, comes the answer, there are other lives than these, and among them that of being unable to choose between Madman and Slave, and of alternating fiercely between them. Tristram, torn between his two loves, was such a person, and Empedocles, unable to live with men or with himself, was another. Borrowing a name from the hero of Clough's poem, we may call him Dipsychus or the Divided Soul.

Confronted by this dilemma, the Youth is about to sink down in despair when there meets his eyes, rising as a kind of mirage from the desert, what seems to be an oasis and turns out to be a pleasure grove, with a throng of noisy merry-makers, feasting and drinking far into the night. To the Youth it looks as if these

---

9. *A Summer Night*, 74–75.

persons have created something analogous to the forest glade, and such may have been their intention when they began. But as he enters and joins with the throng, he soon discovers that this grove is very different from that which he had known as a child. The feminine figures are not those of mother and sister but are languorous, seductive women—Circe, the New Sirens, Eugenia of the *Horatian Echo*, and the Modern Sappho. Further, the buildings of the grove are no longer the beloved abbeys and castles of his youth but are classic palaces with porticos, balustrades, and marble columns. Even the grove itself is false and metallic. In *Mycerinus* "the deep-burnish'd foliage overhead / Splinter'd the silver arrows of the moon," and a hundred lamps turned night into day. The spring or fountain, which was the central feature of the forest glade, has now been replaced by the foaming goblet or bowl, and it is from this source that the joy of the Revellers (for so we may call them) flows. But their joy is not of the kind that the Youth had previously known. Rather it is a hard, mirthless laughter that is all too conscious of the desert just beyond the trees and that quickly collapses into gloom. And this fierce alternation between laughter and gloom, rapture and ennui, shows that by coming into the grove the Youth has not escaped from the dilemma of Madman and Slave but has merely transferred it to another situation.

Indeed, it is now clear to the Youth that the desert is not to be avoided by any change of place but that he carries it with him wherever he goes. And as he considers what has happened to the river of his life, he sees that although on the surface it consists of thin and meager streams which wander across the desert, far beneath the surface there is a subterranean river which flows, silent and strong, directly toward the sea. This river—"The unregarded river of our life"—"The central stream of what we feel indeed"—[10] is Arnold's symbol of the Buried Life. Though it constitutes our true or genuine self, we are for the most part

10. *The Buried Life*, 39; '*Below the Surface-Stream.*'

unconscious of it while we are on the burning plain. But once we become conscious of it, then there arises within us

> an unspeakable desire
> After the knowledge of our buried life; . . .
> A longing to inquire
> Into the mystery of this heart which beats
> So wild, so deep in us—to know
> Whence our lives come and where they go.[11]

For this purpose the Youth goes somewhat apart from the surface life in which he is then engaged. If he is a Slave, he stands apart from the world's work and becomes a Quietist. If he is a Madman, he pauses in his wild career, ascends some eminence, and becomes a Sage. Or if he is a Reveller, he wanders away from his companions into some quiet part of the garden where, as a Strayed Reveller, he can commune with his own soul.

> Sink, O youth, in thy soul!
> Yearn to the greatness of Nature;
> Rally the good in the depths of thyself![12]

The life of the Madman is imaged in Arnold by the straight-line movement of his flight, the life of the Slave by the circular movement of his treadmill existence within the city, the life of Dipsychus by the eddying or fluctuating movement of alternation, and the life of the Reveller by the sinuous movement among the palms. But the lives of Sage, Quietist, and Strayed Reveller are imaged by the still point, the moment of stasis, far above and yet plumbing far below the world's surface. Only at such moments and to such a point do there come, "vague and forlorn, / From the soul's subterranean depth upborne," airs and floating echoes of our true or buried self. Arnold's poems mark the moments at which such echoes come. They are the times when he stands aside from his surface self and communes with his own soul. Initially,

11. *The Buried Life*, 47–53.
12. *The Youth of Man*, 116–18.

their aim is simply to intimate the existence of what cannot publicly be revealed, but ultimately it is to bring to the surface the buried self so that it may unite with the surface stream and flow, clear and whole, into the wide-glimmering sea.

The third phase of Arnold's myth, then, is the phase of reconciliation, first, with the self and then with the world. The river joins its various streams and then it merges with the sea. As a result, the transition to the third phase is not ordinarily dramatic. Rather it is a moment of inward illumination in which, thinking that we are still in a desert, we suddenly discover that we are not, but are in a path leading to the City of God or in an estuary leading to the sea. These two places represent the alternative goals of Arnold's myth, and as we have already noted, they have very different implications. The one is religious, the other naturalistic. The one is to be gained by effort, the other without any effort at all. The one appears to be a final goal, with the suggestion that once it has been reached life's journey is done. The other is not so much a goal as a stage in the world-process, the great cyclical movement which Arnold calls "the general life."[13] For although to man's limited vision the sea is death, to his more extended vision it is the All, the vast continuum of nature into which all things flow and out of which they again return. Finally, corresponding to these two goals are two characters who inhabit the third phase of Arnold's world. They are called the Servants or Sons of God and the Children of the Second Birth. At this point it is not necessary to say very much about them. The former are last seen making their way to the City of their Father, and the latter returning to the home of their mother. It is obvious that they are closely related to the two poems written, at Rugby and at Eaglehurst, by the thirteen-year-old boy.

This, then, is Arnold's imaginative world, and in the chapters which follow we shall simply be retelling, in a different mode, the story we have told here. In the first chapter we shall return

13. *Resignation*, 191, 252.

to the Children of the Forest and under that symbol shall examine Arnold's relation to his predecessors, the English Romantic poets. In the next four chapters we shall move up to the burning plain, which is the point at which Arnold's poetry properly begins, and examine the various stances which he found it possible to assume in the modern world. Finally, in the last three chapters we shall see him turning away from the burning plain, first, by means of a vision of the buried life in *The Scholar-Gipsy*, secondly, by means of a deliberate but mistaken act of self-annihilation in the Preface of 1853 and the poems which follow from that, and thirdly, by means of a prolonged but creative act of self-transformation in the elegies. In this final chapter occasion is taken to explain why the structure of all Arnold's poetry is elegiac and why this necessitates his particular imaginative world.

1 THE CHILDREN OF THE FOREST

We are like children rear'd in shade
Beneath some old-world abbey wall,
Forgotten in a forest-glade,
And secret from the eyes of all.
                    —Stanzas from the Grand Chartreuse

In 1833, when Arnold was ten years old, Dora Wordsworth gave a picnic for the Arnold children on the large island in Rydal Lake.

> You must fancy [wrote Mrs. Arnold] Dora presiding in a sort of stone-built arch, fringed and embowered with trees, and floored with fresh moss, which the children had plucked to form a soft carpet for our feet. Above, the blue sky seen through the trees; on one side the shrubby plants of heath and whortleberry and broom, rising, with rock scattered about, into a kind of mount; while on the other side the ground sloped down to the lake, which glittered through the trees, and gave us, as the clear waters washed up to the rocky shore, the music I most love. To complete the picture, you must fancy Mr. Wordsworth stretched on the grass, and Mrs. Wordsworth, with an animation and sweetness which makes her plain face so agreeable, reading to us some of his MS. poetry.[1]

1. F. V. Morley, *Dora Wordsworth: Her Book* (London, 1924), pp. 107–08.

That this is a picture for the "fancy" Mrs. Arnold intuitively recognized, for it is a very image of the forest glade. In it poetry, nature, and children are in harmonious union, and the union is presided over by the goddess of the glade, Dora Wordsworth. Arnold will reproduce the scene in his elegy on Wordsworth, and it will certainly symbolize for him the whole world of his childhood years. For in 1833 his parents had built a summer house at Fox How in the Lake District, and ever thereafter all possible vacations were spent in that lovely region. Tom, Arnold's brother, has told of the idyllic days sailing boats on the tarns, angling in the streams, climbing and roaming the fells—re-enacting, one might say, the poetry of Wordsworth. "Fair seed-time had my soul," said Wordsworth. So too had Arnold's, but it was very brief. "Bliss was it in that dawn to be alive, / But to be young was very Heaven!" True enough when said of the French Revolution, but hardly true of the "hungry 'forties." For what Mrs. Arnold did not realize when she painted her picture was that it was already an anachronism. By 1833 the period of Romantic nature poetry was over. The first Reform Bill had been passed, and the railroads would soon be cutting through to Keswick. Arnold, like everyone else, had to grow up and put his childhood behind him, but the transition was the more difficult for his generation because of a parallel crisis in the cultural life of England.

Arnold does not identify the forest glade exclusively with the world of the Romantic poets. It is also associated with the bright clear world of early Greece, as represented by Orpheus, Marsyas, Callicles, and others; with the birth of Christianity, as suggested in *Dover Beach* and *Obermann Once More;* with the Middle Ages, as represented by all the imagery of kings and castles, abbeys, knights, and hunt; and with the Renaissance, as in Glanvill's story of the Scholar-Gipsy, "born in days when wits were fresh and clear, / And life ran gaily as the sparkling Thames." It really does not matter with what historical period it was associated, for the main point is that it was always located in the past. The time present of Arnold's poems is the burning plain, and the forest glade is a lovely world which has long since passed away.

This is an important point because the most continuing criticism of Arnold's poetry is that it represents the decline and fall of the Romantic ideal. Book after book comes out in which we are told that Arnold failed the needs of the poetry of his day because he did not maintain the Romantic faith, did not assert the Romantic vision.[2] It is an odd example of a-historical criticism. We do not ordinarily require of poets that they continue to believe what their immediate predecessors believed or write over again the poetry that had been written forty years before. Normally, we allow to each school the right to create poetry in its own mode, and the only group to which we do not accord this right are the Victorians. They are still criticized from the point of view of Romantic poetry, and yet it was not Romantic poetry that Arnold was attempting to write. Thus, we ought to find out what it was he was attempting to do and why he departed from the Romantic tradition.

One answer (it is essentially the Romantic one) is provided by the very lovely poem *The Forsaken Merman*. The story which the poem tells is that of a kindly sea-creature who has been abandoned by his human wife so that she may pray with her kinsfolk in the little grey church on the shore. The poem is a lament spoken by the Merman himself, and it falls into three parts, corresponding to the three regions of Arnold's world. First, there is the recollection of the happy days together in the "kind sea-caves," then the distressful present on the cold windy shore, and finally the hope of future reunion on some moonlight night in spring. Primarily, the poem turns upon a contrast between the first realm and the second, and it is significant that in developing

2. John Bayley, *The Romantic Survival* (London, 1957); R. A. Foakes, *The Romantic Assertion* (London, 1958); D. G. James, *Matthew Arnold and the Decline of English Romanticism* (Oxford, 1961).

this contrast Arnold has reversed the sympathies which he found in his source.[3] His source, a Danish tale, is marked by an unpleasant religiosity which suggests that the mother was right in leaving her husband and children in order to save her immortal soul. But in Arnold she was clearly wrong. For the world to which she goes has all the bleakness and grimness of some middle-class dissenting town in the north of England. The world which she has left, on the other hand, is a rich aristocratic world of the "kings of the sea," with red gold thrones, ceilings of amber, and pavements of pearl. It is an open, timeless world of slow movement and shadowy lights, of the soft vegetative needs of living and growing things. The town, on the other hand, is a closed world of hard, confining objects—the white walls of the town, the narrow paved streets, the small leaded panes, the "shut" door of the church, and the eyes of the mother "seal'd" to the holy book. In the terms of Arnold's world the mother has made herself a Slave, and the poem as a whole seems to denote an England which, through a fit of Evangelical piety, has forfeited its ancient heritage of poetic beauty and poetic truth and has given itself to the prayer book and the spinning wheel. In the third part of the poem the poet envisions a time when this Evangelical rigor may relax and England may give herself to beauty once again, but at the moment she cannot, and she has brought this condition upon herself.

So too in Arnold's other poems which present an undersea world—the Eaglehurst poem, the sonnet *Written in Butler's Sermons*, and *To Marguerite—Continued*. All present a world which

3. C. B. Tinker and H. F. Lowry, *The Poetry of Matthew Arnold: A Commentary* (Oxford, 1940), p. 131. Another version of the tale, not mentioned by Tinker and Lowry, appears in Benjamin Thorpe's *Northern Mythology, comprising the Principal Popular Tradition and Superstitions of Scandinavia, North Germany, and the Netherlands* (London, 1851–52), 2, 171–72. This version has the interest of giving the name of the wife as Margaret, the form employed by Arnold. Unfortunately, I have not been able to discover that it was published before 1851.

is either deeply united in love or else is longing for union, and in every case this union is thwarted by some social force. In the Eaglehurst poem it is the castled cliff which bars the entrance of the sea to the land; in the sonnet it is Butler's analytic intellect which chops up man's nature into separate powers; and in *To Marguerite—Continued* it is "a God" who sunders the islands by a salt, estranging sea. In the last case it is probably a cosmic power that is meant rather than institutional religion, but taking the three poems along with the little grey church of *The Forsaken Merman*, one may say that church, castle, and academic hall are responsible for the fragmentation of the modern world.

In these poems, then, Arnold agrees with his Romantic critics that the burden of evil lies on society itself. Not so in the bulk of his poems, however, particularly those which make use of his usual symbol of the river. An example is *The Hayswater Boat*, a poem from the 1849 volume which opens as follows:

> A region desolate and wild.
> Black, chafing water: and afloat,
> And lonely as a truant child
> In a waste wood, a single boat:
> No mast, no sails are set thereon;
> It moves, but never moveth on:
> And welters like a human thing
> Amid the wild waves weltering.
>
> Behind, a buried vale doth sleep,
> Far down the torrent cleaves its way:
> In front the dumb rock rises steep,
> A fretted wall of blue and grey;
> Of shooting cliff and crumbled stone
> With many a wild weed overgrown:
> All else, black water: and afloat,
> One rood from shore, that single boat.

It is not difficult to see what Arnold was attempting to do here. He was attempting to write a poem in the manner of the early Wordsworth or Coleridge in which he would beget a sense of wonder as to how the little boat came there, so far from shore. Did some pygmy throng steal from the mild hollow of the hill, use the boat, and steal away again? The fancy is quickly dismissed, but in Wordsworth or Coleridge it would not have been dismissed before it had invested the scene with a sense of mysterious powers abroad in the land. In Arnold it does not have this effect, and the reason is that Arnold's imagination was not really seized by the mysteriousness of the little boat but by its perilous situation. It "welters like a human thing" on the black waste of waters. With the "mild hollow" or "buried vale" already behind it, it is now confronted by the threatening cliff and is in imminent danger of being swept over the brink to where "far down the torrent cleaves its way." In this context the final question, "What living hand hath brought it here?" is not a Romantic fancy implying beneficent powers, but a metaphysical demand as to who placed this lonely child in this intolerable situation.

The implication, then, of Arnold's usual symbolism is that leaving the glade is a traumatic experience which the individual suffers and cannot avoid. Even in *The Forsaken Merman*, though the departure from the coral halls was a deliberate act attributed to a human figure, it was passively suffered by the children, and the imagery of waves, tides, and seasons suggests that it could not have been otherwise. For generally in Arnold's poems, even in those which do not make use of the river, there is something corresponding to this element—some streamy, compulsive force, such as the trade winds in *Human Life*, which "drive" the ships from the fair coasts where they willingly would linger, which denotes Fate under the aspect of Time. It is Time, then, which drives us from the forest glade. In terms of the individual no one ever doubts this: one cannot remain a child forever. But in terms of history we sometimes forget it: we like to linger in the forest glade. Yet we cannot do this. Innocence gives way to experience, the pastoral vision to the tragic sense. This was particularly true in the case of the Romantic poets, whose vision of life had something fragile and precarious about it which led it to crumble almost as soon as it was produced.

For after all, when we charge Arnold with losing the Romantic faith, we must remember that this faith had already been lost by the very men who created it. It was in the *Elegiac Stanzas Suggested by a Picture of Peele Castle* that Wordsworth first entered that world of "deep distress," of "fortitude, and patient cheer, / And frequent sights of what is to be borne," which was Arnold's habitual dwelling-place. It was in *La Belle Dame sans Merci* that Keats found himself upon the "cold hill side" of a purely phenomenal world, and in the close of the *Ode to a Nightingale* that he was tolled back from ecstatic union with the bird to "my sole self" and found that "fancy cannot cheat so well / As she is fam'd to do, deceiving elf." It was in the *Ode to the West Wind* that Shelley fell upon the thorns of life and bled, and in *The Triumph of Life* that he looked steadily upon the procession of those who had bled before him. And it was in *Dejection: An Ode* that Coleridge, who had ascended the highest, also fell the lowest in the loss of that active, sacred power wherewith, a pure and joyous soul, he had created a pure and joyous world around him. Of the whole generation Wordsworth had said,

> We Poets in our youth begin in gladness;
> But thereof come in the end despondency and madness;

and of his generation this was approximately true. But of Arnold's it was not. They rather began in despondency and thereof came in the end, at best, a *modus vivendi*. In a poem entitled *Despondency* Arnold says,

> The thoughts that rain their steady glow
> Like stars on life's cold sea,

Which others know, or say they know—
They never shone for me.

As with Prufrock on the mermaids ("I do not think that they will sing to me"), this is the negative point at which Arnold began. In his view, it was the point at which his age required him to begin, for it was the point at which the Romantic poets left off.

Arnold formally announced his post-Romantic position in the Greek motto which he prefixed to both the first and the third volumes of his poetry. It is a fragment from Choerilus of Samos, a little-known writer of learned epics: "Ah, blessed he who was a servant of the Muses, one skilled in song, during that time when the meadow was yet unmown! But now, when all the spoils have been divided and the arts have reached the goals of perfection, we are left behind, the last of all in the race."[4] John Duke Coleridge, reviewing Arnold's work in the *Christian Remembrancer*, declared that this "utterance of a repining and weary soul, coming naturally enough from a Greek in the train of Lysander, at the close of the Peloponnesian war, [was] not the key-note we should have desired for the songs of a Christian Englishman at the present day."[5] Neither was it the keynote that Arnold would have desired; it was merely the only one that he found possible. For in his view, both the religion of Christianity and that of Romanticism were dead, and he was writing not out of a rich and mythic past, but out of an exhausted present—out of a situation where the oracles are silent and "the great god Pan is dead."

Nonetheless, as the nostalgia of the motto suggests, anyone living in this situation and looking back at the Romantic and Christian faiths would naturally wish to go back, and on several occasions Arnold did try. One might say that *Lines Written in Kensington Gardens* was such an attempt. Here the poet escapes

4. *Choerili Samii quae supersunt*, ed. A. F. Näke (Lipsiae, 1817), p. 104. I am indebted to Peter Rose of Yale University for the translation.
5. *The Christian Remembrancer*, 27 (1854), 331.

from "the huge world, which roars hard by" into a perfect imitation of the forest glade.

> In this lone, open glade I lie,
> Screen'd by deep boughs on either hand;
> And at its end, to stay the eye,
> Those black-crown'd, red-boled pine-trees stand!

But though he boldly declares, "Scarce fresher is the mountain-sod / Where the tired angler lies, stretch'd out," it is all too clear, when some child toddles across the glade "to take his nurse his broken toy," what kind of glade it is and to whom it properly belongs. The poem, though a pleasant one, does not really create the true Wordsworthian feeling, and one may say that it stands to the poetry of Wordsworth as Kensington Gardens stands to the Lake country. It is an imitation created in the city.

A more elaborate attempt to return to the forest glade is found in *Stanzas from the Grande Chartreuse*. Many readers have noticed how, in this poem, the image of the children reared "beneath some old-world abbey wall" merges with and becomes indistinguishable from the monks in the monastery of the Grande Chartreuse. The children hear the troops and hunters calling them to action or pleasure, and they are asked, "O children, what do ye reply?" Their reply is that the call comes too late. "Too late for us your call ye blow, / Whose bent was taken long ago." It is in vain to ask how, if they are children, their bent could have been taken long ago, for the poem continues in a way which completely merges their abbey with the monastery and themselves with the monks and the poet. Thus, the poet in ascending the mountain to the monastery was in some sense reascending to his own childhood, in this instance to his childhood religious faith, and it will be noted that the process of the ascent involves a retraversing of the gorge in which his faith had died. The details of the first five stanzas are, of course, topographically precise in their rendering of the actual scene, but the sense of an arduous climb through dark, encompassing forest, "past limestone scars with ragged pines," recreates the feeling of perilous transition; while the cry,

> hark! far down, with strangled sound
> Doth the Dead Guier's stream complain,

points specifically to the constriction of the River of Life which encompasses the death of the child. In *Parting*, one of the Switzerland poems, Arnold also has "the torrents drive upward / Their rock-strangled hum," and again when he emerges on the top of the mountain, he is a "child." But in *Stanzas from the Grande Chartreuse* the children are all dead. Their protective glade is a "close of graves," and the whole emphasis in describing the life of the monks is that it is a "death in life." They move about the corridors in gleaming white, like ghosts, sleep at night in the wooden beds that are later to be their coffins, and are, indeed, in all essentials in them already. And so the poet asks of himself, "What dost thou in this living tomb?" And in the richly complex metaphor which follows, in which a Greek on some northern strand (the poet) looks at a fallen Runic stone (the monastery) and thinks of his own fallen gods (Byron, Shelley, and Obermann), the vanished faith modulates from Christianity into Romantic melancholy. For it is the latter which, in line 97, constitutes the "faith" of the poet and which sciolists deride as "a pass'd mode, an outworn theme." Thus, Arnold's poem has been a complex effort to reascend simultaneously to his childhood, to medieval Christianity, and to the poetic ideal of the Romantic poets. But it is all in vain. The Thunderer (presumably the *Times*) fulminates at him to join the modern world, and as the troops and hunters call to the children, they shrink back together with the cry, "Pass, banners, pass, and bugles, cease; / And leave our desert to its peace." The word *desert* has caused some perplexity, but that is the term by which the area around the Grande Chartreuse is known.[6] Arnold takes advantage of the fact to have his vision quickly crumble and leave him back where he began, in the desert of the modern world.

Initially, then, the reason why it is impossible to go back to the forest glade is that "Time's current strong" will not permit. But ultimately, the problem is a more fundamental one. It is that the forest glade does not exist: it is an illusion. The Christianity of the monks was "a dead time's exploded dream"—not merely dead but also exploded—and so too was the faith of the Romantic poets. This faith asserted, in the famous doctrine of the One Life, that man stands in a loving relation with God, nature, and his fellow men. But Arnold said that this was not true. God does not exist, nature is indifferent, and human beings find it impossible to communicate with one another. Thus, the truth is, not that man is in a loving relation with a harmonious world, but that he is utterly and absolutely alone.

> Alone, alone, all all alone,
> Alone on a wide, wide sea.

What Coleridge asserted as a momentary condition brought on by an act of sin was to Arnold the normal condition of all men. In *Isolation: To Marguerite* he tells his heart that it has

> long had place to prove
> This truth—to prove, and make thine own;
> 'Thou hast been, shalt be, art, alone!'

He freely admits that the Romantic poets, who thought otherwise, were "happier men" than he,

6. Two works which seem to have furnished Arnold with details about the monastery and its environs are John Murray, *Hand-Book for Travellers in France* (3d ed. London, 1847), pp. 503–07, a book which Arnold normally took with him on his travels, and Albert Du Boys, *La Grande-Chartreuse* (Grenoble, 1845), pp. 55–149, listed among books in his library (*Catalogue of Books from the Library of the late Professor Matthew Arnold at St. Paul's Vicarage, Oxford*).

> for they, at least,
> Have *dream'd* two human hearts might blend
> In one, and were through faith released
> From isolation without end
> Prolong'd; nor knew, although not less
> Alone than thou, their loneliness.

But though they were through faith released from isolation, their faith was in some sense a dream, and though they did not know their loneliness, they were no less alone than those who did. They had the advantage of the dream, but Arnold had the advantage of knowing all his life what they knew only at the end, namely, that it was a dream and that man truly is alone.

The process of Arnold's poetry, then, is primarily a process of dispelling the dream. For though the gorge is the symbol of transition from forest glade to burning plain, the actual process of transition is that of a deepened and more realistic understanding. Frequently it takes its departure from a poem of Wordsworth's, for while Arnold is the principal continuator of Wordsworth in the Victorian age, he primarily uses him as a background against which his own divergence can be seen.[7] An example is the little poem *To a Gipsy Child by the Sea-Shore*, which may be regarded as a critique of Wordsworth's doctrine of the child and specifically of the *Immortality Ode*. It was written in 1843–44, while Arnold was on holiday in the Isle of Man. He was standing on the quay at Douglas watching the incoming steamer, when suddenly he found himself looking into the eyes of a little gipsy child, who was gazing backwards over his mother's shoulder. What he seemed to see in the child's eyes was a foreknowledge of all the pain to be suffered upon this earth. Where Wordsworth's child came "trailing clouds of glory . . . / From God, who is our home," the gipsy child came with "the soil'd glory, and

7. U. C. Knoepflmacher, "Dover Revisited: The Wordsworthian Matrix in the Poetry of Matthew Arnold," *Victorian Poetry*, 1 (1963), 17–26.

the trailing wing" of "lost angels." All around him nature was blithe and gay:

> Lo! sails that gleam a moment and are gone;
> The swinging waters, and the cluster'd pier.

But this "superfluity of joy" in external nature did not distract him from the spiritual truth which his "soul-searching vision" inwardly discerned. Hence the "clouds of doom" massed round his brow, in defiance of the glancing day, and hence his posture, "half averse / From thine own mother's breast, that knows not thee." Like Wordsworth's "best philosopher," he knew intuitively all that was known by warrior, exile, philosopher, or king, but what he knew was not his divine origin but his mortal end.

A recent critic, in discussing the relationship between Arnold and Wordsworth, has asserted just the contrary of what is here implied. He has said that whereas Wordsworth finds a place in his poetry for evil, writing poems about idiot boys and unmarried mothers, Arnold has suffered a "dissociation of sensibility" which allows him to speak only of nice things in his poetry and confines his unmarried mothers—like the famous Wragg—to his prose.[8] But surely this is not true. Surely it is one of the glories of Wordsworth's poetry that when evil enters into it, it undergoes a healing process which all but transforms it into good. Thus, his idiot boy is not really an idiot in the sense that we would shudder at if it were true of our own child. Rather he is one of nature's innocents, bound by ties of love with all the human and natural world about him, with his mother, the little horse, and Betty Foy. And on the other hand, it so happens that Arnold did write a poem about an idiot boy, who was not only a real idiot but was rendered so by a blow from his father's hand. The thing that impressed Arnold about this story (which he tells in his sonnet *A Picture at Newstead*) was that the father had had the fact of himself and his idiot child painted in a picture so that

8. Bayley, *The Romantic Survival*, pp. 11–14.

his sin should not be glossed over but should stand forth, exposed to the world. "Methinks," says Arnold,

> the woe, which made that father stand
> Baring his dumb remorse to future days,
> Was woe than Byron's woe more tragic far.

It was also a far more tragic woe than Wordsworth's.

Or take the case of the unmarried mother. Once again it is well known that Martha Ray in Wordsworth's *The Thorn* is not really a part of the world of social evil. Her lover was merely "unthinking," and as to the suspicion that she murdered her child, the poet rejects it.

> But to kill a new-born infant thus,
> I do not think she could!

Moreover, the soft carpet of moss which has grown over the grave and which visibly stirs when suspicious townsfolk try to disturb it, is a symbol of the soft garment of pathos and beauty which nature and the poet have thrown over the grief with the passage of time and with its passage into the realm of art. Not so with Arnold's Wragg. It is the very attempt of Mr. Roebuck to obscure with his rhetoric the bleak fact of England's hideousness which has led Arnold to cull from the newspaper the ugly paragraph in question: "A shocking child murder has just been committed at Nottingham. A girl named Wragg left the workhouse there on Saturday morning with her young illegitimate child. The child was soon afterwards found dead on Mapperly Hills, having been strangled. Wragg is in custody." On which Arnold comments:

> Nothing but that; but, in juxtaposition with the absolute eulogies of Sir Charles Adderley and Mr. Roebuck, how eloquent, how suggestive are those few lines! "Our old Anglo-Saxon breed, the best in the whole world!"—how much that is harsh and ill-favoured there is in this best!

Wragg! If we are to talk of ideal perfection, of "the best in the whole world," has any one reflected what a touch of grossness in our race, what an original shortcoming in the more delicate spiritual perceptions, is shown by the natural growth amongst us of such hideous names,—Higginbottom, Stiggins, Bugg! In Ionia and Attica they were luckier in this respect than "the best race in the world"; by the Ilissus there was no Wragg, poor thing! And "our unrivalled happiness";—what an element of grimness, bareness, and hideousness mixes with it and blurs it; the workhouse, the dismal Mapperly Hills,—how dismal those who have seen them will remember;—the gloom, the smoke, the cold, the strangled illegitimate child! "I ask you whether, the world over or in past history, there is anything like it?" Perhaps not, one is inclined to answer; but at any rate, in that case, the world is very much to be pitied. And the final touch,— short, bleak and inhuman: *Wragg is in custody.* The sex lost in the confusion of our unrivalled happiness; so (shall I say?) the superfluous Christian name lopped off by the straightforward vigour of our old Anglo-Saxon breed![9]

The Mapperly Hills have no softening vegetation to throw over the body of the child, and neither has Arnold. He, like the father in the picture, finds "profit for the spirit" in insisting upon the bleakness and grimness of the whole episode.

Nor is he reluctant to use such episodes in his poetry. For Arnold does have an unmarried mother in his poetry, and what is more, she has committed "a shocking child murder." Her name is Philomela.[10] (The Ilissus was luckier in names, it seems, but not in deeds.)

9. *Essays in Criticism: First Series* (1902), pp. 23–24; Super, *3*, 273–74.
10. I have cheated a little here. As Arnold tells the story, it was Procne who was the unmarried mother. However, Philomela did murder her own child.

O wanderer from a Grecian shore,
Still, after many years, in distant lands,
Still nourishing in thy bewilder'd brain
That wild, unquench'd, deep-sunken, old-world pain—
Say, will it never heal?

The answer is that it will not, and specifically it will not be healed by the Wordsworthian expedient of the forest glade.

And can this fragrant lawn
With its cool trees, and night,
And the sweet, tranquil Thames,
And moonshine, and the dew,
To thy rack'd heart and brain
Afford no balm?

Clearly, it cannot because, morally speaking, the forest glade is an illusion. If one were to take Wragg, says Arnold, and place her in the Lake District, do you not think she would still see, in her mind's eye, the harsh, bare Mapperly Hills where she did her deed? And if Philomela, in the form of the bird, were to wander to this lovely English scene, would she not

behold,
Here, through the moonlight on this English grass,
The unfriendly palace in the Thracian wild?

Assuredly, she would. Nature, lovely as she is, is no solution to moral or human problems.

Arnold had already said as much in his sonnet *To George Cruikshank on Seeing, in the Country, his Picture of 'the Bottle'.* The problem here was drunkenness. Wordsworth in *The Excursion* had implied that the dalesmen were immune to such evils through the benign influence of natural surroundings, but Harriet Martineau, who also lived in the region, declared that they were not. "Nowhere," she said, "is drunkenness a more prevalent and desperate curse than in the Lake District."[11] Arnold addressed his sonnet to George Cruikshank because that artist, recently converted to the temperance cause, had issued on September 1, 1847, a series of eight engravings, entitled *The Bottle*, which depicted in lurid terms the downward path of Adam Roy and his wife Lucy. As Arnold says that he saw the picture "in the Country," and as he was at Fox How during the month of September and early October, when the engravings were selling by the tens of thousands (and when their story was being dramatized in eight theaters simultaneously), it was doubtless at that moment that he wrote the sonnet.[12] Indeed, it is very likely that he saw the picture at the home of Miss Martineau, who was a friend of the Arnold family and who was even then planning a series of lectures to the local population with two "terrifying demonstrations" of the effect of gin on the human stomach. One may suppose that Arnold was not much taken by her remedy of social agitation, but neither was he inclined to adopt that of his other neighbor, Wordsworth, and leave it all to the Vale. Asking what shall calm us when the "prodigy of full-blown crime" intrudes into the valley, he says,

> Shall breathless glades, cheer'd by shy Dian's horn,
> Cold-bubbling springs, or caves?—Not so! The soul
> Breasts her own griefs . . .

William Michael Rossetti, in reviewing this poem in *The Germ*, objected to the conventional diction of "breathless glades" and "shy Dian's horn," but in a sense this is the very point. Nature, says Arnold, has about the efficacy of eighteenth-century pastoral when it comes to coping with the moral issues of the soul. "The soul breasts her own griefs," and no cave, glade, or bubbling spring can breast them for her.

We are obviously moving here between nature as a reality

11. *Excursion*, V, 411–30; Harriet Martineau, *A Complete Guide to the English Lakes* (2d ed. Windermere and London, n.d.), p. 143.
12. Pocket Diary, 1847 (Yale collection).

and nature as a symbol, but there is no difficulty. Arnold is saying that nature as a reality is no solution to human problems and that the forest glade is no symbol of the human condition. The true symbol is the burning plain, and if we ever find ourselves in a forest glade and look at it penetratingly, as Philomela did, our eyes will pierce through the comely exterior to the harsh reality which lies beneath. This, as we have already noted, is the normal process in Arnold's nature poems, to meditate upon the glade until it dissolves in illusion and one perceives, behind its fair appearance, the arid wasteland that he inly knows.

This being so, it is not very useful to talk about Arnold's "idea" of nature. He has three different ideas, corresponding to the three phases of his world, and the process of his poems is to shift us from one idea to another. Thus, if he knows some Independent preacher, who still lives intellectually in the forest glade, preaching that we should be "in harmony with Nature," he will cry out in anger that Nature is cruel, stubborn, fickle, and unforgiving. But in another poem he may appeal from this conception to a loftier one, which consists primarily in cosmic movement, particularly the movement of the stars, the endless flowing of great rivers, and all that is denoted by the phrase "the general life." Each successive conception is more adequate than the one before, and we move through Arnold's world by the process of exchanging one conception for another.

Sometimes we do this purely in visual terms, as did Philomela, or by turning the eye inward so that it becomes the "soul-searching vision" of the little Gipsy. This is the case with Tristram, who, as he gazes into the fountain in which he hopes to cool his fevered brow, sees far within (but reflected from his own soul) the image of Iseult, the source of his fever. And so he flings off, with the narrator commenting,

> The solitudes of the green wood
> Had no medicine for thy mood.

But more often Arnold penetrates through appearance to reality

by exchanging the visual sense, which is suitable only for appre-
hending the surface of the world, for the more profound auditory.
Thus, in *Philomela* it is the nightingale's song which teaches the
poet that the scene before him is not so purely pastoral as he
supposed. Indeed, the very form of the line, "That wild, un-
quench'd, deep-sunken, old-world pain," with its accumulation
of epithets seems to take us back through time and down through
reality to a deeper stratum of nature than that apparent to the
eye. Similarly, in the *Stanzas in Memory of the Author of 'Ober-
mann,'* though Obermann lives in a virgin mountain scene—

> Yet, through the hum of torrent lone,
> And brooding mountain-bee,
> There sobs I know not what ground-tone
> Of human agony.

This tone is not merely the voice of Obermann, it is also the voice
of nature. Anyone who listens carefully to nature will hear it,
and if he would be a true poet, he has a duty to express it. That
is why the nightingale is the very symbol of the artist, uttering
again and again, as if her heart would break, the eternal passion
and eternal pain of life. And that is why Arnold sometimes won-
dered whether Wordsworth, who spoke so powerfully of the joy
in nature, was a true poet of the natural world or not.

He expresses his hesitation in a series of poems written around
1849–50. In the *Stanzas in Memory of the Author of 'Obermann,'*
dated November 1849, he said that "Wordsworth's eyes avert
their ken / From half of human fate," but whether he meant by
this the tragic half or the social half is uncertain. A few months
later, in poems written immediately following Wordsworth's
death (and doubtless influenced by the emotion attendant upon
that event), he was inclined to attribute to him somewhat more.
In *Memorial Verses,* the elegy of April 1850, he declared, of the
stream Rotha, that "few or none / Hears thy voice right, now he is
gone." Here Wordsworth is not only a true interpreter of nature
but is almost the only true one. And in *The Youth of Nature,*

composed probably in the summer of 1850, Arnold carried this idea further by suggesting that with the death of Wordsworth we have lost the beauty of nature altogether. It lies in the poet's eye and is not objectively present in the world. Ultimately, he rejects this view but, paradoxically, in such a way as to reject Wordsworth along with it. For in the course of developing his theme he so moves from the opening shimmering scene of a lake "lovely and soft as a dream," to an austere, enigmatic goddess of Nature, who is remote, mateless, and inaccessible, as essentially to repudiate Wordsworth's conception in favor of his own. And this is what he also does, more deliberately, in *Resignation*.

Resignation, the concluding poem in Arnold's first volume, is based upon two walks which the poet took over the Wythburn fells, the first in childhood with a family group, the second ten years later with his sister Jane (called Fausta in the poem). The burden of the work is a somber philosophy of resignation which is supposed to be validated by the surrounding scene but which actually finds little to support it in the depiction of the earlier, childhood walk. As the "motley band" of children flowed in its "wavering, many-colour'd line" up the gracious slope, it found all the features of the childhood forest glade—the "mild hollows, and clear heathy swells," "cool farms, with open-lying stores, / Under their burnish'd sycamores," shade and rustic cheer, and a bright brook which guided them down to where "We bathed our hands with speechless glee, / That night, in the wide-glimmering sea." Of course, before they reached the sea they had to cross the burning plain:

> The town, the highway, and the plain.
> And many a mile of dusty way,
> Parch'd and road-worn, we made that day.

But this was their childhood experience. When they returned ten years later in 1843, two things had happened: their father had died very suddenly in the prime of his life, and Jane's engagement to a young Master at Rugby had been abruptly broken off just three weeks before the wedding.[13] Hence the theme of resignation. The effect of this upon the poem is that it becomes a kind of inverted *Tintern Abbey*. For where Wordsworth had revisited the banks of the Wye and reported that its beauty had sustained and nourished him during the intervening years, Arnold rather found that the experience of the intervening years had revised his estimate of natural beauty. Nature was not really so gracious as he had supposed. Rather, he reported to Fausta,

> the mute turf we tread,
> The solemn hills around us spread,
> This stream which falls incessantly,
> The strange-scrawl'd rocks, the lonely sky,
> If I might lend their life a voice,
> Seem to bear rather than rejoice.

As these are the very hills tramped by Wordsworth—indeed, tramped by him in the company of the Arnolds—one is inclined

13. These facts were first set forth by Kathleen Tillotson, "Dr. Arnold's Death and a Broken Engagement," *N&Q, 197* (1952), 409–11; cf. Norman Wymer, ibid., pp. 503–04, and his *Dr. Arnold of Rugby* (London, 1953), pp. 191 ff.; T. W. Bamford, *Thomas Arnold* (London, 1960), pp. 169–70.

In my note on *Resignation* in *Poetry and Criticism of Matthew Arnold* (p. 542) I sided with E. K. Chambers in supposing that the date of the two walks was later than 1833 and 1843. Since then I have had the privilege of seeing the unpublished journal of the poet's mother (in possession of Miss Dorothy M. Ward), which states, under the date July 1833: "After a busy Trustee meeting we left Rugby for Allan Bank, where you will recollect our pleasant intercourse with Thorney Howe [home of the Fletchers]—& Jane Matt & Tom will remember their walk to Keswick from Withburn & how their poor young legs were tired by the stiff [stalks?] of the heath[er?] on the mountains, & how they eat [illegible], and bathed to refresh themselves —but how poor Jane was still tired, & obliged to lie down—and was far from well at that comfortless Cockermouth—Mr. Hamilton was with us— and do you not recollect how fine the view was from the high ground as we were returning between Whitehaven, & Scale Hill." Though the account is not perfectly clear, it suggests that they bathed at Derwentwater and probably took a conveyance from Keswick on. Cf. Rev. H. D. Rawnsley, *Literary Associations of the English Lakes* (Glasgow, 1894), 1, 151–52; 2, 215–17; (ed. of 1906), 2, 117.

to read the line, "If I might lend their life a voice," to mean—as distinct from the voice which Wordsworth lent them. For the poem is, at the very least, a demurrer from Wordsworth's nature philosophy.

Almost everything that we have been saying is drawn together and summarized in *Dover Beach*. The poem opens with a scene of pure natural loveliness: the sea calm, the tide full, the moon lying fair upon the straits. There is no sign of man except a single light which gleams for a moment and then is gone, and the great, reassuring cliffs of England stand, glimmering and vast, out in the tranquil bay. But, as Shakespeare tells us in *King Lear*,[14] "The murmuring surge / That on th'unnumber'd idle pebble chafes / Cannot be heard so high," and so, as the poet descends in imagination into the scene and exchanges the flat visual sense for the more penetrating auditory, he becomes aware of an element of discord of which he had not been conscious before. The sea is not calm, there is a "long line of spray"; the moon does not lie fair upon the straits, it "blanches" the land with a ghostly pallor; and the bay is not tranquil, for if you listen, you hear

> the grating roar
> Of pebbles which the waves draw back, and fling,
> At their return, up the high strand,
> Begin, and cease, and then again begin,
> With tremulous cadence slow, and bring
> The eternal note of sadness in.

Wordsworth, writing from the opposite shore at Calais, had also declared, "It is a beauteous evening, calm and free;" and he also had turned from sight to sound and called to the child who was with him, "Listen!" But what he heard was—

---

14. IV.6.21–23. Arnold was well aware that the Dover cliffs are known as "Shakespeare's cliffs" because of their association with *King Lear*. (Letter to his mother, August 4, 1859, University of Virginia collection.) "Darkling," of course, is used in *King Lear*, I.4.237.

> the mighty Being is awake,
> And doth with his eternal motion make
> A sound like thunder—everlastingly.

Not so for Arnold. He moves the reader, not from natural beauty to transcendent Being, but from the illusion of natural beauty to the tragic fact of human experience.

In the second part of the poem the movement is repeated, but this time in terms, not of the natural scene, but of human history. For though the sea speaks eternally of sadness, it speaks to various people in various ways. To Sophocles in the classical age it spoke in a humanistic sense, of the turbid ebb and flow of a purely human misery. But to Arnold in the waning of the Christian age it speaks in a religious sense, of the slow withdrawal of the Sea of Faith. With mention of this Sea the poem retreats for a moment and recreates for the reader the sense of joyous fullness with which it first began. For in a lovely, feminine, protective image the Sea "round earth's shore / Lay like the folds of a bright girdle furl'd," following the ancient cosmology of Ocean Stream. But now, following the new cosmology of an open, exposed, precarious universe, it retreats "to the breath / Of the night-wind, down the vast edges drear / And naked shingles of the world." Readers have sometimes complained that the imagery of the poem is not unified, that we have no sea in the last section and no darkling plain in the first. But the naked shingles *are* the darkling plain, and that we have no sea in the last section is the very point of the poem. The sea has retreated from the world and left us "inland far," but unable, as in Wordsworth's poem, to

> see the Children sport upon the shore,
> And hear the mighty waters rolling evermore.

By two routes, then, through nature and through history, the poem has brought us to the reality of the darkling plain. For this is where the reader is finally placed, not in any religion of nature, which is an illusion, or of Christianity, which is gone—not, indeed, in any world which "seems" to lie before us like a "land of dreams," but here in this harsh, bitter actuality of our imaginative present. The image of the ignorant armies is drawn from Thucydides' famous account of the night-battle of Epipolae, a scene which Dr. Arnold apparently made a commonplace among his pupils as a symbol of the intellectual confusion of the modern age. But whether we imagine ourselves with Thucydides on the heights of Epipolae, or with Gloucester on the cliffs of Dover, or with Oedipus at Colonnus, all can say, "We are here as on a darkling plain." That is the true image to describe the human condition.

One would not go far wrong, then, if he took from this most famous of Arnold's poems its most famous phrase and said that this is the central statement which Arnold makes about the human condition: "We are here as on a darkling plain." No Romantic poet ever made such a statement, and no other Victorian prior to Hardy made it with such uncompromising severity. It is only the modern poet who has followed Arnold in his vision of the tragic and alienated condition of man. In this sense, Arnold may be called a modern poet, and it is certain that he would have accepted the designation. He considered that his poems, more than those of his contemporaries, represented "the main movement of mind of the last quarter of a century." "It might be fairly urged," he wrote to his mother, "that I have less poetical sentiment than Tennyson, and less intellectual vigour and abundance than Browning; yet, because I have perhaps more of a fusion of the two than either of them, and have more regularly applied that fusion to the main line of modern development, I am likely enough to have my turn, as they have had theirs."[15] In this statement we see Arnold once again applying his threefold analysis, this time to the poetic faculty: Tennyson's sentiment, Browning's intellectual vigour, and his own fusion of the two. He does so more formally, and in a historical context, in the essay "Pagan

15. *Letters of Matthew Arnold, 1848–1888,* ed. G. W. E. Russell (New York, London, 1895), 2, 10.

and Mediæval Religious Sentiment": "The poetry of later pagan-
ism lived by the senses and understanding; the poetry of me-
diæval Christianity lived by the heart and imagination. But
the main element of the modern spirit's life is neither the senses
and understanding, nor the heart and imagination; it is the
imaginative reason."[16] Arnold goes on to say that "there is a cen-
tury in Greek life,—the century preceding the Peloponnesian
war, from about the year 530 to the year 430 B.C.—in which
poetry made, it seems to me, the noblest, the most successful
effort she has ever made as the priestess of the imaginative rea-
son, of the element by which the modern spirit, if it would live
right, has chiefly to live." Of this effort the four great names are
Simonides, Pindar, Æschylus, and Sophocles, and it is to the
poetry of these men that Arnold would recall the England of his
day. For Romantic poetry, in Arnold's view, was not a part of the
central European tradition. It was very lovely but it had some-
what the character of a dream. It testified to the purity of the
heart's affections, but it did not take into account the great tragic
facts of human experience. For this reason it could not endure
the test of time or the touch of reality, and it could not serve the
deepest needs of the day. Therefore, Arnold directed the atten-
tion of his age to the poetry that could serve those needs, to the
tragic and heroic poetry of Homer, Æschylus, Sophocles, Dante,
and Milton. It goes without saying that Arnold himself could not
produce such poetry. He could not produce poetry that was even
so great as that of Wordsworth and Keats. But the kind of poetry
which he tried to produce was that of the imaginative reason,
and for this purpose it was necessary to combine with the imag-
ination, which alone was cultivated by the Romantic poets, the
opposing faculty of the senses and understanding.

Only so could one attain the balance and comprehensiveness
of view which was the hallmark of the great poet. Homer, ac-
cording to Arnold's sonnet *To a Friend*, was the "clearest-soul'd

16. *Essays in Criticism: First Series* (1902), pp. 220–21; Super, *3*, 230.

of men," and Sophocles "saw life steadily, and saw it whole." But what Sophocles saw, when he saw life steadily and saw it whole, was "the turbid ebb and flow of human misery." And what Homer saw, according to a sentence of Goethe which Arnold liked to quote, was "that in our life here above ground we have, properly speaking, to enact Hell."[17] Thus, clarity of view requires integrity of spirit, for to have such views and then to stand by them is not easy. When Arnold says of Obermann, "Thy head is clear, thy feeling chill, / And icy thy despair," we are to understand that his despair was icy because his head was clear, and that his head remained clear although his despair was icy. Similarly, when Arnold speaks in *Resignation* of the poet's "sad lucidity of soul," we are again to understand that his soul was sad because it was lucid and that it remained lucid although it was sad. The poet's first concern, as Arnold never ceased to declare, is with truth. He has to tell the truth about the world in which he lives, and for this purpose he requires, along with imagination, a clear, analytic intelligence. "Woe was upon me," he wrote to Clough, "if I analysed not my situation: and Werter, Réné, and such like, none of them analyse the modern situation in its true *blankness* and *barrenness,* and *unpoetrylessness.*"[18]

17. Goethe to Schiller, December 13, 1803, quoted by Arnold in *On Translating Homer* (New York, 1906), p. 149 (Super, 1, 102) and *Letters, 1,* 64.
18. *Letters to Clough,* p. 126.

2 THE STRAYED REVELLER

And if I laugh at any mortal thing,
'Tis that I may not weep.
　　　　　　—Byron, Don Juan

"We are here as on a darkling plain." If this is the central state-
ment of Arnold's poetry, then its central problem is the problem
of evil. How are we to live on the darkling plain? Should we rail
against the gods in Titanic or Promethean defiance, or should we
knuckle under and submit? Should we eat, drink, and be merry,
as the Epicurean suggests, or should we withdraw into the citadel
of our own soul, like the Stoic? The possibilities are not unlimited,
and as Arnold canvasses them in his mind, his poetry becomes a
kind of debate between Madman, Slave, Reveller, and Sage.

This debate manifests itself in two features of Arnold's poetry
which have often been noticed. The first is that many of his
poems center around a formal speech or discourse in which one
of the characters sets forth his attitude toward the world. Ex-
amples are the tirade of Mycerinus, the discourse of Empedocles,
the speech on poetry of the Strayed Reveller, the love duet of
Tristram and Iseult, the reported words of the New Sirens, the
lecture of the Old Vizier to the sick king of Bokhara, and the even
longer lecture of Obermann in *Obermann Once More*. All these

characters are pronouncing on that question which, says Arnold, "most interests every man, and with which, in some way or other, he is perpetually occupied"—the question *how to live*.[1] This does not mean that their speech is the last word on the subject or that it constitutes the total meaning of the poem. Often it is severely modified by the presence of other characters or by the speaker's own subsequent fate. But it does contribute to our impression of a dialectic, and this is further strengthened by the second feature of Arnold's poetry, namely, that he often builds his poems around a dramatic contrast between two or three characters who represent varying ways of life. Thus, in *Memorial Verses* Wordsworth is contrasted with Byron and Goethe, and in *Stanzas in Memory of the Author of 'Obermann'* Obermann is contrasted with Goethe and Wordsworth. In *A Summer Night* the Madman is explicitly contrasted with the Slave, and in *Tristram and Iseult* there is a similar opposition between "the gradual furnace of the world" and "some tyrannous single thought." The whole scheme of *Resignation* is built around a contrast between the daemonic questers at the beginning of the poem, the gipsies, and the poet, and that of *Rugby Chapel* turns upon a similar opposition between the mass of men, the few, and the Servants or Sons of God. In this way Arnold's poetry becomes a kind of Great Consult, comparable to that in *Paradise Lost*. For just as Milton's devils— who have also been expelled from a forest glade—pick themselves up off the burning lake and then proceed into Pandemonium to debate what to do, so too do Arnold's characters, and voices not unlike those of Moloch, Belial, and Mammon will there be heard.

Milton acutely perceived that Moloch would be the first to speak, and it is so in Arnold too. For the most natural and elementary reaction to the burning plain is that of Byronic or Promethean defiance, and therefore the earliest character which we find in Arnold is the Madman. We see him first in Arnold's Rugby prize poem, *Alaric at Rome* (1840), and in the poem with

1. *Essays in Criticism: Second Series* (New York, 1900), p. 142.

which he won the Newdigate at Oxford, *Cromwell* (1843). The former illustrates, as Arnold later wrote to Edmund Gosse, that he had been reading a good deal of Byron, and the latter that he had been reading a good deal of Carlyle. But apart from these academic set-pieces, there is a considerable body of early poetry which seems to have taken as its model the worst features of Romantic and Elizabethan bombast. We find it, for example, in the Yale Manuscript, where there are some half a dozen blank verse fragments, amounting to perhaps seventy lines in all, which date, apparently, from about 1843–46. The piece published by Professors Tinker and Lowry under the title *Rude Orator* is a fair sample. To the orator, who has rashly pronounced mankind happy, the poet replies with "such a damning catalogue of Ills . . . , such Instances / Raked from the swarming Gulf of Sorrow's Hell"[2]— but at this point the verse breaks off, seemingly inarticulate with rage. Another fragment gives another catalogue of ills:

> Sacrilege — we kiss
> Cheeks that decay to fatten us, and thrive
> Upon our fathers' ashes: — Lust; — we grow
> By appetite: — Injustice; — we forgive
> Or punish, and the cross grain'd sentence twists
> Into the avoided Issue: Tyranny — [etc.]

The passage has some concentrated power, but another, which asks, "What are Man's works . . . Seen from the dizzy Summit of an Alp?"[3] is pure pseudo-Elizabethan bombast.

Most of this verse remained unpublished, and indeed the significance of Arnold's first volume, *The Strayed Reveller, and Other Poems* (1849), is that he is here turning away from the voice and manner of the Madman to that denoted by the title poem. Still, in four of the sonnets included in that volume one can recognize the older vein. They are: *To an Independent Preacher, To the Duke of Wellington, Written in Butler's Ser-*

2. Tinker and Lowry, p. 337; Yale Manuscript, fol. 1r.
3. Yale Manuscript, fols. 25r, 27r.

mons, and *Written in Emerson's Essays.* All are "undergraduate" sonnets, if not actually in date at least in their character as blasts against authority. For all are attacks on some stupid thing that somebody has said or done, and in style they "somewhat loudly sweep the string." We know most about the last two, those on Butler and Emerson, which seem to form a contrasting pair. The subject of the former was Bishop Butler's three sermons "Upon Human Nature," contained in the volume of *Fifteen Sermons* published in 1726. The other had reference to either the first or the second series of Emerson's *Essays,* or perhaps to both, published in England in 1841 and 1844 with prefaces by Carlyle. Both Emerson and Butler dealt with moral themes but from diametrically opposed points of view, the former asserting the mystery and unity of the human soul, the latter chopping it up into "Affections, Instincts, Principles, and Powers." But the point is that in Arnold's day the *Sermons* was used as a required text at Balliol along with the *Ethics* of Aristotle, whereas the *Essays* was neglected. Arnold, like many an undergraduate both before his day and since, thought that the required text ought to be omitted and the omitted text required. Indeed, his exasperation on this point was such that even thirty years after the event it may be felt to breathe through the lectures which he delivered on "Bishop Butler and the Zeit-Geist" in Edinburgh. "In Scotland," he says, "I imagine you have in your philosophical studies small experience of the reverent devotion formerly, at any rate, paid at Oxford to text-books in philosophy, such as the *Sermons* of Bishop Butler, or the *Ethics* of Aristotle . . . Your text-book was right; there were no mistakes *there.* If there was anything obscure, anything hard to comprehend, it was your ignorance which was in fault, your failure of comprehension. Just such was our mode of dealing with Butler's *Sermons* and Aristotle's *Ethics.*"[4] Arnold's choice of Edinburgh as the place in which to deliver this lecture was not accidental, for Edinburgh was the

---

4. *Last Essays on Church and Religion* (New York, 1894), pp. 235-36.

native city of the person who had been his tutor in Butler and Aristotle, Archibald Campbell Tait, who later succeeded Dr. Arnold as headmaster of Rugby. Indeed, Arnold's opening sentence, that Scotland of course knew nothing of this habit of mind, is clearly ironical, for in his opinion Scotland was its very source. Tait, though an excellent tutor in many ways, was a dry, logical Scots "Metapheesician" who could be especially infuriating when he was expounding eighteenth-century commonsense philosophy to a group of ardent undergraduates. He was the sworn enemy of anything poetical or mystical, and as he had the fortune in those years to be tutor to a very lively set of undergraduates—"not very easy to manage intellectually," said Dean Lake, who was one of them—his lecture sessions were often a tussle. But "there was no getting round him," according to J. C. Shairp. "His shrewdness, his dry and not unkindly humour, were too much for [the undergraduates]; and if any one, more forward than the rest, tried to cross swords with him, he had in his calm presence of mind an impregnable defence."[5] Impregnable, that is, except against sonnets written outside of class and lectures delivered thirty years later in his native city.

It seems likely that in his irritation against Tait, Arnold was led to take a more hostile view of Butler and a more favorable view of Emerson than he actually felt, and that part of the responsibility for this must be borne by another Scot, Thomas Carlyle. For a passage in Carlyle's "The Hero as Poet" (1841) is probably the real source of the organic view of human nature which is opposed to Butler's mechanistic view, and Carlyle's preface to the English edition of the first series of Emerson's *Essays* is certainly the main source of the Emerson sonnet.[6] Indeed, that sonnet is singularly lacking in Emersonian serenity, singularly filled with Carlylean bluster. Today the main irony of

5. Randall T. Davidson and William Benham, *Life of Archibald Campbell Tait* (London, 1891), 1, 104, 107, 72.

6. Thomas Carlyle, *Works*, Centenary Edition (London, 1896–99), 5, 106; R. W. Emerson, *Essays* (London, 1841), pp. v–xii.

the poem is that readers are quite divided as to whether Arnold is championing Emerson's transcendental view of man or whether he finds it so palpably at variance with the truth that it constitutes a bitter mockery. In view of Arnold's later praise of Emerson as one of the great "voices" of his youth, it is probably the former, but the sonnet is an ambiguous production. The reason for this is that the world which refuses to heed the "voice oracular" of Emerson and which passes by with "a smile of wistful incredulity," gains by this smile a strategic advantage over the angry young man who exclaims, "O monstrous, dead, unprofitable world." The echo of Hamlet is unmistakable, but in this instance to fall a-cursing like a very drab is not so effective rhetorically as simply to adopt a smile "scornful, and strange . . . and full of bitter knowledge." Arnold felt this, and he tinkered with his last line in order to remedy it, but his rhetorical questions are still more easily answered in favor of "mockery" than "truth."

The problem was, of course, that in the 1840s one could not act like a combination of Hamlet, Byron, Teufelsdröckh, and Werther without exciting ridicule. "My tears the world deride," complained Arnold in *Stanzas from the Grande Chartreuse*, and it was one of his chief poetical problems. It seemed grossly unfair that Byron should have been able to parade "the pageant of his bleeding heart" across Europe and that Shelley's "lovely wail" should have been wafted through Italian trees, whereas he, whose "restless heart" had not "one throb the less," should not be allowed this privilege. His melancholy, sciolists told him, was "a pass'd mode, an outworn theme," and so, simply by virtue of having lived one generation too late, he was denied the natural outlet for his grief that the Romantic hero enjoyed.

> The nobleness of grief is gone—
> Ah, leave us not the fret alone!

The solution, of course, was to learn a lesson of those who passed by with a smile "scornful, and strange . . . and full of bitter knowledge," and Arnold began to learn this lesson rather

early. We may see him doing so in a letter which he wrote to
Clough from Rugby in March 1845. It was in the wee small
hours of the night and so he quoted a turgid passage on Night
which has been preserved in the Yale Manuscript on the same
page as the Emerson sonnet.[7] In the letter he ridiculed the pas-
sage by altering the phrase, "the Poets rash & feverish Melan-
choly," into "the 'Usher's' rash and feverish Melancholy," in
allusion to his present humble occupation as an assistant master
at Rugby. In other words, in the year or two which had elapsed
since the writing of the passage he had achieved sufficient distance
from it to be able to parody it, and of the conclusion he says,
"Which last two Lines, I perceive, hang loosely around the
Point," a comment which is perfectly true. In 1848, of some other
lines rather similar in style, he observes, "Why here is a mar-
vellous thing. The following is curious." And even the rather
good sonnet *To a Friend* cannot be quoted to Clough without the
comment, "There's for you but this style is not hard tho: rather
taking."[8] As the lines quoted are those which speak

> Of that lame slave who in Nicopolis
> Taught Arrian, when Vespasian's brutal son
> Cleared Rome of what most sham'd him,

we may assume that the style which was "not hard tho: rather
taking" was the Miltonic sonnet style.

The lesson which Arnold seems here to be learning with regard
to style he had learned much earlier with regard to the conduct of
his own life. For it is well known that even from early boyhood
he had adopted the lofty, supercilious manner which became his
trademark as a young man and which corresponds to the scornful
smile of the world in the Emerson sonnet. It will be useful to
look at this manner before we return to the poetry, and we may
begin with a well-known episode at Winchester School. One
morning at breakfast Arnold was asked by the headmaster how

7. *Letters to Clough*, p. 57; Yale Manuscript, fol. 24v.
8. *Letters to Clough*, pp. 93, 90.

he found the work, and he replied in his breezy manner that he found it "quite light." His answer was overheard by some of the other boys, and as a result he became extremely unpopular, so much so that at the end of the year he was subjected to an ordeal known as "Cloister peelings," in which the culprit was stood at the end of the great school and, amid howls and jeers, was pelted with balls made out of the rolled-up insides of buns, called "pontos."[9] But the end of the story is that he recouped his failure by winning the declamation contest at the end of the year, and the passage which he chose for recitation was the speech which Byron puts into the mouth of Marino Faliero:

> I speak to Time and to Eternity,
> Of which I grow a portion, not to man.
> Ye Elements! in which to be resolved
> I hasten, [etc.]

much in the manner of Empedocles. Here, then, is the tragic stance and the dandiacal stance together, each revealing the true meaning of the other, the one refusing to be perturbed by school-boy tasks and the other saying, if ye think that I am not perturbed, then, like the people in Tennyson's *Ulysses*, ye "hoard, and sleep, and feed, and know not me." Arnold's attitude always presupposes an audience which either does or does not understand, and its main purpose is to be sufficiently oblique so that those who are sympathetic will understand and those who are not will not.

Precisely the same pattern of apparent idleness and actual success persisted at Rugby and Oxford. At Rugby he is said to have made faces behind his father's back, but in the end he won the poetry prize with *Alaric at Rome* and got an Exhibition to Balliol. At Balliol he was very idle. "Matt has gone out fishing," wrote Clough, "when he ought properly to be working," and the result was that he took an inglorious second-class degree. But

9. Thomas Arnold, Jr., *Passages in a Wandering Life* (London, 1900), pp. 14–15.

the next year he recouped by winning a fellowship at Oriel, where the emphasis was rather on intellectual distinction than knowing your "books." Still, he insisted on running off to Paris in pursuit of the French actress Rachel rather than behaving as a young fellow of Oriel ought to behave. "Matt is full of Parisianism," wrote Clough on his return; "theaters in general, and Rachel in special: he enters the room with a chanson of Beranger's on his lips—for the sake of French words almost conscious of tune: his carriage shows him in fancy parading the rue de Rivoli;—and his hair is guiltless of English scissors: he breakfasts at twelve, and never dines in Hall, and in the week or 8 days rather (for 2 Sundays must be included) he has been to Chapel *once.*"[10] The thing to remember is that Rachel was the great French tragic actress, and that if Arnold was in fancy parading the Rue de Rivoli, he was on his way to *Andromaque.*

Or, take an episode in 1845, when Arnold was an assistant master at Rugby. Rugby, with its terrible earnestness and its memories of his father, always brought out the worst in Arnold, and he used to write to Clough from there in his most elaborately fooling vein, mocking the Evangelical "Trimmer-X-Hannah-More type" of reformer of whom A. C. Tait, the new headmaster, somewhat unpleasantly reminded him. In one letter he intimated that his "present Labours may be shadowed forth under the Figure of Satan, perambulating, under the most unfavorable circumstances, a populous neighborhood, thro: which I have lately passed distributing Tracts: which reminds me that I do not give satisfaction at the Masters Meetings. For the other day when Tait had well observed that strict Calvinism devoted 1000s of mankind to be eternally, —and paused—I, with, I trust the true Xtian Simplicity suggested '——'." And on he went into a mock self-examination somewhat in the manner of a female Dissenting missionary: "True, I give satisfaction—but to whom? True, I have yet been late on no Morning, but do I come behind in no

10. *The Correspondence of Arthur Hugh Clough,* ed. F. L. Mulhauser (Oxford, 1957), 1, 134, 178–79.

thing? True, I search the Exercises, but the Spirits?"[11] and so on. But if we turn to Arnold's pocket diary for this period, we find that the one thing which he bothers to record therein is the very matter which he here seems so lighthearted about, namely, whether he did or did not get to morning prayers on time. The entries read, "Prayers in time" for March 1 and "D[itt]o" for the 2nd to the 5th. But on the 6th he was "late." Next day "in time" and "d[itt]o" for the 9th to the 17th, then "late" again. Clearly, he was not really so indifferent to the matter as he pretends. In the same diary, shortly before the time when Clough makes us think that not going to chapel was a kind of joke with Arnold, we find again that whether he went or not is the principal matter which he records.[12]

The usual interpretation of these and similar anecdotes is that Arnold as a young man adopted the dress and manner of the dandy, a pose made fashionable by the novels of Bulwer and Disraeli, but that the "real" Arnold, deep within, was profoundly serious and tragic. It is usually added that we may find the pose in Arnold's life and the real person in his poetry. There is, of course, some truth in this, for it is clear that many persons among Arnold's family and friends were surprised, when his first volume of verse was published, at the depth and earnestness of its thought. Some did not even know that he had been a poet. Miss Fenwick, the friend of Wordsworth and the Arnold family at Fox How, had supposed the volume was by Tom, for, writes Mrs. Arnold, "it seems she had heard of the volume as much admired, and as by one of the family, and she had hardly thought it could be by one so moving in the busy haunts of men as dear Matt."[13] Edward Quillinan, Wordsworth's son-in-law, confided to Henry Crabb Robinson, "To tell you the truth much as I do like the Arnolds, & more than like some of them, Jane & her Mother for example, I never suspected there was any *poetry* in the family till

11. *Letters to Clough*, pp. 59, 55, 56.
12. Pocket Diary, 1845 (Yale collection).
13. Mrs. Humphry Ward, *A Writer's Recollections* (London, 1918), p. 42.

I read M.A.'s."[14] Even J. C. Shairp, a good friend from Balliol days, says, in the stanza devoted to Arnold in his poem *Balliol Scholars,*

> So full of power, yet blithe and debonair,
>   Rallying his friends with pleasant banter gay,
> Or half a-dream chaunting with jaunty air
>   Great words of Goethe, catch of Béranger.
> We see the banter sparkle in his prose,
> But knew not then the undertone that flows,
>   So calmly sad, through all his stately lay.[15]

And May Arnold, the younger sister of Matthew, writes, "His Poems seemed to make me know Matt so much better than I had ever done before. Indeed it was almost like a new Introduction to him. I do not think those Poems could be read—quite independently of their poetical power—without leading one to expect a great deal from Matt; without raising I mean the kind of expectation one has from and for those who have, in some way or other, come face to face with life and asked it, in real earnest, what it means. I felt there was so much more of this practical questioning in Matt's book than I was at all prepared for; in fact it showed a knowledge of life and conflict which was *strangely like experience* if it was not the thing itself." And again to another correspondent: "It is the moral strength, or, at any rate, the *moral consciousness* which struck and surprised me so much in the poems. I could have been prepared for any degree of poetical power . . . ; but there is something altogether different from this, something which such a man as Clough has, for instance, which I did not expect to find in Matt; but it is there."[16]

It is true, then, that there were a number of people who were

14. *The Correspondence of Henry Crabb Robinson with the Wordsworth Circle,* ed. Edith J. Morley (Oxford, 1927), p. 696, quoted in Tinker and Lowry, p. 222.

15. *Macmillan's Magazine,* 27 (1873), 381.

16. Ward, *A Writer's Recollections,* pp. 44, 45.

unable to understand Arnold's pose and who did understand his poetry. But we should not make a sharp distinction between the two, for it is also true that the pose continues into the poetry and that the poetry is not designed to be intelligible to everyone. Indeed, it is designed for a very select group of hearers. This group consists of Arnold's sister Jane ("K", as she was called) and, with a lesser intimacy, his brother Tom, Clough, Shairp, and Froude. "You—Froude—Shairp," he says, writing to Jane, "I believe the list of those whose reading of me I anticipate with any pleasure stops there or thereabouts."[17] Shairp must have been behaving himself particularly well at this time, for on another occasion Arnold "said a lovely poem to that fool Shairp," and he took it not in and so was off the list. Clough was usually on (presumably he was the "thereabouts" in the sentence above)—"You [i.e., Jane] and Clough are, I believe, the two people I in my heart care most to please by what I write"—but because Clough was "sometimes—with regard to *me* especially—a little cross and wilful,"[18] he was sometimes off. Indeed, it is remarkable to what extent Arnold's only true confidant was Jane. "You were my first hearer—you dear K—and such a sympathising, dear—animating hearer, too." And on another occasion: "There is no one and never will be anyone who enters into what I have done as you have entered into it, dearest K,—and to whom I so want to communicate what I do." It would be too strong to say that Jane was to Arnold what Dorothy was to Wordsworth, but she could occasionally see and describe nature in a way that gave him a strange feeling of correspondence. "It was odd," he wrote, "— as your letter about the country you went through on the Italian side of the Alps was being read, it brought to my mind delightfully just what had been present to it when many of the poems of mine which are nearest to me were composed—and then came your sentence saying what you had seen had brought

17. *Unpublished Letters of Matthew Arnold*, ed. Arnold Whitridge (New Haven, 1923), pp. 20–21.
18. *Letters to Clough*, pp. 113, 148, 145.

these Poems to your mind. That was a correspondence to give one real pleasure . . ."[19]

These, then, are the persons for whom Arnold's poems were really intended. Once he went outside this group, however, his poems had to be deformed in order to confront the public. In his childhood his productions had gone directly into the *Fox How Magazine*, the handwritten periodical of the Arnold children, and there had achieved a limited circulation among the family. But at a certain point they seem to have gone underground, and one may assume that this point was when they ceased being jocular, which most of the juvenile poems are,[20] and adopted the serious but ranting style which we have already observed. Now, however, if they are to be made public again, they must adopt the public pose which Arnold had already adopted in his own life. Thus, rather than distinguish between the life and the poetry and say that we find the pose in one and the real self in the other, it would be better to say that both the pose and the real self appear both in the life and the poetry, and that which is pose and which is real is a difficult question. When we find Arnold writing in his notebook, anent his habitual banter and persiflage, "To desire to be *natural* in conversation, & not to have the *force* necessary to supply the demands this desire makes on your collectedness invention & spirit,"[21] we see that for him, to be "natural" was in a sense less natural than to be "unnatural." Arnold had a real inclination towards elegance and a real inclination towards earnestness, and his stances are ə means of combining the two.

The whole complex is well embodied in Hamlet, and anyone who has read the letters of Arnold to Clough cannot help being impressed by the degree to which Arnold thought of himself in terms of this role. He seems to have found in Hamlet's assumption of the burden of evil a symbol of his own position, and he

19. *Unpublished Letters*, pp. 21, 24–25.
20. MS poems in the possession of Arnold Whitridge.
21. Yale Manuscript, fol. 17r.

felt a kinship with Hamlet's alternate desire to rhodomontade like the player king and then to fence in mincing phrases with Rosencrantz and Guildenstern. Or, to change the play, he alternately wishes to be Hotspur in the heat of the battle being offered a pouncet-box by some finical dandy and then to be that dandy offering the pouncet-box to Hotspur in the heat of the battle. He will patronize the Alps in supercilious phrase and then will modulate through a whole series of mock-serious or mock-tragic languages, from the cant of the Evangelicals ("True, I search the Exercises, but the Spirits?") to pure Carlylese ("patent Simulators ceaselessly revolve") to Elizabethan bombast ("I am a reed, a very whoreson Bullrush") to the clear, tragic cry, "O my Clough —in this house they find the Lodger in Apricot Marmalade for two meals a day—and yet?—" the dash expressing untold depths of cosmic desolation at the thought that man can live by Apricot Marmalade alone. Or, in another letter: "Down again dressed for dinner [and so a dandy!]—after dinner to the Price's—but thou'dst not think, Horatio, how ill it is here—"[22] and again the dash to indicate that, if the reader wishes to supply the words "about the heart," he may, but the writer himself would be embarrassed by so direct a reference to that palpitating organ.

The point of dress is central. Where Hamlet is down-gyved because he has "that within which passeth show," Osric is buttoned up because for him all life consists in show. Osric, Beau Brummell, and the Count d'Orsay are pure, classical form. Teufelsdröckh, on the other hand, the hero of that great antidandiacal treatise *Sartor Resartus*, saw in dandies and the world of clothes generally the great enemy of soul-searching, and he cries with Lear, "Come, unbutton here." But the perfect model for Arnold is the "modern" hero, Béranger, Baudelaire, or the late Lord Byron, who described himself in *Don Juan* as "a broken dandy, lately on my travels." The slight openness, flowingness, and looseness of his garments (but of the very finest quality) indi-

22. *Letters to Clough*, pp. 56–57, 113.

cates that he too has that within which passes show and that the
disturbance of his soul must have been very great to have de-
ranged such impeccable garments. He is in between Hamlet and
Beau Brummell and has utilized his Brummell in order to make
his Hamlet effective. So, too, has Baudelaire. His elegant costume,
all in black—steely, polished, faultless—contains no element of
disarray, which he would have scorned as revealing weakness.
"Un dandy," he says, "peut être un homme blasé, peut être un
homme souffrant; mais, dans ce dernier cas, il sourira comme
le Lacédémonien sous la morsure du renard"[23]—he will smile
like the Spartan lad who, rather than reveal his theft, allowed
the fox to gnaw his vitals to the death. Nevertheless, unlike the
Spartan lad, Baudelaire's sufferings are revealed by the very
rigidity of the etiquette employed to conceal them, and also (the
one sign of weakness) by the choice of Hamlet's color black. In
truth, all poetic dandies are "broken dandies, lately on their
travels," and the only question is how muted do they want their
groans to be? Do they groan through clenched teeth, through
smiling lips, or does the sweat stand visibly forth upon their
brow? The young man who published *The Strayed Reveller, and
Other Poems* under the pseudonym "A" wanted his groans to
be through smiling lips.

The nature of Arnold's stance is perfectly illustrated by the
poem which he placed at the forefront of his volume, *Mycerinus*.
Mycerinus is a young Egyptian king who has endeavored to live
all his life in perfect virtue; now, however, he learns from the
oracle that he has but six more years in which to live. As his fa-
ther "loved injustice, and lived long," it is apparent to the young
king that the gods are either impotent or amoral, and he rails bit-
terly against them. At the end of his tirade he concludes, "The
rest I give to joy," and with this announcement that by six years
of an intense Epicureanism he intends to compensate, insofar as

23. "Le Dandy," *Le Peintre de la vie moderne*, in *Oeuvres complètes*,
Bibliothèque de la Pléiade (Paris, 1961), p. 1178.

he can, for a lifetime of misguided asceticism, he moves off, "girt with a throng of revellers . . . / To the cool region of the groves he loves."

But the Epicureanism which the king elects is only an apparent Epicureanism, and Arnold has devised a technique of the utmost delicacy for indicating that this is so. By the three-fold repetition of the phrase, *It may be*, he suggests—but only suggests—that the king is not so much a Reveller as a Strayed Reveller, that he revels with but half his mind, and that his real inward thoughts are on the transformation which this whole experience has occasioned within his soul.

> It may be that sometimes his wondering soul
> From the loud joyful laughter of his lips
> Might shrink half startled, like a guilty man
> Who wrestles with his dream; as some pale shape
> Gliding half hidden through the dusky stems,
> Would thrust a hand before the lifted bowl,
> Whispering: *A little space, and thou art mine!*
> It may be on that joyless feast his eye
> Dwelt with mere outward seeming . . .

But then, just as Arnold introduces the third member of the parallel structure, he fails to repeat the introductory phrase and so gives to the lines which follow just that least tinge of assertion which enables us to take them as true, and as the heart of the poem:

> he, within,
> Took measure of his soul, and knew its strength,
> And by that silent knowledge, day by day,
> Was calm'd, ennobled, comforted, sustain'd.

What Mycerinus has learned is that he was not originally a truly virtuous person, since he practised virtue in the expectation of some reward. Now he knows that the reward of virtue lies, not in the approval of the gods, but simply in the knowledge of one's own rectitude; and in that knowledge he is "calm'd, ennobled, comforted, sustain'd." He is not an Epicurean but a Stoic sage.

By virtue of this new view he is also in harmony with nature. In the first section of the poem, where the king was a theist, there was no landscape, only a godscape, which turned out to be an illusion. In the second section there was the desert and the oasis, perfectly symbolic of both the good points and the bad points of the Epicurean way. And finally, after the intimation of the king's true position, the grove ceases to be an unchanging tropical paradise and becomes an almost English scene. For one thing, it knows the alternation of the seasons, and the king, who once was absolute for heaven and then was absolute for earth, is now in perfect harmony with this somber scene of birth and death, renewal and decay. He is so because all things are muted now, all things are whole. The brilliant lights of heaven in the first section, and the no less brilliant if factitious lights of the grove in the second, are subdued into the dusky stems, the mild dark, the autumnal clouds, and still night of the final section. And the loud sounds of cries, prayers, oracles, and tears in the first section, and of laughter in the second, are muted in the third to the whisper of the pale shape of death, the silent knowledge of the king, the sigh of winter, the dull sound of distant revelry, and the murmur of the moving Nile. The Nile, indeed, is the central symbol. "Insurgent" at the beginning of the poem, as a "tyrannous necessity" which might sweep both gods and man before it, it has now been reduced, by the king's accommodation to it, to the equable movement of the eternal process of nature. It is at once the symbol of the deepest current in the king's own soul and of the cyclical process in nature by which all things die and are renewed. And the fact that the king's revelry does not quail in winter, or pall in summer, or wither in spring, or grow dark in autumn, but "mixes with the murmur of the moving Nile" suggests that he has become so much a part of this process that he will in some sense outlast death and so defeat the oracle. The open ending of the poem confirms our feeling that he does.

But there is one point which should not be obscured in emphasizing the Stoicism of the king: however true it may be that his Epicureanism was merely apparent, the appearance of that Epicureanism was just as important to him as was the fact of his Stoical endurance. "It may be," says Arnold, that he was really a Stoic,

> but not less his brow was smooth,
> And his clear laugh fled ringing through the gloom,

for if his revelry was but a mask, it was a mask very necessary to preserve his soul from hurt. He had been wounded once by laying himself open to attack in an amoral world, and he did not intend that he should be wounded again. Though the revelry really engaged his soul not at all, the armor of the smooth brow and ringing laugh was essential to him. The only question was whether it would be misunderstood. We are told that when the mirth waxed loudest, the sound of revelry floated over the steaming flats "to tell his wondering people of their king," but we are not told whether the people wondered simply in the sense of being surprised or whether they also wondered in the sense of musing upon their king's behaviour and having some inkling, perhaps, of what it meant.

The question is important because there is some evidence that the poem has an autobiographical significance. Arnold was known as the "Emperor" among his family and friends because of his lofty ways, and we are told by his brother Tom that when the Emperor was twenty-four years old (i.e., in 1846, which is about the date when the poem must have been written) he "knew that he was in a certain sense doomed—an eminent physician having told him that the action of his heart was not regular, and that he must take great care of himself."[24] As his father had

24. [Thomas Arnold, Jr.], "Matthew Arnold," *Manchester Guardian* (May 18, 1888), p. 8. The article, signed "By one who knew him well," is identified as Tom's by Alan Harris in the *Times Literary Supplement*, April 18, 1958. For the "Emperor" see Clough, *Correspondence*, 1, 290 n.

died just four years before of angina pectoris, this was advice that Arnold would have to take seriously, and we may believe what Max Müller, a friend of the family says, that Arnold "knew for years that though he was strong and looked very young for his age, the thread of his life might snap at any moment."[25] Thus, Arnold may have seen in this story of the young king a fable of his own situation. He had found the story in Herodotus, where it is simply a tale of oriental cunning—the king outwits destiny by turning night into day and so lengthening his six years into twelve. But Arnold deepened the tale by his understanding of why the king might have acted as he did. The question was whether the "wondering people" of his family and friends would also understand or whether they would wonder only in the sense of being surprised.

Finally, before leaving *Mycerinus* we should note that it is written in two distinct poetic styles. The first half, the tirade of the disappointed king, is an angry, blustery outburst couched in the sounding stanza of Wordsworth's *Laodamia*. The second half, the narrative of the king's revelry and of his inner harmony with nature, is in blank verse and is infinitely quieter, subtler, and more expressive. Most readers would probably agree that they could almost dispense with the first half if it were not necessary as the *donnée* which makes the second half intelligible. But the point is that in turning from the stance of an angry young man to that of a smiling Epicurean Arnold was also turning from one poetic style to another. The poem is not merely his explanation of himself to his family and friends—his equivalent of Hamlet's "How strange or odd soe'er I bear myself, / As I perchance hereafter shall think meet / To put an antic disposition on"—it is also his advice to the players—"Do not saw the air too much with your hand, thus, but use all gently." It confirms what we read in *Quiet Work*, the sonnet which Arnold placed even before *Mycerinus* as a kind of motto to the volume as a whole. The piece

25. F. Max Müller, *Auld Lang Syne* (London, 1898), p. 124.

is not specifically about poetry, but, standing as it does at the forefront of the volume, it seems to warn the reader that although the poetry he will find therein may not be so impressive as that of some other poets, it may be more enduring in the end. It stands to Byron and the Spasmodic poets as Mycerinus at the end of the poem does to Mycerinus at the beginning.

This new attitude toward poetry was also the burden of the sonnet *Shakespeare:*

> Others abide our question. Thou art free.
> We ask and ask—Thou smilest and art still,
> Out-topping knowledge. For the loftiest hill,
> Who to the stars uncrowns his majesty,
>
> Planting his steadfast footsteps in the sea,
> Making the heaven of heavens his dwelling-place,
> Spares but the cloudy border of his base
> To the foil'd searching of mortality;
>
> And thou, who didst the stars and sunbeams know,
> Self-school'd, self-scann'd, self-honour'd, self-secure,
> Didst tread on earth unguess'd at.—Better so!
>
> All pains the immortal spirit must endure,
> All weakness which impairs, all griefs which bow,
> Find their sole speech in that victorious brow.

This sonnet has received a great variety of interpretations, and indeed, it is almost a classic instance of a poem which can be interpreted variously if one considers the text alone. But if one considers the historical background, then there can hardly be any doubt at least as to the general tenor of its meaning. There are two things which one principally needs to know. The first is that in the years immediately preceding 1844, when the sonnet was written, there was a great deal of research done on the life of Shakespeare which was singularly unproductive of results—so unproductive, indeed, that the stage was all set for attributing the works of Shakespeare to Bacon, as was done for the first time in 1856. The result of this "foil'd searching of mortality" was that it became a commonplace among writers on Shakespeare to remark upon how very little was known about England's greatest poet and how regrettable this was. Thus, Walter Bagehot begins his essay, "Shakespeare—the Man" (1853), with the words, "The greatest of English poets, it is often said, is but a name. 'No letter of his writing, no record of his conversation, no character of him drawn with any fulness by a contemporary,' have been extracted by antiquaries from the piles of rubbish which they have sifted."[26] As usual, of course, this paucity of information did not prevent the biographers from going to work, and in the very year in which Arnold's sonnet was written there appeared two full-dress lives of Shakespeare, one by John Payne Collier and the other by the popular writer Charles Knight. We may guess that one or the other of these works provided Arnold with the occasion for his sonnet. Probably it was Knight's, for in 1849 Arnold cautioned his sister Jane not to tell Miss Martineau "that I think her friend Knight a tiresome coxcomb in his writings about Shakspeare."[27] Also, Knight's engraved title page does much to explain Arnold's phrase, "victorious brow," and the epigraph to his work, a statement by the eighteenth-century antiquary, George Steevens, sharply emphasizes Arnold's theme: "All that is known with any degree of certainty concerning Shakspeare is—that he was born at Stratford-upon-Avon—married and had children there—went to London, where he commenced actor, and wrote poems and plays—returned to Stratford, made his will, died, and was buried." Perhaps, too, Arnold had been reading Barry Cornwall's biographical memoir of Shakespeare in the 1843 edition of his *Works,* for Cornwall repeats these same sentiments in language which strikingly anticipates that of the sonnet.[28]

26. *Literary Studies* (London, 1879), *1*, 126.
27. *Unpublished Letters,* p. 17.
28. *The Works of Shakspere . . . with a Memoir, and Essay on his Genius,* by Barry Cornwall (London, 1843), *1*, i. I have quoted the passage in *Poetry and Criticism of Matthew Arnold,* p. 538.

In the light of these facts it is clear that the primary meaning of the opening line of Arnold's sonnet, "Others abide our question. Thou art free," is that other poets submit to our inquiry about their personal biography but you do not. "We ask and ask—Thou smilest and art still." Or, at the very best, Shakespeare "spares but the cloudy border of his base" (his laundry bills!) to "the foil'd searching of mortality." But whereas all the other critics had lamented this fact, Arnold says, "Better so!" and if we wish to know why he rejoiced that so little was known of Shakespeare we must take a second line of inquiry.

For the second critical commonplace about Shakespeare in the early nineteenth century was that he was the very type of the objective poet who does not reveal his personality in his writings but loses himself in the characters he creates. In the phrase which Arnold will use in *The Strayed Reveller*, he "becomes what he sings." The basis for this idea was an eighteenth-century concept of the imagination as grounded in Sympathy: through Sympathy one enters into the characters he would depict. But in the 1820s Hazlitt, followed by Keats, distinguished between two types of imagination, one founded on Sympathy and the other on Self-Love. The former Keats called Negative Capability and the latter the Egotistical Sublime. Negative Capability involved, among other things, the ability to transform oneself almost at will into all sorts and conditions of men. Lacking a proper nature of one's own, one could take on the nature of an Iago, a Desdemona, a Hamlet. The Egotistical Sublime, on the other hand, lacked this ability. It had so powerful a nature, and was so deeply self-absorbed, that it could not enter into others, rather transformed them into some aspect of itself. The one projected itself into a multifarious world and took on the colors of its subject, the other assimilated the world into itself and imbued it with the color of its own mind. In Hazlitt's view, Wordsworth, Milton, and Byron were examples of the latter, whereas Shakespeare was the supreme example of the former. Schiller had already anticipated this view of Shakespeare in his essay *On Naive and Senti-*

mental Poetry. Naive poets, in Schiller's view, were generally classical and objective, sentimental poets generally subjective and modern, but there were certain moderns who were naive, and Schiller makes his point by telling about his early difficulties with Shakespeare. "Misled by my acquaintance with recent poetry so as in every work to look first for *the poet,* to meet him heart to heart, and to reflect with him upon his object, in short to look at the object only as it is reflected in the subject, I found it intolerable that here the poet never showed himself and would never let me question him."[29] In this way too, then, "Others abide our question. Thou art free," and this, of course, is the reason why Arnold says "Better so!" Better that Shakespeare did not parade the pageant of his bleeding heart across Europe, as did Byron and the other Romantic poets. Like other men, he presumably knew "all pains [which] the immortal spirit must endure / All weakness which impairs, all griefs which bow," but with him these did not find expression in his works. Rather they found "their sole speech in that victorious brow." The word *brow* has been the subject of a good deal of comment. Felicitously suggesting the brow of the mountain, which has been the central image of the poem, it also goes back to the facial image started by "smilest," and it is surely intended to recall the brow of Shakespeare himself as depicted in the Stratford bust and the Droeshout portrait. For we recall that the brow was a common symbol with Arnold of the degree of perturbation in the human breast. Mycerinus' brow was smooth, clouds massed round the brow of the little gipsy, Tristram's brow was fevered, Empedocles' was constricted as if by a band. There are forty-two uses of the word *brow* in Arnold's poetry, of which seven refer to mountains and twenty-two are used to characterize a person. That Shakespeare's brow is victorious means exactly what we see when we turn to the engraved title page of Knight's life of Shakespeare and see repro-

29. The translation is that in Bernard Bosanquet, *A History of Aesthetic* (London, 1934), p. 299; cf. Paull F. Baum, *Ten Studies in the Poetry of Matthew Arnold* (Durham, 1958), p. 7 n.

ductions of five different busts and portraits, all of them, by a peculiarity in the highlighting, allowing the brow to stand out very prominently—very high, white, and blank—as if the subject were an absolutely placid Warwickshire burgher without a care in the world. We must remember that Tennyson's Shakespeare in *The Palace of Art* was "bland and mild" and that the Stratford bust, when whitewashed by Malone, must have given an impression unusually masklike and enigmatic. Even today, looking at this bust, one feels that he is confronted by some archaic Greek statue, and that the slightly fixed smile in an otherwise impassive countenance will tell us no more about the man than any *kouros* in the National Museum at Athens. Or, one should say, no more than his works, for the victorious brow is also the symbol of that which emanated from the brow, the perfectly objective works in which Shakespeare accomplished a victory over the pains and griefs which he must have known, by transmuting them into imperishable art.

There is one final problem about the sonnet. Although Arnold is clearly writing out of the critical tradition which makes Shakespeare the type of the objective poet, he does not use Negative Capability as the means by which that objectivity was secured. His Shakespeare is not the "chameleon poet" who has no proper self and who loses his identity in the identity of others. So much may be seen from the single line, "Self-school'd, self-scann'd, self-honour'd, self-secure." On the contrary, his Shakespeare is as solid and unchanging as the mountain by which he is imaged. If one wanted a term to describe him it would be the Egotistical Sublime, and this too, of course, is the type to which Arnold belonged. When Arnold wrote to Clough praising Rachel, he said, "Greater in what she is than in her creativity, eh?" unconsciously admitting that it was not as a dramatic actress that he admired her but as a tragic personality. And so in *The Strayed Reveller*, although he curiously employed the idea that the poet "becomes what he sings," he employed it to symbolize subjective, rather than objective, poetry, and he said that the process of writing such poetry was accompanied with pain. The reason, one may believe, was not merely because of the pain which the poet vicariously experienced but also because the idea of parcelling out one's being among other people was, to Arnold, a painful idea. Whereas to Keats and Shelley this idea seemed to involve some pleasurable sense of dilation of being, to Arnold it involved a loss or fragmentation. Thus, in 1848–49, when he wrote to Clough that Keats and Browning (two fine examples of Negative Capability) would not learn that one "must begin with an Idea of the world in order not to be prevailed over by the world's multitudinousness,"[30] he was unconsciously reiterating the doctrine of the Egotistical Sublime. For what is an Idea of the world but one's own subjectivity, and what is the world's multitudinousness but the variety of characters that a Shakespeare can create? Thus, in praising Shakespeare for not parading the pageant of his bleeding heart across Europe, Arnold was not praising him for being an objective poet but for having suppressed his subjectivity. Like Mycerinus, "Thou smilest and art still."

The themes of *Mycerinus* and *Shakespeare* flow together in a complex way in the title poem of the 1849 volume, *The Strayed Reveller*. The protagonist of this poem is a youthful follower of Bacchus—or Iacchus, as Arnold calls him—who, descending from his hut in the high valley to join the rout of worshipers round the temple, has seen, through the beeches on his left, the palace of the goddess Circe, "smokeless, empty!"

> Trembling, I enter'd; beheld
> The court all silent,
> The lions sleeping,
> On the altar this bowl.

He took up the bowl and drank and sank down sleeping on the steps of the portico, and while he slept there swept through his soul a "wild, thronging train," a "bright procession / Of eddying

30. *Letters to Clough*, pp. 81, 97.

forms." By evening, when the effect of the wine had worn off, he roused and saw Circe, just returned from hunting with Ulysses, standing over him and smiling indulgently. Who was he? she asked. Was he, as Ulysses suggested, one who had followed through the islands some divine bard and learned his songs? But the Youth does not answer directly. Rather he gives a statement about the nature of the poet's vision which he says he learned from the old Silenus, who came lolling that way at noon. The statement, which extends for 130 lines, says among other things that the poet's vision is attended with pain.

> But I, Ulysses,
> Sitting on the warm steps,
> Looking over the valley,
> All day long, have seen,
> Without pain, without labor,

sometimes a wild-haired Mænad, sometimes a Faun, and sometimes, for a moment, the divine, beloved Iacchus. And then, as the vision fades, he calls for the cup again, and the poem closes, as it opened, with the invocation,

> Faster, faster,
> O Circe, Goddess,
> Let the wild, thronging train,
> The bright procession
> Of eddying forms,
> Sweep through my soul!

It would be idle not to admit that the interpretation of this poem presents difficulties, for readers have arrived at very different conclusions as to what it means. But perhaps the simplest way to begin is with a consideration of the central statement which the Youth makes about poetry. This statement seems to involve one of those fables in which the Gods present man with all the gifts that he could desire except one crucial gift, the absence of which is the essence of the human condition. In this case, they present the poets with a vision which is like their own in being universal in extent. The Gods "turn on all sides" their shining eyes, and what they see ranges from the life of the poor Indian harvesting his melons, to that of the wandering Scythians and the merchants of Bokhara, to the prophet Tiresias, the Centaurs, and the ancient heroes nearing the Happy Isles. All these things the poets also see, but whereas the Gods see them directly, from their height on Mount Olympus, the poets see them only by projecting themselves imaginatively into these characters:

> —such a price
> The Gods exact for song:
> To become what we sing.

That is the first difference, and by this Arnold seems to intend the inescapable condition of artistic creation. But there is a second difference, which is that all the scenes envisioned by the Gods are happy, whereas those envisioned by the poets are profoundly troubled. The Gods see the Indian harvesting his melons on the tranquil lake, but the poets see that already, in the unkind spring, worms have gnawn these melons to the heart. The Gods see the Scythians in the spring or summer, the poets at the end of a long, harsh winter. The poets see the heroes and the merchants in the "former violent toil" which preceded their nearing the Happy Isles of rest and wealth, and they see the Centaurs, not in the moment when they stand, with heads reared proudly, sniffing the mountain wind, but in that moment when they feel

> the biting spears
> Of the grim Lapithæ, and Theseus, drive,
> Drive crashing through their bones.

Tiresias is seen by the Gods sitting

> On the warm, grassy
> Asopus bank,
> His robe drawn over
> His old, sightless head,

but the vision of the poets pierces through that robe to

> His groping blindness,
> His dark foreboding,
> His scorn'd white hairs.

Indeed, the Gods in their remoteness and impersonality seem to have a kind of flat visual sense which stops at the surface of things and so gives an impression that all is well, whereas the poets' vision penetrates through the surface to the reality of suffering which lies beneath. The vision of the Gods is pictorial, limited to a single moment of time, whereas that of the poets is historical, following out a scene to its tragic issue or harking back to its laborious preparation. In 1848–49 Arnold was reading Lessing's *Laocoön*, which makes the same distinction with reference to poetry and sculpture.[31]

Arnold is not talking about artistic media, however, but about conceptions of art, and we may gather that, as in the song in *Empedocles on Etna* where Callicles opposes the bland complacency of the Olympians to the tortured writhing of Typho, he is drawing a contrast between two kinds of poetry, one which is objective, serene, and rather shallow, and another which is profound, inward, and tortured. Which of the two, if either, we ought to prefer he does not say. If we were to judge by the loveliness of the scenes, it would be the classic, but if by the honestness of the effort, it would be the romantic. In any case, once the latter has been done it seems impossible to return to the former, and Arnold is certainly saying that the only kind of poetry open to the modern world is that which probes, in a truly inward way, the root of suffering in all conditions of men. And he adds that since the poet can do this only by projecting himself imaginatively into the beings he would depict, he becomes, through this vicarious experience, a kind of Christ who suffers with the suffering of all mankind.

31. Ibid., p. 97.

These things, Ulysses,
The wise bards also
Behold and sing.
But oh, what labour!
O prince, what pain!

That the poet must sacrifice some portion of his life for the sake of his art is an idea very common in the nineteenth century, though it necessarily takes a variety of forms. It may be simply that the poet is a marked man, a *poète maudit*, different from other men and alienated from society by the special vision that has descended upon him. Or, as in the Freudian version of this idea developed by Edmund Wilson in *The Wound and the Bow*, he may suffer from some disability which lies very close to the sources of his power. Or it may be simply that the poet's way is not the world's way, and he who can succeed in the one cannot succeed in the other, sometimes with Emersonian ideas of compensation implied. This seems to be suggested in Arnold's sonnet *To a Friend*, where Homer is the "clearest-soul'd of men" almost because he was physically blind and Epictetus achieved the inner freedom of a Stoic almost because he was born a "halting slave." So in Oscar Wilde's *Picture of Dorian Gray* the actress who can beautifully render the role of Juliet on the stage cannot render it once she begins to be Juliet in real life. "I might mimic a passion that I do not feel," she says, "but I cannot mimic one that burns me like fire." Such, too, we recall, was the lesson learned by the Lady of Shalott. Like the Strayed Reveller, she enjoyed a vision of human life which was universal in extent, ranging from knight to churl, from marriage to funeral, but she enjoyed this vision under a curse, which was that she might not participate directly in human life but must remain detached from it, viewing it only through the mirror of her imagination and weaving it into the web of her art. Fondly imagining that her mirror is but a shadow and her web but the shadow of a shadow, she tries to escape from this world of shadows into the reality of brilliant light and loud

noise which is symbolized by Sir Launcelot. But her tragic dis-
covery is precisely that of the actress in *Dorian Gray*, that in
losing art she loses life also, and that the grey, autumnal world
into which she enters on leaving her tower is far more truly a
world of shadows than was the vividly colored, variously moving
world of her magic mirror and her magic web. Tennyson has
emphasized the themes of appearance and reality, detachment
and involvement, but he agrees with Arnold that the gift of the
poet entails some sacrifice of the poet's life.

It is the desire of the Strayed Reveller, however, to achieve the
gift without the sacrifice, and in the final section of the poem he
asserts that he has found a way. Through a draught from Circe's
bowl he has been able, "without pain, without labour," to see, all
day long, the moving forms of his Dionysian world. The ques-
tion is, how has he done this and what does his doing it mean?

We may say, in the first place, that the Youth's descent, in
earliest dawn, to join the crowd of worshipers round the temple
of Iacchus is not an act in harmony with his deepest nature, for
his dwelling place, in the hut at the head of the high valley, was
a place of fresh natural beauty and the temple of Iacchus was in
the town and surrounded by a rout of people. It clearly represents
the world in opposition to the solitude in which the Youth had
lived, and his descent into the town is the usual Arnoldian sym-
bol for the descent onto the burning plain. But as he descends
and sees on his left, through the beeches, the palace of Circe,
smokeless, empty, he is as one before whom a life-choice has
suddenly opened.

> Two roads diverged in a wood, and I—
> I took the one less traveled by,

which in Greece, as in New England, was the road of poetry.
Drinking from the bowl of poetic inspiration, he feels the same
sense of giddy intoxication which any youthful poet feels when
the world of poetic forms opens suddenly before him. True, his
intoxication might be interpreted differently, for once again we

have the problem of the audience which understands and that which does not understand. Doubtless many who misinterpreted Arnold's life would misinterpret him here, and would see in Circe the witch who transformed men into swine and in the Youth one who was a Reveller indeed. But there is little to support this view in the poem. The Youth is not transformed into a swine, and Circe is presented sympathetically. It is true, of course, if she is a muse, that she is a muse with a difference, for as she smiles down upon the Youth with an amused maternal indulgence and urges him to drink again, she takes on the lineaments of the subtle *femme fatale* who had so many young men in thrall in the literature of the nineteenth century. But this is the very point: these young men are artists, and the *femme fatale,* whether she be the Aphrodite of Tennyson or the Mona Lisa of Pater or the Salomé of Wilde, is the symbol of a pure formal beauty, a beauty so pure, so free from didactic intent, that she may paradoxically be associated with evil if only to make the point that she is not the servant of good. To the respectable world of bourgeois morality such a figure will always seem like an insidious tempt- ress who lures young men to their destruction—to what St. Paul, in a passage which was a favorite with Arnold's father, calls "revelling,"[32]—and it was the poet's intention that she should have this ambiguous character. This, too, is why he called his Youth a "strayed" reveller, because the word *astray,* like the word *reveller,* has the Biblical connotations of sheep who have strayed from the paths of righteousness. But in this sense "Strayed Reveller" would be a tautology, and it is evident that in the more profound sense the Youth is one who has "strayed" from the world of revelry into the world of poetry, from the tem- ple of Iacchus into the palace of Circe, where he revels with wine of a different vintage and with a harlot of another order.

If we ask of what order, we must turn away from the poem for a moment to the letters which Arnold was writing to Clough

32. Gal. 5:21; I Pet. 4:3; cf. Isobel MacDonald, *The Buried Self: A Back- ground to the Poems of Matthew Arnold, 1848–1851* (London, 1949), p. 8.

at approximately this period and in which he was developing his poetic theory in the earliest form in which we know it. This theory is rather surprising to those who are acquainted only with Arnold's mature humanistic criticism, for it is a theory which places him directly in the line leading into Rossetti, Pater, Swinburne, and Wilde, and it goes a long way towards explaining the sympathy, otherwise rather surprising, which those writers always felt for Arnold. For Arnold has here taken up the view that the writer should not regard himself as a "Reformer," but as an "Exhibition," and that he and Clough would be well advised to "keep pure our Aesthetics by remembering its one-sidedness as doctrine," that is, to recognize the difference between aesthetics and doctrine and so keep both the one and the other pure. The French have done this, and the writers whom Arnold most admires at this time are George Sand, Racine, and the "finisht classicality" of Béranger; those whom he most deplores are Wordsworth, Clough, and the English Spasmodics. For he sees that English poetry is in a moment of crisis, Romantic agony combining with Victorian earnestness to produce a puzzle-headed poetry in which writers solve, or attempt to solve, their personal problems and then impose their solutions upon the world. In Arnold's view, poets should not mine the drifts of metaphysical ore but should forge the golden word and let it sing. "More and more," he writes, "I feel bent against the modern English habit (too much encouraged by Wordsworth) of using poetry as a channel for thinking aloud, instead of making anything."[33] This was his view from about 1845 to 1849.

It is evident that the kind of poetry which Arnold praises in these letters and the kind of poetry which he dispraises are very closely related to the two kinds typified in *The Strayed Reveller* by the vision of the Gods and the vision of the poets. For one thing, he continually uses images of breadth for the former and images of depth for the latter. "Not deep the Poet

33. *Letters to Clough,* pp. 59, 69; *Unpublished Letters,* p. 17.

sees, but wide," he says, quoting from his own *Resignation,* and
what he means by this is indicated very clearly when he accuses
Clough of being "a mere d——d depth hunter in poetry," that
is, of "trying to go into and to the bottom of an object instead of
grouping *objects* . . ." Clough could furnish the thought to write
a single speech in Racine's *Phèdre,* but he could not write *Phèdre*
as a whole because he does not have the breadth to achieve
the balance and harmony of a dramatic composition. That is why
Arnold, in the sonnet *To a Friend,* praises Sophocles as one who
"saw life steadily, and saw it whole" and why he emphasizes
that the Europe which Homer saw means, etymologically, "The
Wide Prospect." In a kinder mood he will acknowledge the val-
iancy of Clough's effort "to get breast to breast with reality,"
but he will declare that he is unable to follow him because the
precept " 'much may be seen, tho: nothing can be solved'—
weighs upon me in writing." Indeed, Clough's habit of treating
the universe as a nut to be cracked is what particularly irritates
Arnold, for "to *solve* the Universe as you try to do is as irritating
as Tennyson's dawdling with its painted shell is fatiguing to me
to witness: and yet I own that to *re-construct* the Universe is not
a satisfactory attempt either—I keep saying, Shakspeare, Shak-
speare, you are as obscure as life is: yet this unsatisfactoriness
goes against the poetic office in general: for this must I think
certainly be its end."[34]

In this last passage we see that there is an extreme of the kind
of poetry for which Arnold has been contending which is nearly
as bad as the extreme which he has been opposing, and that
really he seeks some middle way between the superficial pictorial
vision of the Gods and the agonized probing of the poets. This
is apparent in several other of his remarks. Asked by Clough
whether the "fury" of Burns was artistic, he replies that "fury
is not incompatible with artistic form but it becomes *lyric* fury
(Eh?) only when combined with the gift for this," that is, for

34. *Letters to Clough,* pp. 99, 81, 86, 63.

form. And in the sentence already partly quoted he says, "The trying to go into and to the bottom of an object instead of grouping *objects* is as fatal to the sensuousness of poetry as the mere painting, (for, *in Poetry*, this is not *grouping*) is to its airy and rapidly moving life."[35] Evidently, "*lyric* fury" is in between "fury" and "artistic form"; "the grouping of *objects*" is in between "trying to go . . . to the bottom of an object" and "mere painting"; and "*re-constructing* the Universe" is in between "solving the Universe" and "dawdling with its painted shell." All have in common that they are the right middle way for the poet to go to work. Indeed, we may see in these comments that whereas Arnold had been drawn by the analogy *ut pictura poesis* into a rather purely imagistic conception of poetry, he is now becoming more aware of the differences which separate his own art from the art of the painter. We have already noted that he was reading Lessing's *Laocoön* by the autumn of 1848, and although the poem *Epilogue to Lessing's Laocoön*, did not appear until the volume of 1867, it is very likely that it was conceived in 1848–49 and so reflects Arnold's thinking in the period roughly contemporaneous with *The Strayed Reveller*. The question which it raises is why the arts of music and painting have so much more often achieved success in their spheres than poetry has in the sphere proper to it. The answer, of course, is that the poet's sphere is the more difficult, combining that of the painter with that of the musician and adding something more, proper to itself alone. The painter's sphere is simply the outward semblance of things as seen in a single moment of time and from a single point of view. The musician's sphere is comparatively larger. He takes a motive of human feeling, such as that expressed by the words *Miserere, Domine,* and, where the words express this motive briefly and by way of statement, music elaborates it almost to infinitude and itself becomes the penitential moan which it expresses. (It is revealing that at this point Arnold does not give to words the

35. Ibid., pp. 69, 99.

power to be as well as mean.) The sphere of poetry, then, includes both the objective world of visible things and the subjective world of feeling, both the world of space and the world of time, and though it expresses neither of these so well as the art which is devoted to one alone, it has the additional task of capturing that sense of the whole which Arnold calls "the movement of life."

It is obvious that the three arts of painting, music, and poetry, as developed in the *Epilogue to Lessing's Laocoön*, correspond to the three phases of Arnold's world. Painting corresponds to the forest glade (its subject is even the pastoral one of grazing kine), music to the burning plain (its subject is the *Miserere, Domine*), and poetry to the life-circulation of the wide-glimmering sea (the "tide" of humanity circling about the Ride in Hyde Park). In *The Strayed Reveller* the arts correspond to the vision of the Gods, the vision of the poets, and the vision of the Youth, who also effects a synthesis of the first two. Seated as he is on a portico high over the valley, he shares the aloofness and distance of the Gods and he does not in any sense become what he sees. Rather what he sees becomes some aspect of him, for his vision is not the realistic and varied one of the Indian, Scythian, merchant, prophet, hero, and Centaur, but is composed entirely of the Dionysian forms of his own mind. He does not project himself into the world, rather he assimilates the world unto himself. It flows through his mind rather than he flowing through it, and yet, neither is it the static, superficial, painted world of the Gods. It consists of forms, but these forms swim, waver, eddy, fade, and sweep. They move faster and faster. They are actually the forms of a Dionysian rout, and they are also the forms of the great life-circulation of nature. For as the Youth invokes earth, air, fire, and water, and cries out to Ulysses, "Thou . . . waved-toss'd Wanderer! Who can stand still?" it is evident that his questing imagination will take him much further than have the purely physical wanderings of much-enduring Ulysses. So much is expressed by the circular form of the poem, ending where it began with "the wild, thronging train, / The bright procession / of eddying forms." But the circular form also emphasizes the perfect stillness of the Youth. He, Circe, and their cup constitute a series of bright, hard, classical images which make up the substance of the poem: Circe, standing with her right arm against the column, her left propping her cheek; the Youth sunk in slumber, his white, delicate neck bending down to the margin of the cup; and the cup itself, the very symbol of Dionysian energy in an Apollonian form—

> See, how glows,
> Through the delicate, flush'd marble,
> The red, creaming liquor,
> Strown with dark seeds.

This is what Arnold would call "*lyric* fury." Just as the hurt of Mycerinus glows through his Epicurean stance, so the passion of the modern subjectivist poet glows through his sharp, chiselled, Parnassian forms.

3 THE WORLD AND THE QUIETIST

The time is out of joint; O cursed spite,
That ever I was born to set it right.
                                    —Hamlet

When the Revolution broke out in France in February 1848, both Arnold and Clough were vastly excited—though Clough much more than Arnold. The latter was unfortunately just then reading the *Bhagavad-Gita*, and although that poem does not discountenance action (quite the contrary), it does discourage setting one's heart upon the fruits of action. Arnold apparently recommended this point of view to Clough, for on March 1 he had to write, "I am disappointed the Oriental wisdom, God grant it were mine, pleased you not. To the Greeks, foolishness."[1] The last remark probably explains why Critias, in the poem *The World and the Quietist*, was given a Greek name and placed in opposition to the white-robed slave in the Persian palace. For essentially, the conflict between them is between the Eastern and the Western civilization, between contemplation and action, and Arnold takes his stand with the contemplative life of the East. To Critias, who is impatient with this position, Arnold replies that he knows that the world has decided in favor of action. With

1. *Letters to Clough*, pp. 69, 71, 75.

"credulous zeal" it calls for labourers to turn "life's mighty wheel."

> Yet, as the wheel flies round,
> With no ungrateful sound
> Do adverse voices fall on the world's ear.
> Deafen'd by his own stir
> The rugged labourer
> Caught not till then a sense
> So glowing and so near
>   Of his omnipotence.
>
> So, when the feast grew loud
> In Susa's palace proud,
> A white-robed slave stole to the Great King's side.
> He spake—the Great King heard;
> Felt the slow-rolling word
> Swell his attentive soul;
> Breathed deeply as it died,
>   And drain'd his mighty bowl.

In the letter of March 1 Arnold admits, "Certainly the present spectacle in France is a fine one: mostly so indeed to the historical swift-kindling man, who is not over-haunted by the pale thought, that, after all man's shiftings of posture, restat vivere."[2] The "pale thought" is clearly related to Hamlet's "pale cast of thought" by which "enterprises of great pith and moment / . . . their currents turn awry / And lose the name of action." It is also related to the "pale shape" which thrust in between Mycerinus and his bowl, and to the white-robed slave who performed the same office for the Persian king. But the white-robed slave, who can transform a Reveller into a Strayed Reveller by giving him pause, can do the same for the labourers who turn life's mighty wheel. By means of his "adverse voice," which speaks the "slow-rolling word," he can communicate a contrary motion to the

2. Ibid., p. 68.

mighty wheel which gives it the stasis of the "mighty bowl." Indeed, it is only in this way that the rugged labourer gains a sense of his "omnipotence" and so is transformed from a slave into a king. He is a king in the sense that he understands, and so rules, the nature and destiny of his own soul.

In these images from *The World and the Quietist* we have almost all the symbols which it will be necessary to use in discussing Arnold's social poems in the 1849 volume. Chief among them are the voice, the wheel, and the Slave. To speak first of the wheel, it is Arnold's chief symbol of the workaday world. When the wife of the Forsaken Merman retreats to the town, it is her "whizzing wheel" that symbolizes her busy but empty life, and as the whizzing wheel mingles with the "humming streets" of the "humming town," one can see that the town itself becomes a kind of wheel in the dull round of its activity. With its white walls and narrow streets, its shut doors and leaden panes, it also becomes a kind of prison, and it is clear that the two images merge in Arnold's mind. In *A Summer Night*, where he most fully develops the contrast between Madman and Slave, he uses the open image of the sea for the one and the closed image of the city for the other. In the city the windows "frown, / Silent and white, unopening down, / Repellent as the world," and this image then modulates into that of the prison.

> For most men in a brazen prison live,
> Where, in the sun's hot eye,
> With heads bent o'er their toil, they languidly
> Their lives to some unmeaning taskwork give,
> Dreaming of nought beyond their prison-wall.

In *Tristram and Iseult* the brazen prison becomes "the gradual furnace of the world," and in *Resignation* it is the "iron round [which] hems us all in," essentially what Carlyle calls the "ring of Necessity."[3] In sum, Arnold's image of the life of the Slave in-

3. *Sartor Resartus*, Bk. II, chap. 2.

volves a concept of the city as at once a furnace, a prison, and a mighty wheel.

In the eyes of the world this wheel is supposed to be an instrument of progress, and so Arnold does occasionally imagine it as the wheel of a chariot which carries us across the desert to our goal. Thus, in the Butler sonnet our unified powers provide "aërial arches all of gold, / Whereo'er the chariot wheels of life are roll'd / In cloudy circles to eternity." And in the sonnet to the Duke of Wellington, the Duke is praised because, through his faith, "the wheels of life / Stand never idle, but go always round." The Duke was able to do this, however, not through sheer energy, but because he "saw one clue to life, and follow'd it." This clue, which suggests that we should consider life as a kind of labyrinth or maze, was the "vision of the general law," that is, of the whole scope and tendency of human history. Other people, the mere sons of pleasure, setting their hands to the wheel, spun sand, and thus reduced the straight-line movement of progress to the circular movement of the Slave. In *Resignation* Fausta is entranced with this straight-line movement to some final goal and is impatient that she and her brother should be retracing their journey of ten years before. But the poet points out that the fierce questers whom she admires are really the slaves of their own passions, and that they, by adopting a circular path, have put themselves in harmony with the life-circulation of nature. As Wellington has had a vision of "the general law," so they have participated in the "general life," and this has set them free. Carlyle perceived that the way from the Everlasting No to the Everlasting Yea was to transform the ring of Necessity into the ring of Duty, which one does essentially by acceptance. This, too, is what Arnold has done. Instead of trying to transform the world through social action, he tries to understand it and place himself in harmony with it. This involves transforming the circular image of the wheel into the life-circulation of nature. In terms of the human image, it involves transforming the Slave into a "white-robed slave" or Quietist. For the white-robed slave stands to the true Slave in the same relation as the Strayed Reveller stands to the actual Reveller. Like the "halting slave" Epictetus in the sonnet *To a Friend*, he is one who assumes the guise of the Slave in order to be truly free.

The world of the Slave and the wheel Arnold analyzes more fully in his later criticism. In "The Function of Criticism at the Present Time," for example, he sees as the characteristic of his age that it lives in the aftermath of the French Revolution, and that this Revolution was dominated by a desire for the immediate practical application of the ideas which inspired it. Whereas in earlier periods it had been possible to entertain ideas simply for their own sake, in the period 1825 to 1850 ideas seemed to exist only for the purpose, first, of being believed, and then, of being acted upon. One was supposed, first, to take one's stand, and then, to put one's shoulder to the wheel. Thence came Tractarian movements and Evangelical movements and church reform. Thence came factories and railroads and iron bridges. Thence came the extension of the franchise, the new Poor Law, the regulation of the conditions of labor, the municipal corporations act, and a better system of education. What men had regarded earlier as the problem of evil, and had speculated upon, they now regarded as the "condition-of-England" question, and acted upon. To most persons this question was the more urgent because of the dangerous example set by France. Three times within little more than half a century France had known revolution, and in the decade after 1830 England was very fearful that she might also take this path. Therefore all good men, writers as well as statesmen, were moved by a sense of alarm. Tennyson in his early work seemed to hesitate between the symbol of a feminine figure immured in an ivory tower and that of a masculine figure sallying forth into the world, but in *The Palace of Art* he suggested a moratorium on art until the social problems of England were solved. Carlyle was increasingly impatient with belles lettres. In the series of works which made him probably the most potent voice in England in the 1840s—*Sartor Resartus, The*

French Revolution, Critical and Miscellaneous Essays, He-
roes and Hero-Worship, and *Past and Present*—he called upon
his countrymen to leave the playing with ideas and to realize
the idea in the actual. "Up, up! Whatsoever thy hand findeth to
do, do it with thy whole might. Work while it is called Today;
for the Night cometh, wherein no man can work."[4] In this way
the doctrine of work became the unofficial credo of the age.

This is the world in which Arnold grew up, and it is clear that
he found it an exciting but also an enervating place in which to
live. We see him, in his Oxford days, a member of the "little
interior company" described by his brother Tom and including
Tom, Clough, and Theodore Walrond. "We used often to go
skiffing up the Cherwell," wrote Tom, "or else in the network of
river channels that meander through the broad meadows facing
Iffley and Sandford. After a time it was arranged that we four
should always breakfast in Clough's rooms on Sunday morning.
These were times of great enjoyment. Sir Robert Peel was in
power; he was breaking loose more and more from the trammels
of mere party connexion, and the shrewd Rentoul [Rintoul], who
then edited the *Spectator,* welcomed in the Conservative chief the
only true statesman that England had seen since the days of Can-
ning. The *Spectator* of the day before used to arrive at breakfast-
time, and the leading articles were eagerly read and discussed."[5]

For more extended discussion there was the Decade, an in-
formal debating society which included the little interior com-
pany and, in addition, Benjamin Jowett, Arthur Stanley, John
Duke Coleridge, J. C. Shairp, and several others. It handled
subjects somewhat graver than those discussed at the Union, and
all those who have reported on it seem to agree that Clough was
its most brilliant speaker. No other member of the society, ac-
cording to Tom, "spoke in so rich, penetrating, original, and
convincing a strain . . . He was not rapid, yet neither was he slow

4. Ibid., chap. 9.
5. T[homas] Arnold, Jr., "Arthur Hugh Clough: a Sketch," *Nineteenth
Century,* 43 (1898), 106–07.

or hesitating; he seemed just to take time enough to find the right word or phrase wherein to clothe his thought. My recollections have grown sadly dim; but I remember one debate when he spoke to a resolution that I had proposed in favour of Lord Ashley's Ten Hours Bill. In supporting the resolution he combated the doctrines of *laissez faire* and the omnipotence and sufficiency of the action of Supply and Demand, then hardly disputed in England, with an insight marvellous in one who had so little experience of the industrial life, and at the same time with a strict and conscientious moderation."[6] At another time he spoke on "the future politics of the world, the connexion of the world and of the Church," of which Frederick Temple said that "the grandeur of the thought and the splendour of the language quite carried him away." Of Arnold it is only recorded that he failed to appear when he was supposed to have spoken on behalf of Wordsworth against the contention that "Alfred Tennyson is the greatest poet of his age."[7]

Tennyson had himself belonged to a similar debating society at Cambridge, the Apostles, and we are told that he was actually read out of the organization for refusing to produce an expected paper on "Ghosts." It appears, then, that poets are not good members of debating societies, and yet, both the Decade and the Apostles were images of the mighty world, which, in the 1840s, was a place of contending voices. In the most vivid picture which Arnold has left us of his undergraduate days, the exordium to his lecture on Emerson, he declares: "Forty years ago, when I was an undergraduate at Oxford, voices were in the air there which haunt my memory still. Happy the man who in that susceptible season of youth hears such voices! They are a possession to him for ever. No such voices as those which we heard in our youth at Oxford are sounding there now. Oxford has more criticism now, more knowledge, more light; but such voices as

6. Ibid., p. 107.
7. *Letters to Clough*, p. 21 n.; William S. Knickerbocker, "Matthew Arnold at Oxford," *Sewanee Review*, 35 (1927), 414.

those of our youth it has no longer." The voices which Arnold mentions are those of Newman, preaching in St. Mary's pulpit every Sunday afternoon and seeming "about to transform and to renew what was for us the most national and natural institution in the world, the Church of England"; the voice of Carlyle, not sorely strained then, but "fresh, comparatively sound, and reaching our hearts with true, pathetic eloquence"; through Carlyle the voice of Goethe, "the greatest voice of the century," bringing to us "the large, liberal view of human life in *Wilhelm Meister*"; and finally, from over the Atlantic, the clear, pure voice of Emerson.[8] To these we should add (and Arnold himself did so in another essay) the voice of George Sand: "Days of *Valentine*," he cries, "days of *Lélia*, days never to return! They are gone, we shall read the books no more, and yet how ineffaceable is their impression! How the sentences from George Sand's works of that period still linger in our memory and haunt the ear with their cadences!"[9] She too was one of the voices that were in the air at Oxford.

But what is a voice? In Arnold's thought it seems to mean two things. It may be a summons to the will, a clarion call to action, or it may be simply that which gives voice to, or articulates, experience. The distinction is important because it is clear that Arnold listened to the voices at Oxford in one way, whereas Clough and Tom, the two persons who were nearest to him at the time, listened to them in another. They listened to them as calls to action and belief, whereas he listened to them simply as voices—*vox et praeterea nihil.*

Take, for example, the voice of George Sand. We are told that what particularly entranced Arnold about her was the vision which her novels presented of a life of personal and artistic freedom. But in a letter of 1845 he shows himself perfectly aware that to adopt her vision would be to lose the very freedom of which she spoke. "A Code-G.-Sand would make G. Sands impos-

8. *Discourses in America* (1896), pp. 138–39, 142–43.
9. *Mixed Essays* (New York, 1883), p. 242.

sible," he wrote, and he appealed to Clough not to join "my misguided Relation," Tom, in becoming an "Emotee."[10]

So, too, with Goethe. What moved Arnold most in *Wilhelm Meister*, he says, "was that which, after all, will always move the young the most,—the poetry, the eloquence." But what moved Tom most was the vision, presented in the second part of the novel, of "an organised society closely linked with the past, directed by a 'Bond' of wise and good men," and he immediately wondered whether this vision "might not contain the true medicine for the world's maladies." Therefore, in November 1847, his head filled, as he himself says, with fancies of "some kind of Pantisocracy, with beautiful details and imaginary local establishments such as Coleridge never troubled himself to formulate,"[11] he shipped out to New Zealand to become the nucleus of a new society. The sequel is strangely pathetic but not entirely unpredictable. Clearing a plot of ground for which he hoped to exchange his own less desirable site, he found that he could not exchange it and so went on to Tasmania, where he was converted to Roman Catholicism. He then returned to England, was reconverted to the Anglican faith and finally converted back to Catholicism, ending his life as one of Newman's co-workers in the Catholic University of Ireland.

For Tom, then, listening to George Sand and Goethe had led to their antithesis in Newman. What was the case with Arnold? Like Tom, he did not arrive in Oxford till 1841, just after the affair of Tract 90, and so saw the Movement only in its decline. But he attended the Sunday afternoon sermons at St. Mary's and, on occasion, followed Newman out to Littlemore to hear him preach. He always thought that these sermons were Newman's best work, and he probably did so because he heard them in the compelling accents of a living voice. Indeed, it is likely that the metaphor of the voice, which he uses in the lecture on

10. Ward, *A Writer's Recollections*, p. 12; *Letters to Clough*, p. 59.
11. Arnold, *Discourses in America* (1896), p. 144; T. Arnold, Jr., *Passages in a Wandering Life*, pp. 151, 64.

Emerson, is really derived primarily from Newman, whom alone he would have heard speak, and is only by courtesy extended to the others, whom he would have read on the printed page. For when we remember that J. C. Shairp in his poem *Balliol Scholars* speaks of Newman simply as a "voice," and that Froude in his famous description of Newman's preaching emphasizes the silvery intonation of his voice,[12] we realize that among this group of young Oxford men, most of whom did not know Newman personally but merely heard him preach, it was customary to think of him primarily as a voice. The question is, what kind of voice, a summons to the will or a voice and nothing more? To his brother Tom, Arnold gave assurances that it was the latter, that he attended the Sunday afternoon sermons simply for the sake of their literary style. By Newman's opinions, said Tom, "he was never touched in the smallest degree."[13] On the other hand, we know that this is exactly what Arnold would have said, simply as part of his literary stance, and we know too that in the lecture on Emerson he does not speak so indifferently. "Who could resist," he says, "the charm of that spiritual apparition, gliding in the dim afternoon light through the aisles of St. Mary's, rising into the pulpit, and then, in the most entrancing of voices, breaking the silence with words and thoughts which were a religious music,—subtle, sweet, mournful? I seem to hear him still."[14] And so, in the poem entitled simply *The Voice* and containing the invocation, "O unforgotten voice!" we inevitably wonder if the voice is not that of Newman. The poet speaks of hearing this voice again after many years and of its coming upon his heart "anxiously and painfully . . . drearily and doubtfully,"

> And oh, with such intolerable change
> Of thought, such contrast strange.

12. Shairp, "Balliol Scholars," *Macmillan's Magazine*, 27 (1873), 376, J. A. Froude, *Short Studies on Great Subjects* (London, 1917), pp. 284, 286.

13. T. Arnold, Jr., *Passages in a Wandering Life*, p. 57; Ward, *A Writer's Recollections*, p. 12.

14. *Discourses in America* (1896), pp. 139-40.

When, we are compelled to ask, could this have been? When could Arnold have heard Newman a second time under conditions so drear? Undoubtedly it was in April 1848, when Newman, now a Catholic, delivered a series of Lenten sermons in several of the churches in London.[15] Arnold was in London at the time and it is unlikely that he would not have attended. It would have been his first opportunity to hear Newman since his conversion, and hence the "intolerable change of thought," the "contrast strange." We know, too, that the sermons, which Newman gave on the urgent invitation of Cardinal Wiseman and much against his will, were poorly attended, a dismal failure, almost the only failure in preaching which Newman ever experienced. As a result, his voice might well have been described as anxious and painful by one who had known him in his prime. But the interesting point is that in the last stanza we are told what effect that voice had had upon the speaker when he first heard it.

> Those lute-like tones which in the bygone year
>   Did steal into mine ear—
> Blew such a thrilling summons to my will,
>   Yet could not shake it;
> Made my tost heart its very life-blood spill,
>   Yet could not break it.

It was not true, then, if the poem is about Newman, that Arnold attended the sermons simply for the sake of their style, and that by Newman's opinions he was not touched in the smallest degree. He was touched; he felt the voice as a siren's voice, but he had taken the precaution of Ulysses to lash himself to the mast of noncommittment, and so he sailed untroubled by.

15. The suggestion that *The Voice* refers to Newman was first made by Kathleen Tillotson in a review of E. K. Chambers' biography in *Review of English Studies*, 24 (1948), 265. For Newman's Lenten sermons, see Wilfrid Ward, *The Life of John Henry Cardinal Newman* (London, 1913), 1, 205–06; *The Letters and Diaries of John Henry Newman*, ed. C. S. Dessain (London, 1962), 12, 201. In 1855 Arnold wrote to his brother, "Newman . . . is gone off greatly, they say, as a preacher" (Ward, *A Writer's Recollections*, p. 53).

That Arnold was deeply drawn to the Tractarian ideal is also suggested by several other poems. In the late work *Obermann Once More* he has his protagonist declare, " 'Oh, had I lived in that great day' "—the day of the birth-time of Christianity—

> 'How had its glory new
> Fill'd earth and heaven, and caught away
> My ravish'd spirit too! . . .
>
> 'No cloister-floor of humid stone
> Had been too cold for me.
> For me no Eastern desert lone
> Had been too far to flee.'

Of course, Arnold did not live in "that great day," and so such an action was unthinkable. But in one of his early poems he took as his subject a young monk who did live in an Eastern desert lone in the birth-time of Christianity. His name was Stagirius, and he has entered into history because, on being vexed by a devil, he was addressed a letter in three books by St. Chrysostom. In Arnold's poem he is represented as speaking a litany, and the problem of the poem is that we do not know how far to sympathize with the speaker. One reader has taken it as a critique of Romantic melancholy because Stagirius is so interpreted in a work by Saint-Marc Girardin which Arnold read in 1848.[16] But the poem was composed in 1844 at a time when St. Chrysostom was a key figure in the Tractarian movement. All through the late 'thirties and early 'forties books by and about him were being published in considerable numbers as a part of the controversy over the nature of the Church. Arnold's father had a long-standing interest in putting forth an edition of St. Chrysostom, and Arnold himself took two volumes of St. Chrysostom's works out

16. Kenneth Allott, "Matthew Arnold's 'Stagirius' and Saint-Marc Girardin," *Review of English Studies*, n.s., 9 (1958), 286–92. Allott does make the point that the spelling of the name "Stagyrus," in the 1849 edition, probably derived from Saint-Marc Girardin.

of the Oriel library in March 1846 and April 1849.[17] In view of these facts it is difficult to suppose that the poem did not originally have some association for Arnold with the Tractarian movement. Probably it was intended as a serious litany in which the deprecations of the Book of Common Prayer were replaced by those relating to the more subjective evils of the modern spirit. But if so, then the poem becomes another example, like *The New Sirens* and *A Modern Sappho*, of Arnold's taking an ancient type and reinterpreting it in the form in which it appeared in the modern world. A "modern Stagirius," however, could only be a young Tractarian.

If this is what *Stagirius* means, then it is Arnold's most Tractarian poem. For by 1849 he was projecting a work under the title, *To Meta—the cloister & life liveable*, which, if we may judge from what appears to be a fragment, would have represented the cloister as a haven of peace but of the peace that is a living tomb.[18] It was not a "life liveable." This, too, is the view in *Stanzas from the Grande Chartreuse*. That poem resulted from a visit which Arnold made to the monastery of the Grande Chartreuse on his wedding trip in 1851, and we recall that after describing the life of the monks he suddenly declares, "And what am I, that I am here?" The question is put with a certain grim humor because Arnold is well aware that a young Oxford man visiting a continental monastery in 1851 might easily be queried about his intentions. But the reassuring reply comes:

> rigorous teachers seized my youth,
> And purged its faith, and trimm'd its fire,
> Show'd me the high, white star of Truth,
> There bade me gaze, and there aspire.

These rigorous teachers were probably Goethe and Spinoza,

---

17. Arthur P. Stanley, *Life and Correspondence of Thomas Arnold,* 5th ed., (London, 1845), 1, 216; *Register of Books Taken out of the Oriel College Library by the Provost and Fellows* (MS, Oriel).

18. Tinker and Lowry, pp. 12–13, 338–40.

among others, for Tom tells us that in 1842, following their father's death, Matthew "plunged his spirit very deeply . . . in the vast sea of Goethe's art and Spinoza's mysticism. He had already in 1845 drifted far away from Orthodox Christianity, so that the appearance of the translation of Strauss's 'Leben Jesu' in that year [actually 1846]—an epoch-making book for many—found him incurious and uninterested."[19] Probably one should rather say that it found him curious in the French sense and disinterested—just as he was about Catholicism. For in Arnold's view, Catholicism was to Strauss as the forest glade to the burning plain. The latter was a fact with which he had long been familiar, and so he was not upset when it was announced in 1846. The former was an illusion from which he had long been freed, and so he was not inclined to believe it when it was preached at St. Mary's. But he liked Catholicism much better than he did Strauss. All through his prose works he shows to Newman, the Tractarian movement, and the Roman Catholic religion a sympathy which he never shows to the opposite camp.[20] Unfortunately, their religion was not true. As he said in his lecture on Emerson, "Cardinal Newman . . . in his Oratory . . . has adopted, for the doubts and difficulties which beset men's minds to-day, a solution which, to speak frankly, is impossible."[21] If it had been possible, it would have been much to be desired, for at the same time that Arnold rejected the dogma of orthodox Christianity, he greatly admired its ethos and temper. He saw that Newman and the Tractarians were doing in the realm of religion what he wished to do in the realm of culture. They were creating a center of authority whereby the individual could correct and discipline his own nature. But whereas Newman saw this authority as divine, Arnold saw it as human. It was Arnold's view that as time went

19. [T. Arnold, Jr.], *Manchester Guardian* (May 18, 1888), p. 8.

20. *Essays in Criticism: First Series* (1902), pp. 20, 60, 69, 142 ff., 194 ff.; *Second Series* (New York, 1900), p. 238; *On the Study of Celtic Literature* (New York, 1906), p. 22; Super, *3*, 44, 97, 244, 250, 305.

21. *Discourses in America* (1896), p. 139.

on poetry would more and more take the place of religion, and one may say that Arnold's treatment of Newman is a prime example of this process. For what Newman wrote dogmatically Arnold read poetically, and so he assimilated Newman into his own humanistic system.

Hence, Arnold could write to Newman in 1871: "I cannot forbear adding, what I have often wished to tell you, that no words can be too strong to express the interest with which I used to hear you at Oxford, and the pleasure with which I continue to read your writings now." And then, with a quaint apology for not having become a Catholic, he adds, "We are all of us carried in ways not of our own making or choosing, but nothing can ever do away the effect you have produced upon me, for it consists in a general disposition of mind rather than in a particular set of ideas." A few months later he adds, "There are four people, in especial, from whom I am conscious of having learnt—a very different thing from merely receiving a strong impression— learnt habits, methods, ruling ideas, which are constantly with me; and the four are—Goethe, Wordsworth, Sainte-Beuve, and yourself. You will smile and say I have made an odd mixture and that the result must be a jumble . . ."[22] Jumble or not, it was Arnold's peculiar strength that he did not take up with Newman —or with any of the other voices of his youth—and that he could adopt a general disposition of mind without giving himself to a particular set of ideas.

If we turn now from the contrast between Arnold and Tom to that between Arnold and Clough, we find the situation partly different and partly the same. For if Tom is the person who marries in haste and repents at leisure, Clough is the one who does not not marry at all and grows peaked through frustration. Arnold, on the other hand, is the happy bachelor. Arnold "grappled with the same problems as Clough," said Max Müller, "but they never got the better of him, or rather he never got the worse of them."

22. *Unpublished Letters*, pp. 56, 65–66.

Part of the reason for this was that Arnold, according to Tom, "had the temper of an observer and an interpreter," not of a teacher and reformer. He "did not at first care about reforming the world or any part of it, not even middle-class education; his ambition was to understand and estimate aright men and books." Clough, on the other hand, did care about reforming the world. As Dr. Arnold's prize pupil at Rugby he wrote, "I verily believe my whole being is regularly soaked through with the wishing and hoping and striving to do the School good, or rather to keep it up and hinder it from falling in this, I do think, very critical time . . ." This was fine when he had Dr. Arnold to tell him what the good was, but when Dr. Arnold died and he was exposed at Oxford to the contrary voices of Newman, Strauss, and Carlyle, he became confused and did not know what to do. His friend W. G. Ward pressed him hard with the dilemma, either the whole of Roman Catholic doctrine or atheism, and in the exhaustion which followed he seems to have been inclined to give up speculation altogether and devote himself to humble tasks of social betterment which he knew were right. In this he was listening to the voice of Carlyle: "Do the Duty which lies nearest thee . . . Thy second Duty will already have become clearer." But alas, it did not. In the summer of 1848, when Clough was bidding farewell to Emerson, he said, "What shall we do without you? Think where we are. Carlyle has led us all out into the desert, and he has left us there." Emerson noted that many young men in England had made similar comments to him.[23]

Thus Clough became the image of his own Dipsychus. "You ask me," wrote Arnold in 1853,

> in what I think or have thought you going wrong: in this: that you would never take your assiette as something de-

23. Müller, *Auld Lang Syne*, p. 112; [T. Arnold, Jr.], *Manchester Guardian* (May 18, 1888), p. 8; Clough, *Correspondence*, 1, 35; Katherine Chorley, *Arthur Hugh Clough: The Uncommitted Mind* (Oxford, 1962), p. 104 n.; *Sartor Resartus*, Bk. II, chap. 9; E. E. Hale, *James Russell Lowell and His Friends* (Boston, 1899), p. 136.

termined final and unchangeable for you and proceed to work away on the basis of that: but were always poking and patching and cobbling at the assiette itself—could never finally, as it seemed—'resolve to be thyself'—but were looking for this and that experience, and doubting whether you ought not to adopt this or that mode of being of persons qui ne vous valaient pas because it might possibly be nearer the truth than your own: you had no reason for thinking it *was*, but it *might* be—and so you would try to adapt yourself to it. You have I am convinced lost infinite time in this way: it is what I call your morbid conscientiousness—you are the most conscientious man I ever knew: but on some lines morbidly so, and it spoils your action.[24]

It is the fashion now to deprecate Arnold's criticism of Clough, and it is true that he was not handsome in his treatment of his friend. Yet in this instance he was surely right. If Clough could have thrown off this incubus of conscience and given himself to his natural gaiety of spirits, he would have been a fine writer. His first long poem, *The Bothie of Tober-na-Vuolich,* is a delightful treatment of the high jinks of an undergraduate reading party. But only the first half is truly delightful. For as the poem proceeds the hero becomes worried whether the *summum bonum* of life is Beauty, in the form of a high-born maiden, or Utility, in the form of a peasant lass with a fork uprooting potatoes. In pursuit of this question he zig-zags back and forth across Scotland and finally compromises on Elspie Mackaye, who combines Beauty with Utility in that form commonly known as the Good. Together they emigrate to New Zealand. The poem is as nearly resolved as any of Clough's are, and yet it would be truer to say that it is not resolved, merely deferred to another country. In the two poems which follow, indecision is carried further. In *Amours de Voyage,* which is a kind of poor man's *Werther,* the hero toys idly with arms and the woman and ultimately gives himself to neither; and

24. *Letters to Clough,* p. 130.

in *Dipsychus* he toys with the world, the flesh, and the devil, and ultimately remains undecided, not about them, but about whether his own work is a crude melodrama or a sophisticated self-parody. One cannot help admiring the fresh modernity of Clough's work, but in *Dipsychus* he has carried the anti-poem to the point of producing no poem at all.

The basic problem may have been sexual, for Clough's three poems contain more sex than all the works of Tennyson, Arnold, and Browning put together, but overtly it takes the form of religious doubt and social guilt. The dramatic moment in Clough's life came in 1848 when he threw up his tutorship and later his fellowship at Oriel College. The ostensible reason for this was a dispute with Edward Hawkins, the provost, about re-subscribing the Thirty-Nine Articles of the Anglican religion, but the deeper reason seems to have been an impatience with the trifling character of academic life at a time when all the world around him was in ferment. Ireland was in her second year of famine, and England had just passed through its most severe economic crisis since 1825. In February revolution broke out in France, and in April the final convulsion of Chartism was enacted in monster processions through the streets of London. It was in response to this that Clough left Oxford,

> o'ermastered by the stress
> Of yearning for the myriads of his kind,
> Who, buried in the city's wilderness,
> Unknown, uncared for, pined.[25]

So says Shairp in his elegy on Clough, and Arnold says the same in *Thyrsis*.

> Some life of men unblest
> He knew, which made him droop, and fill'd his head.
> He went; his piping took a troubled sound

25. William Knight, *Principal Shairp and His Friends* (London, 1888), p. 89.

Of storms that rage outside our happy ground;
He could not wait their passing, he is dead.

Initially, the revolution was a wonderful tonic to Clough. "If it were not for all these blessed revolutions," he wrote, "I should sink into hopeless lethargy." He declared that in Oxford he had the reputation of being "the wildest and most écervelé republican going," so much so that on March 7 Arnold mischievously addressed him a letter inscribed to "Citizen Clough, Oriel Lyceum, Oxford."[26] It may have been in this very letter that Arnold enclosed the two sonnets *To a Republican Friend,* for the title seems to continue the jest and the sonnets were certainly written just about the first week in March. They seem to have been partly inspired by a "deeply restful" article which Carlyle had contributed to the *Examiner* on March 4. "The source of repose" in this article, Arnold explained to his mother, "is that he alone puts aside the din and whirl and brutality which envelope a movement of the masses, to fix his thoughts on its ideal invisible character." This too is what Arnold attempted to do in his sonnets. But whereas Carlyle had fixed upon the fall of Louis Philippe as the destruction of sham, Arnold fixed upon the problem of what the new regime would be able to do. For it was upon this point that he and his republican friend differed, in other things "agreeing like two lambs in a world of wolves."[27] "God knows it, I am with you," he exclaimed in the first sonnet—with you in the high hopes you entertain for humanity; but in the second sonnet he adds:

Yet, when I muse on what life is, I seem
Rather to patience prompted, than that proud
Prospect of hope which France proclaims so loud—
France, famed in all great arts, in none supreme.

26. *Letters to Clough,* p. 67; Clough, *Correspondence,* 1, 216; Tinker and Lowry, p. 33. The envelope addressed to Citizen Clough is in the Yale collection.
27. *Letters,* 1, 4, 6.

The reason for this patience is expressed in two images of limitation—the "Uno'erleap'd Mountains of Necessity," which represent the limits imposed on man by God or Nature, and the "network," which represents the limits imposed upon him by his fellow man. Clough might well have been irritated by this double barrier, since presumably it was not the purpose of the revolution to o'erleap the Mountains of Necessity, merely to break through the network imposed by man. Arnold himself had admitted as much in a letter a few days earlier. Commenting on the "twaddle" which the *Times* had put forth about "the eternal relations between labour and capital," he opined that these relations would not prove so eternal if the whole nation resolved to live by justice. "If there is necessity anywhere," he said, "it is in the Corruption of man, as Tom might say, only.—" But the corruption of man is not a part of the network, rather of the Mountains of Necessity, and it is ultimately upon this point that Arnold takes his stand. "After all man's shiftings of posture," he declared, "restat vivere"[28]—the problem of living remains. The new social arrangements, however admirable, will still have to be made to work, and the question is, does France, "famed in all great arts, in none supreme," have the depth of soul to do it?

For at this point Arnold's thinking turns to that question of national character which engrossed him so profoundly in later years, and as he compared the English with the French, he felt that the great advantage of the latter lay in the wide diffusion of a high level of general intelligence, so that they were capable of being "*Idea-moved masses*" and of creating a revolution. The English, on the other hand, were relatively insensible to ideas, and though they might be roused by French example, their action, if they were roused, would only be "brutal and plundering." "But I do not say that these people in France have much dreamed of the deepest wants of man, or are likely to enlighten the world much on the subject . . ." Indeed, "taken individually, the French

28. *Letters to Clough*, pp. 68–69.

people, no more than one's own, are up to the measure of the ideal citizen they seem to propose to themselves; this thought constantly presses on me . . ." But the English—the best of the English, that is—have dreamed of the deepest wants of man and could enlighten the world on this subject. Therefore, if we as a nation were to cease imitating the French, particularly the French effort to create rational societies, and were to follow our own national line and drive "our feet into the solid ground of our individuality as spiritual, poetic, profound *persons*," we would be doing a great service both to the world and to ourselves.[29]

Arnold himself has exemplified this process in his two sonnets, for the second, in which he expresses his doubts about the revolution, is a much better poem than the first, in which he expresses his hopes. Partly this is due to the powerful image of the Mountains of Necessity, but more especially it is due to the tone of quieter and more profound meditation established by the line, "Yet, when I muse on what life is . . ." The first sonnet with its smart rhetorical structure of "If . . . if . . . if . . . if . . . then," seems to echo the loud proclaiming of proud hopes from shallow France; whereas the second, which gives the other side of the picture, is spoken by the "adverse voice" of the Quietist.

The events of 1848 undoubtedly caused Arnold to think more intensively about social and political problems than he had done hitherto. His *Horatian Echo*, written in 1847, merely expresses lighthearted indifference to the events of the day:

> Omit, omit, my simple friend,
> Still to enquire how parties tend,
> Or what we fix with foreign powers.
> If France and we are really friends,
> And what the Russian Czar intends,
> Is no concern of ours.

True, this indifference has as its purpose to "cloak the troubles of the heart / With pleasant smile" in the approved fashion of a

29. *Ibid.*, pp. 72, 73; *Letters*, 1, 6, 7, 4.

Strayed Reveller, but it is a fairly frivolous poem. Later in the same year, when confronted by the evil of drunkenness in George Cruikshank's engravings, Arnold rejected both the Romantic view that it will not happen and the Utilitarian view that it can be cured. Instead, he accepted the Stoic view that it must be borne and is of limited significance.

> The soul
> Breasts her own griefs; and, urged too fiercely, says:
> 'Why tremble? True, the nobleness of man
> May be by man effaced; man can control
> To pain, to death, the bent of his own days.
> Know thou the worst! So much, not more, he *can!*

Since Adam Roy, the subject of Cruikshank's engravings, murders his wife with the bottle, reduces himself to imbecility, his son to the poorhouse, and his daughter to the streets, Arnold's reassurance that this is the most he can do is perhaps a little bracing. Yet in 1869 he chose to emphasize this thought by changing the title of the sonnet to *Human Limits:* "So much, not more, he *can.*"

The sonnets *To a Republican Friend* are both more serious and more humane than these earlier works, and essentially they embody the views which we will find later in *Culture and Anarchy*. These views place Arnold in the conservative ethical tradition which, on the one hand, fades off into the severity of Hobbes, Malthus, and Carlyle and, on the other, rises into the idealism of Plato and Emerson. Burke lies close to its center. It is a position so ethically radical that it is politically and socially conservative. It distrusts the new naturalistic schools of Romanticism on the one hand and Utilitarianism on the other, together with their cohorts, the Evangelicals. These three groups were the principal movers in nineteenth-century social reform, but though they often worked together, their methods were different. To the Utilitarians the alleviating of distress was primarily an intellectual problem in which one first ascertained the causes of the evil and then applied the remedies, educational, legislative, or technological, which lay at the disposal of society. To the Romantics and the Evangelicals, on the other hand, the task was primarily an individual matter which had as its basis, not the intellect, but the sympathy or fellow-feeling which one had for a brother in distress. Hence, they gave it the name "philanthropy." The conservative was skeptical of both these efforts. On the one hand, he doubted the means which they employed, and, on the other, he could not highly approve the end. He doubted the means of the Romantics and the Evangelicals because people are not generally altruistic and they do not feel much drawn to so abstract a concept as the brotherhood of man. If they feel charitable impulses at all, it is likely to be towards their own little group—their family, their friends, their parish—the particular people whom they know. And, on the other hand, he doubted the means of the Utilitarian because the laws and arrangements of society are not so easily altered as the Utilitarians suppose. There are eternal laws, laws of Nature and of God, which have prescribed that there always will be a certain margin of distress and that attempts to reduce it, as in the Poor Laws, may actually be mischievous, certainly will be of no avail. But most of all, the conservative could not highly approve of the end which these philanthropic endeavors proposed, an end which, by and large, was the materialistic and relativistic one of personal happiness. It was better to make people good, and this one did by transforming the people themselves, not their external circumstances. It was all very well to give them more means, but how they would use their means was still a question, and the conservative did not think that you were likely to get a good society until you got good people to compose it. This was a matter for the people themselves. It was a question, not of the intellect or the feeling, but of the will, of conforming the will to that absolute standard of excellence which was the law of Nature and of God.

These being Arnold's views, it is difficult to believe that he was very deeply attached to the legislative program of the Whig government with which he was associated. As secretary to Lord Lansdowne, the President of Council, he seems to have spent his time chiefly in reading. "Who prop, thou ask'st, in these bad days, my mind?" and the answer is Homer, Epictetus, and Sophocles—not the proposals of Lord John Russell. In a letter, hitherto unpublished, written to Lord Shelburne, the son of Lord Lansdowne, on the occasion of the latter's death, Arnold says: "Lord Lansdowne took me as his Private Secretary when I had not the slightest claim of any sort upon him, and solely from his interest in my father's memory: I was four years and a half with him and during all that time never had from him one sharp or impatient word: my situation with him gave me, besides many other advantages, comparative leisure for reading at a time of my life when such leisure was of the greatest value to me: he enabled me to marry: and he has treated me with unvarying kindness ever since. And when I speak of his kindness, I can never forget that of Lady Lansdowne also."[30] This personal kindness does not mean, of course, that Arnold agreed with "my man" (as he less formally calls him in the letters to Clough) in every detail, and there is one poem which seems to express the kind of disagreement that they had.

It is called *The Youth of Man*, and it represents the poet as standing with an aged couple who, years before, had declared, "Man is the king of the world!" and had said that these mystics who prate of the beauty of nature are fools, for they do not realize that beauty is not in nature but is in the beholder's eye. But now, old and infirm, their eye is dim, and so they cannot see that the prospect from their castled house, with its grey-walled garden and grey balustrade, is as lovely as ever—the wide valley with cornfield and hamlet and copse, the light still playing on the city spires, and the imperial stream floating silently on to the sea. If Arnold had not republished a tiny segment of this poem under the title *Richmond Hill*, we should never have been able

30. Letter dated February 2, 1863 (in the possession of the Marquis of Lansdowne). For "my man," see *Letters to Clough*, p. 70 n.

to guess that the prospect he describes is the famous one just to the south and west of London. But with this clue we can easily see that it is, and indeed one can go to Richmond Hill and pick out almost the exact spot where the speaker in the poem must have stood. And if he takes along a guidebook of the period, he will learn that on this spot in the 1840s and 1850s stood a residence of the Marquis of Lansdowne, a fact which immediately gives to the poem an autobiographical significance which it did not have before.[31] Clearly, there are fictional elements, but in 1850–51, the probable date of the poem, Lord Lansdowne was seventy years of age and badly crippled with gout. Further, as a disciple of Bentham and Dugald Stewart he undoubtedly held the views on the subjectivity of beauty and on man's power to make his own world, which are attributed to the aged couple in the poem. With Protagoras he would have declared that "Man is the measure of all things," and his young secretary would

31. *The Visitor's Hand-Book to Richmond, Kew Gardens, and Hampton Court* (London, Cradock & Co., [c. 1849]) explains that on Upper Road, leading from Hill Street to Richmond Park, is, on the right, "*Cardigan-house*, which belonged to the late Earl of Cardigan; and a seat of the Marquis of Lansdowne. These two mansions enjoy eminent attraction of prospect over the winding course of the Thames. The upper division of the Marquis of Lansdowne's grounds—in which is an Artesian well 320 feet in depth—is connected by a subterraneous passage under the Petersham road, with the gardens on the lower part of the hill, which extend to the towing path on the banks of the river" (p. 14). Cf. also *The Picturesque Pocket Companion to Richmond and Its Vicinity* (London, [1850]), p. 42. As the poem must be dated either 1850 or 1851 and as the house was occupied in the summer of 1851 by the two Miss Berrys, the friends of Horace Walpole (Edward Walford, *Greater London*, London, 1895, 2, 374), the experience upon which the poem is based, if any, must have occurred in the former year. One may note that *The Youth of Nature* is also connected with Richmond by the fact that its opening lines seem to echo Wordsworth's *Remembrance of Collins composed upon the Thames near Richmond*, which in turn echoes Collins' *Ode on the Death of Mr. Thomson*, the scene of which "is suppos'd to lie on the *Thames* near *Richmond.*" Cf. Walter E. Bezanson, "Melville's Reading of Arnold's Poetry," *PMLA*, 69 (1954), 378–79.

have held precisely the contrary view of the speaker in the poem.

Finally, Arnold's views on society are summarized most effectively in *The Sick King in Bokhara*. The story, as Arnold tells it, is of a certain Moollah—that is, one learned in the sacred law —who, at a time when all the city was suffering from a terrible drought, found a little pool of water under some mulberry trees and, taking it up in a pitcher, concealed the whole of it for himself. But his mother and brother discovered it while he slept and drank it all, and when he rose up, all sick with fever, and found out what they had done, he cursed them—cursed his mother— a crime punishable by death in the Moslem law. Being a good Moslem, the man demanded his punishment, but the King put him by, thinking he must be mad. A second and a third time he returned, and so at last the King had him tried by a congress of the priests, who sentenced him to death as the law required. The man died "with a great joy upon his face," but the King was plunged into grief because he had been powerless to save him.

Arnold found this tale, or rather the elements of it, in Captain Sir Alexander Burnes' *Travels into Bokhara* (1834), and it is not difficult to see what attracted him to the story. Burnes was a young Englishman of liberal humanitarian views, but of limited intelligence, who, although quite tolerant of differences in dress and custom among the nations he passed through, was frequently outraged by anything which violated his moral or religious sensibilities. Thus, his narrative is punctuated by indignant comments on the Bokharan slave trade, the administration of justice, and the fanaticism of the Moslem religion; and the episode of the Moollah is told to illustrate "the rigour of the Mohammedan law." It is concluded by the statement that "to this day verses commemorate the death of this unfortunate man, whom we must either pronounce a bigot or a madman."[32]

Doubtless it was this phrase that made Arnold's hackles rise

32. Vol. 1, pp. 307–08; cf. Tinker and Lowry, pp. 85–89.

and led him to reinterpret the story so that it would not appear that everyone who believed in the existence of absolute values was either a bigot or a madman. He saw in the theocratic state of Bokhara a type of what Newman would call the dogmatic principle, and in the young King and his English sympathizer he saw a perfect instance of the sentimental humanitarianism, whether of the Benthamite or Evangelical variety, which was leading the age into pure ethical relativism. He only needed to sharpen the antagonism between them by modifying certain details in the anecdote as Burnes had told it. In Burnes the crime of the Moollah was not specified. Arnold took the crime of cursing one's mother from another anecdote because that was an act which, although it violated a religious taboo, could not really be said to have done any harm in the Utilitarian sense. And then, since this curse had not been motivated in Burnes, he added the detail of the drought and the man's burning fever to provide him with every extenuating circumstance. In this way he devised a fable which would illustrate, even more neatly than Dostoevky's *Crime and Punishment*, the conflict between redemptive and sociological justice.

To this conflict Arnold added a second theme, closely related, arising out of the young King's grief for the slain Moollah. The King is advised by his aged Vizier that his grief is unwise, for the man was nothing to him and, if we are to grieve for those unrelated to us, we will have no end of sorrow.

> But who, through all this length of time,
> Could bear the burden of his years,
> If he for strangers pain'd his heart
> Not less than those who merit tears?

> Fathers we *must* have, wife and child,
> And grievous is the grief for these;
> This pain alone, which *must* be borne,
> Makes the head white, and bows the knees.

If we consider the matter well, we must realize that all over the world people are suffering from sickness, poverty, slavery, war. "Wilt thou have pity on all these?" asks the Vizier. "No, nor on this dead dog, O King."

It is difficult for the modern reader, raised in the humanitarian tradition, to accept this harsh, un-Christian doctrine as being in any sense "right" within the framework of the poem. Yet so it is. The Vizier is the voice of reason, justice, law, experience, the King of a sentimental humanitarianism which has to learn that it cannot have the world entirely its own way. And in the end, albeit under protest, the King does learn this. He admits that the man was a sinner, not a madman, and that he himself cannot put aside absolute law in order to indulge his own personal whim. Indeed, he confesses that throughout the entire episode he has been sick, and we should note that the King's sickness, like the drought of the land, is a detail added by Arnold to the original story. It is a detail which associates the King with the other sick kings of legend whose lands have been waste as a symbol of their own spiritual illness. The King says he is sick because, in the language of Arnold's later essays, he cannot "do as he likes," but one might better say that he is sick because he wishes to do as he likes and because of his morbidly conscientious feelings towards the sufferings of mankind.

In the Vizier's speech, on the other hand, one can recognize the thought of Burke and the Stoics that one should be guided in his social duties by the bonds which Nature herself has established. We owe a primary obligation to family and friends, a lesser one to race and country, hardly any at all to the brotherhood of man. It was just this narrow prejudice, of course, which the whole liberal movement was attempting to overcome, but that Arnold inclined, at least in these early years, towards the older view may be seen not merely from *The Sick King in Bokhara* but also from a poem which he placed immediately preceding it in the 1849 edition, the *Fragment of an 'Antigone.'* In Arnold's *Fragment,* which is not so much a portion of the Sophoclean drama as a general interpretation of its fable, the dramatic conflict is not between Antigone and Creon but between Antigone and her betrothed Hæmon. The Chorus declares that it can praise the person who, selecting some goal of personal happiness, carves his way to it, so long as justice is not infringed. But it can also praise, and perhaps more highly, the person who, not seeking personal happiness, is guided in his conduct by that "clue" which the Birth-Goddess and the austere Fates first gave him when they marked him out a country, a kinsfolk, and a home. For otherwise, "unguided he remains." The latter person is, of course, Antigone, who in burying the corpse of her brother is being guided by the clue of her blood relation. The former is Hæmon, who is here represented as the relativistic, commonsense hedonist. Hæmon desires nothing more than that Antigone should put aside this absurd taboo about her brother's body and give herself to happiness with him. If she will not, if she persists in suffering death for what is essentially a chimæra, he cannot help regarding her in the same light in which Captain Burnes regarded the Moollah: she is either a bigot or a madman. But the Chorus points out that the obligation to a brother is but the form in which the divine law comes to an individual, and by a series of examples, rising in the importance of the individual and in the generality of the obligation, it shows that Zeus himself could not contravene his own oath in order to save his son Heracles. Zeus is no "sick king," and those of us who would not be, should do our duties to our families and friends. We should, indeed, limit our duties to them. "Be kind to the neighbours," wrote Arnold in the midst of the Revolution of 1848, " 'this is all we can.' "[33]

But why should one limit one's duties to family and friends? Essentially, Arnold would say, because one is a limited, finite being. Christ can suffer with all mankind because he has infinite

33. *Letters,* 1, 7.

resources of divine love and compassion, but mortals do not. Shelley may say, paraphrasing Dante,

> True Love in this differs from gold and clay,
> That to divide is not to take away;

but Arnold did not think so. He thought that every individual had only a certain quantum of love, pity, compassion, feeling, and that it was his duty to husband that quantum carefully and to use it only where he knew it ought to be used. In one of the early love poems he retorts upon some friends who laugh at the way he husbands his impressions:

> Laugh, my friends, and without blame
> Lightly quit what lightly came ....
> I, with little land to stir,
> Am the exacter labourer.

If this were true of the ordinary man, it was more especially true of the poet. The poet has a particular obligation to hoard the riches of his own personality, for the duty of a poet is not to feed the poor but to write poems. "Do not tell me ... ," says Emerson, "of my obligation to put all men in good situations. Are they *my* poor? I tell thee, thou foolish philanthropist, that I grudge the dollar, the dime, the cent I give to such men as do not belong to me, and to whom I do not belong." And Arnold wrote in his notebook, "Our concerning ourselves with other men ought only to be a result of our world-insight & objective prudence – & must not be confounded with our duty of self-discipline & self-cultivation." And in the same notebook: " – the yearning of Christ to the multitude – the solitariness of the philosopher."[34]

Applying this to the present poem, we become aware that although on one level *The Sick King in Bokhara* is about ethical

34. Shelley, *Epipsychidion*, 160–61; Dante, *Purg.* xv; Arnold, *A Memory-Picture*, 1–2, 5–6; Emerson, *Essays* (1841), p. 52; Yale Manuscript, fols. 22v, 5r.

and social problems, on a second level it is about the poet. It is analogous to *The Strayed Reveller*, and the young King is the type of the Romantic poet who projects himself into the sufferings of others, just as the Vizier is the type of the classical poet who remains detached, remote, aloof. It is not wonderful that this should be true, for the Sympathy which was the basis of the Romantic concept of imagination was also the basis of philanthropy. "A man, to be greatly good," says Shelley, "must imagine intensely and comprehensively; he must put himself in the place of another and of many others; the pains and pleasures of his species must become his own. The great instrument of moral good is the imagination; and poetry administers to the effect by acting upon the cause."[35] The King, who at first was a would-be philanthropist, becomes by the end of the poem a practising artist. His original question to the Vizier was, "May I bury him?" and although he apparently meant by this, "May I grieve for him?" for this was the sense in which the Vizier answers it, he ultimately interprets it, "May I memorialize him?" for this is the sense in which he acts.

> I have a fretted brick-work tomb
> Upon a hill on the right hand,
> Hard by a close of apricots,
> Upon the road of Samarcand;
>
> Thither, O Vizier, will I bear
> This man my pity could not save,
> And, plucking up the marble flags,
> There lay his body in my grave.
>
> Bring water, nard, and linen rolls!
> Wash off all blood, set smooth each limb!
> Then say: 'He was not wholly vile,
> Because a king shall bury him.'

35. *A Defense of Poetry*, ed. A. S. Cook (New York, 1890), p. 14.

The fretted brickwork tomb is a symbol of the work of art in which the man is enshrined. Previously, the king had described his summer palaces high in the hills, with great cisterns of water and orchard-closes, with arcades and mosques and all manner of cool and pleasant things, and he had complained that all this was useless if he had not power to save the man he pitied. But now, on another hill, by another close, and on the road to another source of waters, he has created a new oasis amidst the burning plain. And he has perceived that the royal wealth, which could not prevent suffering, can be used to make beautiful in death the "man my pity could not save." Bringing water, nard, and linen rolls, he performed for the martyred Moollah the office which Joseph of Arimathea performed for Christ, and by thus transforming his pity into a *pietà* he healed his own sickness without falling into the opposite evil, the repellent coldness of the old Vizier.

The brickwork tomb shows us that the writing of poetry may itself be a social act. One does not need to join the Mendicity Society or write Oxford Retrenchment pamphlets, as did Clough. One does not need to found Pantisocracies in the wilderness or to join the Roman Catholic Church. One does not even need to repudiate the Articles and pace the barricades in Paris and Rome. One can simply sit in the elegant library at Lansdowne House and read one's Homer and write one's poems, and in so doing one will perform a social act. Doubtless this is part of what Arnold meant by prefixing to his volume the sonnet *Quiet Work*. To anyone who knew Carlyle, with whom the doctrine of work was associated, the phrase "quiet work" was almost a contradiction in terms. But this is what Arnold meant, the work of a Quietist—the work done by a poet, who does not act but is simply a voice, either an adverse voice, calling upon his fellows to consider the other side of the question, or an unforgotten voice, memorializing the meaning of human experience.

Such an idea explains Arnold's stance vis-à-vis the world. In order to be such a voice he needs distance, detachment. But—reversing the usual phrase—though he is not in the world, he is of it. In *Resignation* we see the poet in his usual mountain-top situation, looking out over the varied forms of human life, like Teufelsdröckh in his watch-tower in Illusion Lane.

> From some high station he looks down,
> At sunset, on a populous town;
> Surveys each happy group, which fleets,
> Toil ended, through the shining streets,
> Each with some errand of its own—
> And does not say: *I am alone.*

Teufelsdröckh did say this: "But I, *mein Werther*, sit above it all; I am alone with the Stars."[36] So too did Byron, and Werther, and all the other Romantic heroes. Even Lucretius, in the famous exordium to his second book, declares, " 'It is a pleasure to stand upon the shore, and to see ships tossed upon the sea: a pleasure to stand in the window of a castle, and to see a battle, and the adventures thereof below: but no pleasure is comparable to the standing upon the vantage ground of truth' (a hill not to be commanded, and where the air is always clear and serene), 'and to see the errors, and wanderings, and mists, and tempests in the vale below.' " To which Lord Bacon adds, "—so always that this prospect be with pity, and not with swelling or pride."[37] With this Arnold would now agree, and this seems to be at least one aspect of the thought of *In Utrumque Paratus.* That poem is probably Arnold's reaction to Robert Chambers' *Vestiges of the Natural History of Creation* (1844), the most important work on evolution published during the quarter of a century before Darwin. To most people the book was profoundly disturbing, but Arnold felt that his peculiar position prepared him, as the title says, for "either eventuality." He was prepared for Chambers' evolutionary world pushing up from below or for an idealistic

36. *Sartor Resartus*, Bk. I, chap. 3.
37. Lucret. 2.1 ff., as quoted in Bacon, *Of Truth.*

world handed down from above. The imagery of the poem is closely related to that of the sonnet on Shakespeare, but whereas Shakespeare spared "but the cloudy border of his base / To the foil'd searching of mortality" and was "self-school'd, self-scann'd, self-honour'd, self-secure," the emphasis here is that "proud self-severance from them [i.e. mortality] were disease." That is a line from the new stanza added in 1869, but the earlier version also says,

> Oh when most self-exalted, most alone,
>   Chief dreamer, own thy dream!
> Thy brother-world stirs at thy feet unknown,
> Who hath a monarch's hath no brother's part;
> Yet doth thine inmost soul with yearning teem.
> —Oh, what a spasm shakes the dreamer's heart!
>   'I, too, but seem!'

This is not the language of the old Vizier, where the point was that "who hath a monarch's hath *no* brother's part." It is rather the language of *To Marguerite—Continued*, where in imagery also drawn from the earth-sciences, a deep volcanic fire is felt to connect one human heart with another. It is this "spasm" which now shakes the poet's heart, so that, whereas Teufelsdröckh looked down upon the flood of humanity and exclaimed, "These are Apparitions: what else? Are they not souls rendered visible: in Bodies, that took shape and will lose it, melting into air?"[38] Arnold can say, "*I, too, but seem*"—I, too, am a part of that world of appearance which, rushing out of eternity and into eternity again, demands our sympathy and our aloofness, while we are here.

38. *Sartor Resartus*, Bk. I, chap. 3.

4 TRISTRAM AND THE TWO ISEULTS

Mad for thy love?
           My lord, I do not know;
But truly I do fear it.

                                    —Hamlet

With the publication of *The Strayed Reveller, and Other Poems* it would appear that Arnold had solved all his problems. The problem of human suffering was to be solved by the stance of the Quietist, and the problem of personal anguish by the mask of revelry. By these means Arnold could remove himself from evil and at least pretend that he was untouched by it. And yet, it is this very element of pretence that makes one wonder how lasting the solution will be. Is there not something unreal about it which will crumble at the first actual contact with evil? This is the thought that occurred to James Anthony Froude, the future historian, who, on the day after the volume was published, wrote to his friend Charles Kingsley, "Matthew Arnold has published poems like himself, calm and elegant. A sheet of not deep water, if it is calm, is as good a looking glass as the ocean its own self." A week later he was complaining to Clough in the same vein. "I admire Matt—to a very great extent. Only I don't see what business he has to parade his calmness and lecture us on resignation when he has never known what a storm is, and doesn't know what he has to resign himself to—I think he only knows the shady side of nature out of books."[1]

In a sense Froude was right. It is not merely that Arnold had never been systematically starved and beaten as a child, the way Froude was; it is also that he had never known anything like the storm that Froude was at that moment weathering. For in the very week in which Arnold had published *The Strayed Reveller, and Other Poems*, Froude had brought out his ill-fated novel, *The Nemesis of Faith*. The *Nemesis*—"Faith with a Vengeance," as his friends called it—is the story of a young Oxford graduate, Markham Sutherland, who is reluctant to take orders because he is perplexed by religious doubts. Under pressure from his family and friends he finally does so and is immediately plunged into difficulties. He is forced to flee his parish and goes to Italy, where he contracts a liaison with a married woman. Through their imprudence the lady's daughter dies, and Markham, stricken with grief, is saved from suicide only by the opportune arrival of a countryman (Newman), who places him in a monastery. He finds no faith, however, and the moral of the story is clear: force a young man to believe too much and he will end by believing nothing at all, even by falling into immorality—Faith with a vengeance! As might be expected, the book created a furor. It was denounced from the pulpit and, on the very day on which Froude was writing to Kingsley, was publicly burned by the Rector of Froude's college. Shortly thereafter Froude was deprived of his fellowship and found himself in some difficulties as to earning a living. It is no wonder, then, that he was a little annoyed at Arnold's imperturbable calm and thought that he knew the shady side of life only out of books.

What Froude could not know, of course, was that within three years' time Arnold would be publishing his own Nemesis of Faith in the volume *Empedocles on Etna, and Other Poems* (1852) and that he himself would have married and settled down and come

1. Waldo H. Dunn, *James Anthony Froude: A Biography, 1818–1856* (Oxford, 1961), p. 134; *Letters to Clough*, p. 127 n.

to regret his youthful volume. Arnold was four years younger than Froude, and so it is not surprising that he was three years behind him in development. But it is striking that with Arnold the period of *Sturm und Drang* came after an initial period of Parnassian calm.

For if we compare his new volume, *Empedocles on Etna*, with the volume that preceded it, we find that there has been nothing less than a revolution in Arnold's poetic outlook. In the first place, the aesthetic stance—the stance of the Strayed Reveller and the withdrawn poet—is simply gone as a method of meeting the world's ills. Arnold's new fictional heroes suffer nothing worse than did Mycerinus or the Strayed Reveller, but they do not meet their fate with a smile—they throw themselves into volcanoes or die upon their bed of pain.

Along with this change in stance goes a change in method. In March 1849, when Arnold was still loyal to what he had done in *The Strayed Reveller*, he declared to his sister that he felt "more and more . . . bent against the modern English habit (too much encouraged by Wordsworth) of using poetry as a channel for thinking aloud, instead of making anything." And when Shairp urged him to speak more from himself, he replied that this was what he less and less had the inclination to do, or even the power.[2] But in *Empedocles on Etna, and Other Poems* he does speak from himself, and he does use poetry as a channel for thinking aloud instead of making something. In particular, he has developed a new type of philosophic lyric which, instead of depending on image and situation, depends almost entirely on direct statement. One gains the impression that he is so intent upon thought in these poems that he does not wish to be bothered by problems of expression—even, in some instances, by regular meter. He speaks in a letter of possibly writing a tragedy "in a regular and usual form," so that, if it is successful, he may then be permitted "to use metres in short poems which seem

2. *Unpublished Letters*, p. 17; *Letters to Clough*, p. 104.

proper to myself," presumably the irregular meters which he learned from Goethe and used in *Human Life, A Summer Night,* and other poems. He says, however, that he will write these poems only "when I cannot help it," that is, in answer to urgent personal need.[3]

Beyond this, there is a change in Arnold's imaginative world. In *The Strayed Reveller* we were drenched in the sunlight of the Mediterranean basin. We were in Bokhara or the palace of the Persian king, in the desert with Stagirius or in the pleasure-grove of Mycerinus. We were in the palace of the New Sirens, or listening to a Modern Sappho, or speaking to Circe in her courtyard with its sleeping lions. Except for the sonnets, which are modern, the world of *The Strayed Reveller* is a classical world; but in *Empedocles on Etna,* except for the title poem, there is not a single classical subject. With this volume we move from what Madame de Staël calls "the literature of the South" to "the literature of the North," and its scene is no longer a sun-drenched world but a world of mist, wind, sea, and storm. Indeed, it is with this volume that the image of the Sea of Life becomes an important feature of Arnold's world. Previously, it had appeared only incidentally, but now it is a major alternative to the burning plain, and by this means Arnold is able to emphasize, not the aridity of modern life, but its turbulence. We feel that it was astute of Froude to criticize *The Strayed Reveller* in terms of ocean and storm, for that is precisely what was lacking in Arnold's previous world and what has entered it now.

Finally, as implementing this new imagery there is a new subject, the subject of love, and one is inclined to think that this change lies at the base of all the others. Whether or not Arnold was ever in love before he went over to Switzerland in September 1848 and met a French girl whom we have come to know as Marguerite, we cannot say, but if he was, it has left little impress

3. Yale Manuscript, fols. 5r, 9r, 11r, 12v, [17v]; Ward, *A Writer's Recollections,* p. 43.

upon his poems. Of the poems written before that date there are only three that deal in any way with love, and these, *The New Sirens, A Modern Sappho,* and *Horatian Echo,* are all, as their titles indicate, a rehandling of classical themes. This does not, of course, preclude their having a personal character, but their attitude of weary negligence—the repudiation of passion because it does not endure—seems very bookish and very young. In any case, the theme is distinctly a minor one in a volume whose main subjects are poetry, nature, politics, and religion. In *Empedocles on Etna,* on the other hand, there are only two subjects, love and a larger cosmic theme about the nature of human life. The love poems fall into three groups: those relating to Marguerite, those relating to Frances Lucy Wightman, whom Arnold will later marry, and the narrative poem *Tristram and Iseult.* Doubtless these poems are not so important as *Empedocles on Etna* and the group relating to it, but one has the feeling that the experience behind them permeates the entire volume. One scholar has called *Empedocles on Etna* "Marguerite's book,"[4] and it is probably true that the rumblings of the Greek philosopher on top of his volcano in Sicily were ultimately a part of the same seismic disturbance generated by a small French girl called Marguerite.

Of Marguerite, says one critic, it is fairest to say that we know nothing whatsoever. Strictly speaking, this is true; but, once it has been admitted, we may then go on to detail the few things about her which we like to think we know because they may be so plausibly inferred. The first is that she existed. Family tradition says that she did not, and that the poems about her were fictitious. But in 1932 there was published a letter from Arnold to Clough, written from the Baths of Leuk in Switzerland on September 29, 1848, which contained the following sentence: "Tomorrow I repass the Gemmi [Pass] and get to Thun: linger one day at the Hotel Bellevue for the sake of the blue eyes of one of its inmates: and then proceed by slow stages down the Rhine to

4. H. W. Garrod, *Poetry and the Criticism of Life* (Cambridge, Mass., 1931), p. 36.

. . . England."[5] As the scene of the Marguerite poems is demonstrably that of Thun, the Aar valley, and the Bernese Alps, and as the girl in these poems had blue eyes, scholars have concluded that she was the inmate in question. The suggestion is strengthened by the fact that the meager biographical data fit in perfectly with the story which the poems appear to tell. We know that Arnold vacationed in Thun twice, in September 1848 and again in September 1849. It is logical to assume, then, that the poem *To my Friends, who ridiculed a tender Leave-taking* (later entitled *A Memory-Picture*), which was published in the 1849 volume, referred to Arnold's parting from Marguerite in 1848, and that *Meeting*, which was first published in 1852 and was connected with the former poem by Arnold's own note, referred to his reunion with her in September 1849. A letter written from Thun on September 23 of the latter year indicates that Arnold is planning an excursion of three or four days up into the Bernese Alps, and that he plans to return briefly to Thun before heading back to England. As he announces his plan by quoting a few lines from *Parting*, "I come, O ye mountains! / Ye torrents, I come!" one assumes that the flight to the mountains envisioned in that poem is the same as that projected in the letter; and the return to Thun, which is described in the first stanzas of the next poem, *A Farewell*, would then be the return of about September 27. In between these two poems, though not directly relating to Marguerite, should be placed the *Stanzas in Memory of the Author of 'Obermann,'* for it is dated November 1849 (presumably the date of its completion), and we are told by Arnold that it was "conceived, and partly composed, in the valley going down from the foot of the Gemmi Pass towards the Rhone,"[6] the route which Arnold had followed the previous year and which he would have taken again into the Bernese Alps.

Apart from this circumstantial evidence, however, the strongest reason for believing that Marguerite existed is the simple fact

5. *Letters to Clough*, p. 91.
6. *Poetical Works*, p. 499.

that Arnold was incapable of inventing her. "No Arnold could ever write a novel," he once said, and though his younger brother defied him by doing so, he himself was so completely the type of the Egotistical Sublime that he believed that every other artist was too. "Yes, undoubtedly there was a real Beatrice," he wrote in his essay on Dante, "whom Dante had seen living and moving before him, and for whom he had felt a passion. This basis of fact and reality he took from the life of the outward world: this basis was indispensable to him, for he was an artist." In a similar vein he praised Goethe for always writing so directly out of his own experience, and he said of his own poetry that its literalness and sincerity would always be a source of its charm.[7] If the Marguerite poems are not historical, one can only say that they are the only examples of their kind in Arnold's entire work. He does not have a single other poem, of those involving character and incident, which does not derive either from his own experience or from a literary or historical source.

Fortified by this evidence that there was a real Marguerite, the scholars of the 1930s began to re-examine the poems and discovered, what they perhaps should have seen all along, that there lies behind them an important, complex, and unified experience. The only trouble is that under the excitement of this discovery they went too far and attributed to Marguerite's influence all the poems which had anything to do with love or passion. Even the group of lyrics, also published largely for the first time in 1852 and collected under the title *Faded Leaves* in 1855, which family tradition assigned to Arnold's courtship of Frances Lucy Wightman, was given to Marguerite. The assumption was that if Arnold had deceived us once he would deceive us again, and in any case a poem about a mistress is much more exciting than a poem about a wife. One critic even went so far as to assign to Marguerite the poem *The Voice*, which is almost certainly about John Henry Newman, and another the poem *Urania*, which is

7. Müller, *Auld Lang Syne*, p. 112; Super, *3, 5; Letters, 1,* 11, 59.

about the Muse of Heavenly Beauty.[8] The high tide of Marguerite idolatry attributed to her some twenty or twenty-five poems, whereas most scholars now would give her about a dozen. In my opinion the Marguerite poems are the nine poems which at one time or another appeared in the *Switzerland* series (eight of them mention her name either in text or title); the poem *Destiny*, which was originally published in the midst of the Marguerite group but did not get into the *Switzerland* series because it was never reprinted after that series was formed; *The Buried Life*, whose arch, mocking heroine is recognizably the same as the heroine of the *Switzerland* group; *Tristram and Iseult*, which we know was conceived at Thun; and possibly *The Church of Brou*, which has affiliations with *Tristram and Iseult* and which, with its heroine the Duchess Marguerite, could hardly have been written by Arnold without his at least thinking of the other Marguerite poems. *Faded Leaves*, on the other hand, must belong largely to Mrs. Arnold. Indeed, since Kenneth Allott published the earliest version of the first poem in the series, *The River*, and showed that the river there is the Thames and not the Aar, we know that that poem is hers, and, if that, why not the others too?[9] *On the Rhine* and *Calais Sands* are certainly hers and probably also *Dover Beach*, though about that we are quite uncertain. On the other hand, *The Forsaken Merman*, *The New Sirens*, *A Modern Sappho*, *Horatian Echo*, *Euphrosyne*, and *Requiescat* probably do not belong to either one or the other. Finally, *A Summer Night*, *Human Life*, and *Stanzas in Memory of the Author of 'Obermann,'* though not properly love poems, are very closely related to the Marguerite experience and probably should be placed within her penumbra.

Though the Marguerite poems are not fictional, Arnold gave

8. E. K. Chambers, *Matthew Arnold: A Study* (Oxford, 1947), pp. 48–49; Louis Bonnerot, *Matthew Arnold, poète* (Paris, 1947), p. 69; Tinker and Lowry, pp. 49, 166.

9. Kenneth Allott, "Matthew Arnold's Original Version of 'The River,' " *Times Literary Supplement*, 57 (March 28, 1958), 172.

some attention to trying to form them into a verse narrative that would tell a coherent story. In 1852 all the love poems had been printed simply as individual poems without any indication either that they belonged together or that they should be separated into two groups. Those relating to Mrs. Arnold were placed before those relating to Marguerite, so that a reader who went straight through the volume would have the impression of moving from a quieter and happier love to a more turbulent and tragic one. This was, of course, just the reverse of what had happened, and in 1853 Arnold apparently decided that there was some advantage, either personal or literary, in separating the poems into two groups and isolating them one from another. Thus in *Poems* (1853) he took six of the Marguerite poems and grouped them together under the heading *Switzerland*. Two years later he placed the five poems to his wife in *Poems: Second Series* under the heading *Faded Leaves*. The latter group was not thereafter revised. The *Switzerland* series, on the other hand, varied somewhat from edition to edition both in the number and the selection of poems, though not much in the order. In the final arrangement it had seven poems, but in order to read the series in its entirety, we need to restore, as Numbers 1 and 3, the two early poems which originally formed a part of the group and which were not removed until 1869 and 1877. The complete series would then be as follows: (1) *A Memory-Picture*, (2) *Meeting*, (3) *A Dream*, (4) *Parting*, (5) *A Farewell*, (6) *Isolation. To Marguerite*, (7) *To Marguerite—Continued*, (8) *Absence*, (9) *The Terrace at Berne*.

The setting of these poems is that of Arnold's imaginative world, and therefore its story moves through the three realms of forest glade, burning plain, and wide-glimmering sea. Briefly, it is the story of a man who for one delicious moment enjoys a fresh and rapturous love, is then plunged into a sea of passion, suffering, and loss, and finally, through deepened self-understanding, moves into the solitude and calm that are properly his. It should be emphasized that this story is not told consecutively through the whole series of lyrics, but rather is told in each lyric individually, but with varying completeness and with a shift of emphasis which does give to the series a consecutive character. Thus, the first three poems are concerned with the foreboding of loss, in the next three this loss actually occurs, and in the last three (as also in the middle group) the poet is struggling to move off the burning plain onto the wide-glimmering sea. As a result, the poems cannot be read quite as if they were episodes in a novel, for no poem takes up at the point where the preceding one left off. Often they repeat the preceding one but perhaps carrying the action on a little further. Thus, the *Switzerland* lyrics are really variations on a theme rather than a narrative action consecutively developed.

The initial moment of love is always presented in the poems under the concrete image of the natural scene and the figure of Marguerite herself. Arnold always visited Thun in the fall, but in the opening moment of the poems it is always spring. There are the fresh green fields, the sun-warmed pines and the chestnuts, the lake, the garden, and the Aar flowing at the foot of the garden—the whole silvered by moonlight or bathed by the pure mountain air. In this garden is Marguerite, who is associated with it by the most prominent feature of her costume, the lilac kerchief which binds her soft, brown hair. She is described as having a soft pliant grace, pale rounded cheeks, and sweet blue eyes—also an arch and roguish smile "that tells / The unconquer'd joy in which her spirit dwells." For Marguerite, in this opening moment of the poem, is the very embodiment of the spirit of Joy. As goddess of the forest glade, she is one who flashes upon us in moments of delicious and rapturous surprise. We are standing in the garden when suddenly she emerges from the oleanders and is clasped in our arms. Or we are in a room and she enters heedless, kissed by us. We mount eagerly to her chamber, the door opens, and she is there! She smiles upon the strand and we spring to meet her. Our boat flashes by upon the stream, and for one delicious moment we rise, we gaze, and then she is seen no more. She is always a momentary vision of supreme and joyous delight.

What is it that undoes love in Arnold's world? In *A Memory-Picture* it is Time, and in *A Dream* it is the onward-rushing River of Life. In *Human Life* it is the winds of destiny which "from our side the unsuiting consort rive"; and in *Meeting* and *To Marguerite—Continued* it is "a God." In *Parting* it is "our different past," and in *Absence* it is the "petty dust" of daily life. If we were reading these poems as a story, we should like these inconsistencies cleared up, but reading them thematically, we can see that it hardly matters what particular form the impediment to love should take. The important thing is that initially it should present itself to the poet as an external barrier, and that ultimately he should come to understand that it is as much within him as without.

The poet comes to this understanding partly through the same process which we find elsewhere in Arnold's poetry, of penetrating through the illusory beauty of Marguerite to the reality which lies beneath. The clearest instance of this is in *Parting*, where Marguerite's voice is the very symbol of her limpid and spring-like beauty:

> Say, has some wet bird-haunted English lawn
> Lent it the music of its trees at dawn?

The lines remind us of *Philomela*, where another fragrant English lawn was unable to assuage the pains of Philomela because she saw through it to the horror of the Thracian wild. So here, as Marguerite comes nearer, and as the poet's attention shifts from her voice to her figure, then to her face and lips—"Sweet lips," he says, "this way!" But then (and it must be admitted that to a modern reader the effect is a little comic), he starts back with the cry,

> To the lips, ah! of others
> Those lips have been prest,
> And others, ere I was,
> Were strain'd to that breast.

Under the surface of romantic love he has discovered the fact of sex, and he is precipitated by this discovery onto the burning plain.

That Arnold was making this discovery in these years we may gather from his letters. Writing from the Baths of Leuk in the autumn of his first meeting with Marguerite, he speaks of being glad to be tired of a certain author because it is "one link in the immense series of cognoscenda et indagenda despatched. More particularly is this my feeling with regard to (I hate the word) women. We know beforehand all they can teach us: yet we are obliged to learn it directly from them." And he then quotes some cynical verses of his own such as Hamlet might have composed about Ophelia in the context of the graveyard scene. But what is more, in a letter written to Wyndham Slade from London in the spring of 1850, he makes what seems to be a comment on the Marguerite episode. He has been trying, unsuccessfully, to meet Miss Wightman, and he says: "How strange about die unerreichbare schöne! To have met her to have found something abstossend [repellent], and to have been freed from all disquietude on her account, voilà comment je comprends a matter of this kind."[10] Arnold was writing only a few months after the presumed termination of the Marguerite affair, and so, if he declared that his experience in these matters was to be initially attracted and then repelled, presumably this is what happened in that instance. In any case, it is what happened in the poem *Parting*.

To see Marguerite not as virginal and pure but as soiled, is to make her share in the transformation of nature from forest glade to burning plain. But on the human level she also assumes the role of various inhabitants of the burning plain, particularly of Dipsychus and the Strayed Reveller. In *Isolation* she is Dipsychus, as her feelings "ebb and swell," and in *A Farewell* both she and the poet have this character. This, indeed, is why they cannot love, for

10. *Letters to Clough*, p. 93; Tinker and Lowry, pp. 169–70.

> women—things that live and move
> Mined by the fever of the soul—
> They seek to find in those they love
> Stern strength, and promise of control.

They seek the "trenchant force / And will like a dividing spear" of the strong, Byronic soul. But the poet's soul has something within its depths "too strange, too restless, too untamed," for him to be loved by Marguerite. In *The Buried Life*, on the other hand, this inability to love is related to the fact that both are Strayed Revellers. "Light flows our war of mocking words," says the poet, and with this phrase we perceive that a prime trait of Marguerite has undergone a transformation. From the very first she has been characterized by nothing so much as an arch and roguish gaiety. In *A Memory-Picture* she had "the archest chin / Mockery ever ambush'd in," and in *Parting* she had an "arch smile." But at that time this archness was revelatory of her inner mind. Her "arch smile . . . tells / The unconquer'd joy in which her spirit dwells," and her eyes are "frank eyes, where deep I see / An angelic gravity." But in *The Buried Life* this is not so. Here her archness is a mask, and the poet complains that though he knew the mass of men concealed their thoughts for fear of indifference or ridicule, he did not think that lovers did so. Lovers should be able to speak openly to one another, the real self of one to the real self of the other, and he is convinced that if he and Marguerite did so they would discover that neither one of them was a Dipsychus or a Strayed Reveller. For already in *A Farewell* he had perceived that he and Marguerite but "school our manners, act our parts" in pretending to be Dipsychus. And in *The Buried Life* they are "trick'd in disguises" in their light war of banter and persiflage.

It is altogether delightful to see Arnold complaining that Marguerite will not be open and frank with him, for one thinks how often, when he was playing the dandy, he had inspired the same complaint among his friends. Now, however, he is getting a taste of his own medicine! He is being confronted by one who can outplay him at his own roles, and he does not like it! And so, in the course of his complaints, he develops the theory of the Buried Life. It is very striking that this theory should have been developed in a love poem, for it is in love, and especially the love leading to marriage, that one needs to know who and what he is. In poetry one does not. Poetry even encourages one in the playing of roles, in adopting this or that form of life not because it is your own but so you can enter into and understand it. But in marriage you have to be one single person, and in the happy marriage you have to be the right person. You are looking, says Arnold, for "the twin soul which halves [your] own,"[11] and this means that you must know, not merely the twin soul, but also your own. You must decide whether you are a Strayed Reveller or a Quietist, a Madman or a Slave, or not any one of these but something quite different. Arnold was evidently constrained to make this decision in September 1849.

We may guess that he was forced to do so by the necessity of defining his relations with Marguerite. It was his second visit to Thun, and it must have been clear to him that something had to be decided. "—I am here," he wrote to Clough, "in a curious and not altogether comfortable state: however tomorrow I carry my aching head to the mountains and to my cousin the Blümlis Alp." He then quotes the few lines from *Parting*—"I come, O ye mountains— / Ye torrents, I come"—which indicate that that poem dramatizes the moment of which he speaks. "Yes," he concludes, "I come, but in three or four days I shall be back here, and then I must try how soon I can ferociously turn towards England." The flight to the mountains was evidently for the purpose of self-mastery and self-discovery, for earlier in the letter Arnold had confided to Clough: "What I must tell you is that I have never yet succeeded in any one great occasion in consciously mastering myself: I can go thro: the imaginary process of mastering myself and see the whole affair as it

11. *Too Late,* 4.

127

would then stand, but at the critical point I am too apt to hoist up the mainsail to the wind and let her drive. However as I get more awake to this it will I hope mend for I find that with me a clear almost palpable intuition (damn the logical senses of the word) is necessary before I get into prayer . . . . [My] one natural craving is not for profound thoughts, mighty spiritual workings etc. etc. but a distinct seeing of my way so far as my own nature is concerned . . ."[12]

The image of hoisting up the mainsail to the wind connects this passage with *A Summer Night*, which presents the conflict between languor and passion in terms of two contrasting symbols, the brazen prison of the Slave and the bark of the Madman, scudding before the wind. The symbols are paralleled by two contrasting scenes, one of the city and the other of the sea, and the conflict is resolved by the one element common to both, the bright, calm moon. One cannot say that in this poem, which was probably written in London either earlier or later the same year, Arnold actually attained the "clearness divine" which the moon represents, for it remains "a world above man's head," an ideal to be realized but not realized as yet. The poem shows Arnold going through the imaginary process of mastering himself and seeing the affair as it would then stand, but we have to wait for the *Stanzas in Memory of the Author of 'Obermann'* to see this process realized in his own person.

He composed this poem on the excursion up into the Alps on September 24–27, an excursion which possibly took him round by Lake Geneva and the Rhone valley but certainly brought him back by the Baths of Leuk and the Gemmi Pass. It was a route which he had travelled the previous year, and in taking it now he was revisiting country associated with two Romantic solitaries, Obermann and Byron. Byron had gone that way in 1816, and passages from his journal describing the scene had been spread at large over the pages of John Murray's *Handbook to Switzerland*, which Arnold carried with him. Byron

12. *Letters to Clough*, p. 110.

had even gone to Thun, and one may be sure that if there was a predecessor of Marguerite in the town, he had fallen in love with her. Arnold was uncomfortably aware that his travels in Switzerland, his falling in love, and his writing poetry about it were all reminiscent of Byron. Hence his remark in 1848 that the "whole locality is spoiled by the omnipresence there of that furiously flaring bethiefed rushlight, the vulgar Byron."[13]

Obermann was both better and worse. He was the hero of the Romantic epistolary novel published in 1804 by the French writer, Etienne Pivert de Sénancour. Arnold had encountered him in 1847 in an edition of the work containing a preface by George Sand. The preface acutely analyzes Obermann's malady in relation to the other varieties of Romantic melancholy: Werther, who represents "passion frustrated in its development, that is, man against the world"; René, who represents "the consciousness of superior faculties without the ability to realize them"; and Obermann, who represents "the consciousness of incomplete faculties." The first is the least interesting as being purely external; the last two are distinctly modern. "René says, 'If I could will, I could do it.' Obermann says, 'Why bother willing? I never could do it.'"[14] Nonetheless, it was by this austere and debilitated writer, the patron saint of impotence, that Arnold was so entranced from 1847–49 that Obermann became one of the most important "voices" of his youth. Indeed, with Obermann Arnold could not claim that he had remained entirely free. Sénancour, he wrote to a friend, "produced on me when I happened, at 25, to fall in with his works, an extraordinary impression. My separation of myself, finally, from him and his influence, is related in a poem in my Second Series."[15]

This poem was the *Stanzas in Memory of the Author of*

---

13. Ibid., p. 92; cf. John Murray, *A Hand-book for Travellers in Switzerland* (3d ed., London, 1846), p. 125.

14. [Étienne Pivert] de Sénancour, *Obermann*, nouvelle édition revue et corrigée, avec une préface par George Sand (Paris, 1852), pp. 6–7.

15. Tinker and Lowry, p. 271.

'*Obermann.*' The poem begins by praising Obermann as one of three in the modern world who have known to see their way (the other two are Wordsworth and Goethe), and as Arnold develops the superiority of Obermann even to these, he cries out, "To thee we come then!" thus symbolically re-enacting his election of Obermann two years before as the "master of my wandering youth." But then, as he perceives that the calm of Obermann is really the calm of death, he declares, "—Away!"

> Away the dreams that but deceive
> And thou, sad guide, adieu!
> I go, fate drives me; but I leave
> Half of my life with you.

This act—the act by which Arnold separated himself from Obermann—was certainly the most important spiritual act of his entire life, for it put behind him all the turbulence and unrest, the *Sturm und Drang*, that had troubled him in previous years. It also, of course, involved a separation from Marguerite, for she represented the same kind of spiritual morbidity as did Obermann. Thus, there can hardly be any doubt that when Arnold went back down to Thun, to see "how soon I can ferociously turn towards England," he found his task much easier than if he had not written the *Stanzas in Memory of the Author of 'Obermann'* in the mountains.

In making the decision to leave Obermann Arnold declared, "I in the world must live," but this did not mean that he must be a Slave. Rather it meant that he was to be one of a new group of characters who now appear in his poetry for the first time. He calls this group "The Children of the Second Birth, / Whom the world could not tame." The phrase comes from the third chapter of the Gospel according to St. John, where it is said, "Except a man be born again, he cannot see the kingdom of God." Arnold alludes to this passage in his letter to Clough written from Thun on September 23: "Marvel not," he says, "that I say unto you, ye must be born again. While I will not much talk of these things, yet the considering of them has led me constantly to you the only living one almost that I know of of

> The children of the second birth
> Whom the world could not tame—"[16]

But although Clough is almost the only living example of this group, there is a "small, transfigured band" of them among the dead. Arnold's list—"Christian and pagan, king and slave"— suggests that Thomas à Kempis, Marcus Aurelius, and Epictetus would be among the group, but so too, he now perceives, is Obermann. For the deeper message of Obermann is that it does not matter whether one lives in the world or out of it, so long as he remains "unspotted by the world." Thus, by rejecting a surface conception of Obermann for a more profound one, Arnold has rejected the surface conception of himself for his true or buried life.

Arnold's discovery of his true nature is also reflected in the *Switzerland* poems. There he discovers that he is not the passionate Byronic lover which his relation with Marguerite implies but is essentially a Child of the Second Birth—gentle, mild, and true. He is more preoccupied with ideas and things than with people, and is asexual, passionless, cold. From the very first he has had an intimation that this was true. In *A Memory-Picture* he was ridiculed by his friends for prolonging a tender leave-taking so as to fix Marguerite's image more firmly upon his mind. He was not disturbed by this, however, for he had had experience of a certain poverty of his emotional life which made it necessary that he should husband his impressions carefully. "I with little land to stir, / Am the exacter labourer." Formerly, he had held that this very preoccupation with remembering was the best way to forget, but now, rejecting what Mill calls Carlyle's "anti-selfconsciousness theory," he paints upon the canvas of his memory the picture of Marguerite which is designed to rescue her from the flux of time. For the first year it succeeds. But by the date of *Ab-*

16. *Letters to Clough*, pp. 109–10.

sence he has already forgotten her. The sight of a stranger whose
eyes resemble the eyes of Marguerite suddenly brings her image
to his mind, and he shivers—not because he has forgotten her,
for by this time he is not unwilling to forget, but because he has
forgotten her involuntarily. "This is the curse of life!" he says,
that" we forget because we must / And not because we will." In-
deed, by this time, in the poem *Destiny*, the poet acknowledges
that he has a "heart of ice" yoked with a "soul of fire," and that
this is the reason why each of us "is striving from of old, / To
love more deeply than he can." We are incongruous creatures,
longing to love but, by a kind of spiritual impotence, unable to do
so. And so, in *Isolation: To Marguerite*, the poet confesses
openly to his solitary, moon-like nature:

> —and thou, thou lonely heart,
> Which never yet without remorse
> Even for a moment didst depart
> From thy remote and spheréd course
> To haunt the place where passions reign—
> Back to thy solitude again!

Back with "the conscious thrill of shame" which the moon-god-
dess felt when she forsook her starry heights to hang over En-
dymion's sleep; for he, even more than she, has proved, and
made her own, this truth, "Thou hast been, shalt be, art, alone."
And it is not, as in *To Marguerite—Continued*, because he has to
be, because of some salt, estranging sea, rather because (*pace*
John Donne) every man is an island. For we have now reached
the point where the poet, by accepting his fate, realizes that what
had presented itself as an external barrier to love was really an
inner resistance. The God whose tremendous voice had counseled
him to retire was really the voice of his own soul. The River
which, in *A Dream*, had swept him past his beloved, turned out,
in *The Buried Life*, to be the river of his Best Self. The winds
of destiny which, in *Human Life*, reft from his side the "unsuit-
ing consort," were actually guiding him by his own "inly-written

chart." It was because of his own nature that he was alone, or, "if not quite alone, yet they / Which touch thee are unmating things"—Nature, and Life, and the dreams of ideal love as expressed in Art.

Therefore, in the two poems *Parting* and *A Farewell* the poet rejects the sexual relationship with Marguerite in favor of an asexual relation with Nature and the Ideal. In the former, having perceived that Marguerite's lips have been soiled by contact with others, he flees up the mountain, through the "ice-cumber'd gorges" with their "rock-strangled hum," until, suffering a kind of death and rebirth, he emerges upon the shoulder of the mountain a "child" in its mother's arms.

> Blow, ye winds! lift me with you!
> I come to the wild.
> Fold closely, O Nature!
> Thine arms round thy child.

From this vantage he can gaze down into the valley and witness "the stir of the forces / Whence issued the world"—the life-circulation of nature.

In *A Farewell* the movement of the poem is the same except that here it is conducted in Christian rather than naturalistic terms. Ostensibly, Marguerite has rejected the poet because, as Dipsychus, she longs for a strong, Byronic soul with "will like a dividing spear." But more truly it is he who has rejected her because he has perceived that the true bent of both their hearts is to be gentle, tranquil, true. He believes that some day she too will perceive this, but until she does they must part. And when they are reunited, not in this world but in the next, it will be as disembodied spirits who "greet across infinity." Just as in *Parting* the poet had exchanged his beloved for a mother, so here, "in the eternal Father's smile," he exchanges her for a sister.

> How sweet, unreach'd by earthly jars,
> My sister! to maintain with thee

> The hush among the shining stars,
> The calm upon the moonlit sea!

A biographer could hardly resist the interpretation that Arnold found his relationship with his mother and his sister more satisfactory than that with Marguerite. Certainly it is true that when Jane's first engagement was broken off, Arnold was able to counsel resignation, and that when her second, to William Forster, was announced, he was emotionally upset. In a previously unpublished letter, undated but probably from the winter of 1849–50, he says:

> My dearest K. I must write again before I see Mr. Forster —I have been in a kind of spiritual lethargy for some time past, partly from headache partly from other causes which has made it difficult for me to approfondir any matter of feeling—but I feel quite sure my darling that when I can sink myself well down into the consideration of you & your circumstances as they really are then will you be truly set right in respect of your engagement. At present my objections are not based on *reality*, that I feel.
>
> I am subject to these periods of spiritual eastwind when I can lay hold only of the outside of events or words—the malevolent eastwind which now prevails has something to do with it, and also the state of strain & uneasiness in which in these days & in London it is so hard not to live. You my darling have been a refreshing thought to me in my dryest periods: I may say that you have been one of the most faithful witnesses (almost the only one after papa) among those with whom I have lived & spoken of the reality & possibility of that abiding inward life which we all desire most of us talk about & few possess—and I have a confidence in you & in this so great that I know you will never be false to yourself—: and everything merely fanciful & romantic should be sacrificed to truth.[17]

17. In the possession of Arnold Whitridge.

Obviously, Jane was also, along with Clough and himself, one of the Children of the Second Birth, but now, a few months after he had broken off relations with Marguerite, Jane had announced a relation with William Forster. What was there for Arnold to do but get married himself? His disengagement from Marguerite occurred in September 1849, Jane's marriage to Forster in August 1850, Arnold's to Frances Lucy Wightman in June 1851.

But first we must dispose of Marguerite. The process is completed in the last poem of the Switzerland series, *The Terrace at Berne*, written ten years after the preceding when Arnold was travelling in Switzerland with his wife on business for the Education Office. He is now an established *père de famille* and all his fume and fret are behind him. And so, as he walks in the evening on the famous Enghe Terrace outside of town, he looks over the valleys toward Thun and speculates on what has happened to Marguerite. Is she there the same as ever, or has she died? Or has she long since wandered back to France and become a prostitute, as people like her too easily do? This last supposition has earned for Arnold a great many hard words among the critics, who declare that the thought is unworthy of him. Perhaps it is, but the real trouble is that the critics have so fallen in love with Marguerite that they cannot endure the process of disengagement which is the main movement of the poem. For the thought is entirely one with the process of seeing through the deceptive beauty of Marguerite to the "riotous laughter" which now replaces her smile, the "rouge, with stony glare," which replaces her cheek's soft hue, and the "fluttering lace," which replaces her kerchief. Still, Arnold does not end upon this note. He merely decides to leave Yarrow unrevisited:

> I will not know! For wherefore try,
> To things by mortal course that live,
> A shadowy durability,
> For which they were not meant, to give?

Of course, the whole purpose of the first poem in the series, *A*

Memory-Picture, had been to rescue Marguerite from the flux of time, but now, with the image of "driftwood spars, which meet and pass / Upon the boundless ocean-plain," the poet rejects this effort and declares, "And Marguerite I shall see no more."

There is one further alternative which Arnold might have added in his poem, and that is that Marguerite did not exist at all, but was merely a creature of his imagination. For in this idea, which he set afloat in later years, we must recognize one further effort on his part to erase the image of Marguerite from his life. We do not always realize, perhaps, how deliberately this must have been done. Certainly, when he was first in love with Marguerite everybody at all close to him must have known pretty much all about it. It is impossible to think that Jane did not—or Tom, or Clough, or Walrond, or Slade—and neither would Arnold have allowed his wife simply to read these poems and wonder what to think. No, everybody must have known, and it could only have been very gradually, as people forgot or died or ceased to care, that the tradition was established. Probably it was assisted by a destruction of manuscripts, for it is a striking fact that Arnold's diaries for the crucial years 1848–50 are missing, although those for the years before and after have been preserved. He asked that no biography of him be written, and he has expressed his strong disapproval of publishing to the world the private loves of Keats and Shelley. He has also said that *Vaudracour and Julia,* the comparable poem in Wordsworth's career, was the one work by that poet that he could not read with pleasure.[18] There are, of course, good critical reasons for this, but there may have been biographical reasons as well. Yet with him this was not mere Victorian prudery. It was rather that, by heroic struggle, he had put passion behind him, and he did not wish it to be resurrected, except in the domain of art.

> I struggle towards the light; and ye,
> Once-long'd-for storms of love!

18. *Letters, 1,* vii; *Essays in Criticism: Second Series* (1900), pp. 101–02, 236–37, 162.

If with the light ye cannot be,
I bear that ye remove.[19]

So far as we know, Arnold met his future wife, Frances Lucy
Wightman, in London in the spring of 1850. She was the daugh-
ter of Sir William Wightman, Justice of the Queen's Bench, and
Arnold probably met her through his legal friend, John Duke
Coleridge. At least it was to his house that he was invited in the
spring of 1850 for the purpose of meeting her, and we are told
that his "wheels burned the pavement" and that he "mounted
the stairs like a wounded quaggha." Unfortunately, Lucy's
mother had taken tickets to the opera and she was not there—
die unerreichbare schöne.[20] Ultimately, however, they met, and
the poem *The River*, which is probably to be dated August 1850,
apparently records their courtship on the river Thames, probably
near the Wightman's house at Hampton. Whether *Too Late* and
Separation are really related to this affair or are early lyrics put
in to splice out the series we do not know. The former suggests
that Miss Wightman's hand was already bestowed, which we do
not know to have been the case, and the latter seems much closer
in mood to *A Modern Sappho* and the Marguerite series than to
this. For here the impediment, so far as we know, was purely
external. Sir William was reluctant to allow the pair to marry on
the slender income and uncertain prospects which Arnold had as
Lord Lansdowne's secretary, and they were apparently asked not
to see each other for a while. Arnold had already arranged to go

---

19. *Absence*, 13–16.
20. Tinker and Lowry, p. 169. I deduce that it was at Coleridge's house
that Arnold was to meet the lady because the pavement which his wheels
burned was that of Park Crescent, and according to the *Post Office London
Directory*, 1850, the only one living in Park Crescent whom Arnold knew
was J. D. Coleridge (at No. 26). The date of the episode may be established
by the fact that the opera season "commences towards the close of Feb-
ruary, or early in March, and continues till August. It is not, however, un-
til after Easter that the chief attractions are brought forward." (*London
Life As It Is; or, a Handbook to All the Attractions . . . of the Great City*,
London [c. 1849], p. 36).

abroad with his friend Wyndham Slade at the end of the summer, and *Calais Sands*, the manuscript of which is dated August 1850, records a stratagem whereby he preceded the Wightmans to Calais, lingered on the pier as they arrived, and apparently spent the night, unknown to them, in the same hotel. The poem speaks of his hurrying on next day to the "storied Rhine," and so we may assume that *On the Rhine* records the next stage of his feelings. He is trying vainly to forget, but his despair is not really deep, and by January of the next year the couple were seeing each other again and corresponding frequently. On March 23 Arnold secured his appointment as Inspector of Schools, a week later Sir William gave his formal consent, and the wedding followed on June 10. "It is very difficult," wrote Tom, "to fancy the 'Emperor' married!"[21]

In truth, in getting married Arnold somewhat divested himself of his imperial robes and became a more ordinary mortal. Stanley wrote to Tom that Matt was "greatly improved by his marriage —retaining all the genius and nobleness of mind which you remember, with all the lesser faults pruned and softened down." That is to say, he had actually become the milder and gentler self which he had foreshadowed in the poems. Furthermore, he had married the kind of person that Marguerite would have become had she too died unto her old self and been reborn as Arnold believed her to be. For Frances Lucy (Flu, as she was called) is described by Arnold as having "all my sweetness and none of my airs"—that is, as not being given to role-playing. She is "entirely free from the taint of letters"—presumably, of Byronic stances —and is, in short, "a charming companion."[22] If there is something mildly depressing in hearing a young lover describe his

21. Clough, *Correspondence, 1,* 290 n.; cf. Ward, *A Writer's Recollections,* p. 65.

22. Ward, *A Writer's Recollections,* p. 52; E. M. Sellar, *Recollections and Impressions* (Edinburgh and London, 1907), p. 152; Alan Harris, "Matthew Arnold, the 'Unknown Years,' " *Nineteenth Century, 113* (1933), 509.

bride-to-be as "a charming companion," one can only say that this is the point to which Arnold had come. Ultimately, of course, he would have no doubts—his marriage was a clear success—but who can say if there was not an initial period when he felt some uncertainty whether his famed "self-mastery" was really a process of discovering the best self or of settling for the second best? For the idea of the "second best," of what we have to settle for in this life, is also an important idea in Arnold, and it is not at all certain that marrying the charming daughter of an English judge would not come under this heading.

As poetry, the *Faded Leaves* series is certainly second best. Its very title suggests the album verses of domesticated sentiment. The most that one can say for it is that Arnold is here beginning to distance his experience and to take of it a more contemplative view. In his Dante essay he had asserted that art requires a basis of fact and reality, but he had also gone on to say that art "desires to treat this basis of fact with the utmost freedom; and this desire for the freest handling of its object is even thwarted when its object is too near, and too real."[23] One cannot but feel that this was the case with the Marguerite poems, that their object was too near and too real, and that most of them, except perhaps the famous *To Marguerite—Continued* do not achieve the perfection of art for this reason. But in *Faded Leaves* the poet is adopting a different attitude and a different poetic method. In *Longing*, if the beloved comes to him in his dreams, it will adequately compensate him for her absence during the day, and in *On the Rhine* he will be happy if she beams upon his "inward view." Finally, in *Calais Sands*, the best of the group, he not only achieves felicity merely by gazing upon her unseen from the crowd of "idlers" on the pier, but he is able to utilize the medieval associations of the scene, the Field of the Cloth of Gold and the storied Rhine, to dramatize himself as a knight or page worshipping his queen from afar. This projection of himself leads, of course, into the

23. Super, 3, 5.

story which is his principal artistic shaping of these materials, the narrative *Tristram and Iseult.*

Arnold tells us that he first encountered the story of Tristram and Iseult in a French review article while he was at Thun, and that by the time he got to England the outline of the poem was pretty well formed in his mind.[24] This means that it was conceived at a time when there was only one Iseult in his life, though it can hardly have been completed before there were two. One may well believe that this fact is responsible for some of the ambiguities which the poem contains, but it would not do to press the biographical parallel too far. For in its action the poem dramatizes what Arnold did not do rather than what he did. He did not send Mrs. Arnold and the children off to the southern wing of the castle while he summoned Marguerite from over the sea to attend him in his dying hour. Indeed, he did not languish for Marguerite at all. Instead, he put all that he had thought and felt about her into Tristram and allowed him to die for love, while he recovered himself, wrote his poems, and set to work as Her Majesty's Inspector of Schools.

The poem opens with Tristram lying on his death-bed "on this wild December night." A "dying fire" illuminates the symbols of his former power, his dark green forest-dress and gold harp; and standing by the fire is the one hope of future health, his wife, Iseult of Brittany. Tristram ignores both of these, however, his mind fixed on the grey, gale-swept sea over which Iseult of Ireland is coming to meet him. "Is she not come?" he asks, and when he is told she has not, his mind wanders, in his delirium, over the scenes of his past life. Four scenes are presented, each of them fixed obsessively upon Iseult and three of them ending with the mention of her name. Aided by comments from the narrator, they are the means of telling the story of the two lovers, and they are so selected as to present the main stages in Arnold's poetic myth.

24. R. E. C. Houghton, "Letter of Matthew Arnold," *Times Literary Supplement,* 31 (May 19, 1932), 368.

The first scene is the idyllic moment when Tristram was bringing Iseult of Ireland back to Cornwall to be the bride of King Marc.

> The calm sea shines, loose hang the vessel's sails;
> Before us are the sweet green fields of Wales,
> And overhead the cloudless sky of May.

To which Iseult replies,

> Ah, would I were in those green fields at play,
> Not pent on ship-board this delicious day!
> Tristram, I pray thee, of thy courtesy,
> Reach me my golden phial stands by thee,
> But pledge me in it first for courtesy.

There is no indication with what degree of knowledge or consciousness Iseult makes this request, but the subtle emphasis upon "courtesy" suggests that the pair are being deluded by a false set of values which ignores the real bonds by which they are "pent." If so, disillusionment quickly follows:

> Ha! dost thou start? are thy lips blanch'd like mine?
> Child, 'tis no true draught this, 'tis poison'd wine!

That the golden phial is "no true draught" but "poison'd wine" is paralleled by the fact that it does not release the lovers into the green fields but "binds their souls" in adulterous passion. And so, in the next scene, the scene of their discovery and flight, the "pleasaunce-walks" have become drear, the wind is chill, and Iseult is no longer addressed as "child," rather as "madcap." For she has already begun the life of subterfuge and deceit that she will have to lead as a kind of female Strayed Reveller in the court of King Marc. Tristram, on the other hand, flees the court, and in the two scenes which follow he becomes a kind of Dipsychus, alternating between the solitude of the forest and the heat of the battle, and finding relief in neither. In Part II, when he and Iseult meet again, they will debate which was worse, to be "a pining exile in thy forest," or "a smiling queen upon my throne," but essentially the question hardly matters. For the real issue of the poem is not between them, but between them and Iseult of Brittany; or, as the structure of the poem is actually arranged, between the two Iseults, for each of whom Tristram has felt an attraction.

The narrator presents this conflict in the opening section:

> There were two Iseults who did sway
> Each her hour of Tristram's day;
> But one possess'd his waning time,
> The other his resplendent prime.

The two Iseults are contrasted pretty much as are the conventional dark and light heroines of Victorian fiction—Eustacia Vye and Thomasin Yeobright, Becky Sharp and Amelia Sedley. The one has raven locks, the other is like a snowdrop. The one is proud and imperious, the other patient and mild. The one is a dazzling beauty who lives in the brilliant court of King Marc; the other a simple country princess who dwells with her maidens in a remote castle by the sea. The one, with her "spiced magic draught" which boils and rolls through the veins of her lover, has pagan associations of sorcery and witchcraft. The other is "the sweetest Christian soul alive" and would never do anything that was not good and true. If a man were a bishop, he would surely prefer Iseult of Brittany, but if he were a lusty young knight, he might conceivably prefer the other. Unfortunately, Tristram is—or was—a lusty young knight, and even the narrator admits that the most he would find with Iseult of Brittany would be,

> Hours, if not of ecstasy,
> From violent anguish surely free!

Thus, the question in deciding between Iseult of Ireland and Iseult of Brittany is essentially that of deciding between Passion and Calm. Does one prefer moments of rapture followed by years of anguish or a lifetime of calm which knows neither anguish nor rapture? By the time Arnold finished the poem he knew the answer, but there is just the suggestion that while he was writing it he was not sure.

For in the poem *Lines written by a Death-bed* (later entitled *Youth and Calm*), which was published immediately preceding *Tristram and Iseult* in the 1852 volume, Arnold declares,

> *Calm's not life's crown, though calm is well.*
> 'Tis all perhaps which man acquires,
> But 'tis not what our youth desires.

If this sentiment were applied to Iseult of Brittany, she would receive considerably less favorable treatment than she now does, and there is some evidence that the lines once were associated with her poem. For in 1869 the first paragraph of *Lines written by a Death-bed* was inserted into *Tristram and Iseult* as the description of Iseult of Ireland lying in death (II, 131–46), and it is clear from the surrounding context that it was originally written for that position.[25] It is not likely that the second paragraph (including the lines quoted) was also written for *Tristram and Iseult*, but the fact that Arnold was writing such a poem at the same time and that he could associate it so closely with *Tristram and Iseult* suggests that he was of two minds about the conflict which it presented. For although Iseult of Brittany is certainly not "life's crown," neither is she so clearly a "second best" as *Youth and Calm* implies.

The true hierarchy is that Calm is better than Passion but not

25. The evidence is rhyme scheme, verse form, and various descriptive details. Tinker and Lowry (pp. 42–44) are certainly wrong in their account of this matter and Bonnerot (*Matthew Arnold*, pp. 85–86) is certainly right. Since *Youth and Calm* is in couplets and the first paragraph of *Lines* is in an irregular rhyme scheme, they probably did not originally belong together. *Youth and Calm* may have been written as a kind of pendant to *Stanzas in Memory of Edward Quillinan* (died July 8, 1851), for it appears in Rotha Quillinan's album under the date December 28, 1851, one day later than the *Stanzas*.

so good as Joy and that lasting Joy is not possible in this world. Thus, when the narrator asks of Iseult of Brittany, "And is she happy?" he replies, "Joy has not found her yet, nor ever will." Still, she has many simple pleasures in her children, her domestic companions, and the common objects of her daily life. For if we ask what it is "which shuts up eye and ear / To all that has delighted them before," we learn that it is not sorrow or suffering, rather it is

> the gradual furnace of the world . . . ,
> This, or some tyrannous single thought, some fit
> Of passion, which subdues our souls to it,
> Till for its sake alone we live and move—
> Call it ambition, or remorse, or love—

The antithesis between "the gradual furnace of the world" and the "tyrannous single thought" is the same as that between Slave and Madman in *A Summer Night*. The perplexing thing is that in this poem only the "tyrannous single thought" would seem to apply, and perhaps for this reason Arnold removed this passage of some forty lines from two editions of the poem. But he later restored it, perhaps because it expresses so clearly (too clearly?) a central theme of the poem, "how this fool passion gulls men potently." Some critics have thought that the passage ought to be discounted because it is spoken by the narrator, not by Arnold, and it is certainly true that Arnold would not have said it in quite this way. But he does say essentially the same thing elsewhere, and the effect of what he says (as distinct from its "medieval" tone) is borne out by the stylistic peculiarities of the poem as a whole.

For the three parts of the poem, called respectively "Tristram," "Iseult of Ireland," and "Iseult of Brittany," are written in three different styles appropriate to their several themes. The first is in the ballad manner and irregular four-stressed meter of Coleridge's *Christabel*. One may say that it is appropriate for the romantic beginning of the tale. The second largely replaces the narrative by a dramatic stichomythia between Tristram and Iseult of Ireland which is conducted in stanzas of trochaic pentameter with alternating masculine and feminine endings. It is a stanza which Arnold regularly used for moments of high passion and it is probably associated in his mind with the lyrics of Byron. It is the least successful part of the poem, and I think one may say that it is intended to be. It corresponds, in the structure of the poem, to Mycerinus' bombastic discourse and Empedocles' crabbed diatribe. It presents the fact of violent sexual passion, and the meaning of the poem consists in the attitude taken up by the poem as a whole toward this fact. As Empedocles spoke and then leaped into the volcano, so the lovers do the only thing left to them to do—die and leave the field to Iseult of Brittany. Her section is infinitely quieter and more mature. It is essentially the rhymed iambic pentameter as practiced by Keats or by Cowper.[26] Except for the one passage where the narrator medievalizes, the language is modern, flexible, dignified, and pure. It is a deliberate criticism of both the naive style of the first section and the strident style of the second section, and is simply the best kind of poetry that Arnold was able to write. Its effect is to give to Iseult of Brittany not only the last word but also the best.

Partly through this stylistic weight the characters in the third part of the poem gain an advantage over those in the other two. Essentially, they gain the same advantage that a true or buried self gains over a superficial self, and this may be seen most easily in the case of the two Iseults. Like most nineteenth-century doubles, the two Iseults are not really distinct persons but rather different aspects of the same personality. This is indicated by the fact that Arnold has chosen to entitle his poem simply *Tristram and Iseult*—in the singular—without specifying which Iseult is meant. Clearly, he means both: Tristram (the "man of sorrows") and the "Iseult element" in modern life, namely, woman. This is further confirmed by the fact that the two women—although the conflict is between them—never confront one another in the

26. Cf. Cowper's *The Needless Alarm*.

poem, rather succeed one another in separate sections. Iseult dies
as Ireland to be reborn as Brittany, and the process is subtly sug-
gested by Arnold in the scene where Iseult of Ireland, falling
upon the bed, actually takes on the lineaments of Iseult of Brit-
tany. We are told that "so healing is her quiet now" that she has
achieved in death "a tranquil, settled loveliness, / Her younger
rival's purest grace." A little later she "seems of marble on a
tomb," and this image is then taken up in Part III and applied to
the death-like routine of Iseult of Brittany—

to-morrow'll be
To-day's exact repeated effigy.

Indeed, the emphasis upon Iseult of Brittany's death-in-life—
"she seems one dying in a mask of youth"—is the principal thing
that detracts from the validity of her Calm. But this is somewhat
remedied in the person of her children. For if she dies as Ireland
to be reborn as Brittany, Tristram dies as himself to be reborn
as his own children—the Children of the Second Birth. In the
third section of the poem the action is entirely between Iseult of
Brittany and her children, and thus we once again have a poem
in which a highly sexual relationship is replaced by an asexual
relationship between mother and child.

The children are closely associated with Arnold's most notable
poetic device, the "end-symbol" or "coda." This is an image
which the poet introduces, without comment, at the end of the
work in order to lift the mind into the serenity of the third phase
of his myth. The river in *Mycerinus* is such a symbol, the Oxus
in *Sohrab and Rustum*, and the Tyrian trader in *The Scholar-
Gipsy*. Here each of the three parts has an end-symbol, though
to a certain extent the whole of the third part is end-symbol to
the first two. In every instance the symbol is some aspect of
Tristram commenting upon himself. In the first, which is by far
the clearest, it is the comment made upon his fever-bed by the
scene of his two children sleeping peacefully in the southern
wing of the castle. The emphasis in this picture is upon the cir-

cumscribed, enclosed character of the scene. The children's heads are "turn'd to each other—the eyes closed," and their lashes are "reposed" upon their cheeks. Round their brows "the cap close-set / Hardly lets peep the golden hair," and through their "soft-open'd lips the air / Scarcely moves the coverlet." Only "one little wandering arm" is thrown over the counterpane, and its fingers "close in haste" as on some butterfly.

> This stir they have, and this alone;
> But else they are so still!

The picture has an infantine prettiness that is somewhat cloying, but it is immediately qualified by the Jamesian suggestion that there is more stirring in these little children than the imagery of angel-heads, butterflies, and helpless birds would suggest. If they went to the window and looked out over the moonlit glade, would they not wish to follow their fancy over the park to the bare heaths, the moors, the inlets, and the glittering sea beyond —i.e. to break out of their closed situation into the vast open plain which was the scene of their father's wanderings? "Mad-caps" they are called when this possibility is opened, and as this was Tristram's word for Iseult in the pleasaunce-walk, it is suggested that, though at the moment they are Iseult of Brittany's children, they have it in them to become Iseult of Ireland's too.

Yet in the next end-symbol they have grown up from childhood into youth and see the result of such wandering. For as the lovers lie dead on the bed, they are, as it were, transformed into marble effigies and so can be spoken to by another figure from the world of art, a "stately Huntsman, clad in green," who is wrought upon an arras hanging in the chamber. He is too like the youthful Tristram not to suggest some earlier self passing judgment upon a later. And certainly there is a striking contrast between his scene on the arras, a "clear forest-knoll," and that of the lovers in their chamber bright. For he, in his fresh, youthful vitality, has paused but for a moment before he sweeps on through the glade with dogs and bugle after the rustling boar.

But their chamber is a closed, sterile place of hard, confining objects—the iron-figured door, the huge fireplace, the mullioned windows, and the effigies like "marble on a tomb." To the Huntsman it is an unreal, fantastic world, but as he gazes down upon it, his vision, like that of the children, wanders out through the window, over the court, across the drawbridge, past the moat, and over the reefs to "the unquiet bright Atlantic plain." In other words, he sees both the expanse into which the lovers were released and the prison in which they are now bound, and by this sight he is perplexed and bewildered. Just as the Scholar-Gipsy was urged to "fly our paths, our feverish contact fly," so the Huntsman is urged to cheer his dogs into the brake; for these lovers, once so hot, are now as "cold as those who lived and loved / A thousand years ago."

And yet, the Huntsman is judged by the lovers even as they are judged by him. For as he gazes down upon this scene "with heated cheeks and flurried air," he is somehow naive and rather foolish. He is so unacquainted with passion and death that he thinks the knight but sleeps and the lady kneels to pray, and that he himself was transported there by magic. He is a kind of Hippolytus, inexperienced in love, a follower of Diana not of Venus, and when he "stares and stares, with troubled face," we feel that new and disturbing thoughts are being aroused in him, such as Lord Henry aroused in Dorian Gray at the moment when he was becoming a picture. Momentarily he has stepped out of his eternal world of art into the real world of passion, and though he is told to flee back into his arras again, we doubt that he can ever be the same.

Finally, in the third part, the children of Tristram and Iseult come out of the end-symbol into the narrative itself and are made conscious objects of freedom and control through art. They are allowed to play on the grassy heath whose openness had tempted them by moonlight and been the scene of their father's wanderings. But their mother is careful that they do not wander far. They play "in a green circular hollow in the heath," and though from the hollow's banks one can see far and wide over the lone, unbroken waste, the children do not mount to these banks. They play "in the smooth centre of the opening," and when at length their cheeks have become "flushed" and their hair tumbled out from underneath their hats, as it had not done when they were asleep, Iseult apparently thinks they have gone far enough and calls them to her. They are then wrapt in warm mantles, and the three cluster under a screen made by three hollies, while Iseult tells them "an old-world Breton history." As, while they were asleep in the castle, they did not in fact wander because they saw "fairer in [their] dreams," so now the tale explains their dreams as a means of fixing the dangerous fancy. We are told that as they listened, "their blue eyes / Fix'd on their mother's face in wide surprise; / Nor did their looks stray once to the sea-side," nor to the heaths, nor to the snow, nor to anything else in that series of retreating objects which again ends "where the bright Atlantic gleams." In this way the children are calmed, and once the tale is told, then Iseult took them by the hand and "found the path, / And led them home over the darkening heath." Arnold, disciplining the reader in precisely the same way that Iseult disciplines the children, does not tell us the tale immediately, but makes us wait for eighty-seven lines before at last we hear, in indirect discourse, the story of Merlin and Vivian.

This last of the three end-symbols speaks, not of a child nor of a youth, but of an old man. Once again, it obviously relates to Tristram's case, for it is the tale of one who thought he was wise but foolishly allowed himself to be enslaved by passion. But, watchful as Iseult is, we must not think that she is crudely indoctrinating her children by an object-lesson about their father's passion. No, this is a tale in which she herself delights. It is one of many which she, as a child, "gleaned from Breton grandames" in their huts along the coast, and we are told that she loves these tales for their own sakes, can "forget all to hear them, as of old." Of course, the tale has a special meaning to her as having relevance to her own situation, and it may be that the children gain some inkling of the fact that the answer to Vivian's question, "How may I imprison a man without tower or wall or chain?" is, "By passion." But they must also recognize that it is very pleasant to be imprisoned by one so enchanting as Vivian and that the spot in which Merlin sleeps forever is a lovely spot, full of birds and bright-eyed squirrels and the shy fallow-deer, singularly similar to the heathy hollow in which they listened to his tale. For, as Keats says,

> when a tale is beautifully staid,
> We feel the safety of a hawthorne glade,[27]

and this is what the children felt in listening to the tale of Merlin. Through art they and their mother distanced themselves from their experience, achieved control over it, and transformed it into a thing of beauty. And it is clear that this is what Arnold intended by the episode, for he says that he introduced it into the poem for "relief."[28] "Relief" is an old-fashioned word which we do not like today because it seems to go against the organic theory of art. But it is clear that Arnold meant by it approximately what we have been saying, for he has left us a clue in his essay on Heine to the interpretation of this episode. There he quotes a passage from Heine which he must have been reading about 1848. "My body," says the German, "is so shrunk that there is hardly anything of me left but my voice, and my bed makes me think of the melodious grave of the enchanter Merlin, which is in the forest of Broceliand in Brittany, under high oaks whose tops shine like green flames to heaven. Ah, I envy thee those trees, brother Merlin, and their fresh waving! for over my mattress-grave here in Paris no green leaves rustle; and early and late I hear nothing but the rattle of carriages, hammering, scolding, and the jingle of the piano."[29] Heine's mattress-grave is anal-

27. *I Stood Tip-toe*, 129–30.

28. R. E. C. Houghton, *Times Literary Supplement*, 31 (May 19, 1932), 368.

29. *Essays in Criticism: First Series* (1902), p. 191; Super, *3*, 131. For Arnold's reading of Heine in 1848, see *Letters*, *1*, 11.

ogous to Tristram's fever-bed, and so it appears that the discussion of the loss of Joy, which postponed the telling of the tale, prepared us for it by containing a philosophy of art. For when Arnold says that sorrow and suffering are not incompatible with Joy, whereas the merely painful is, he is all but stating the doctrine of the 1853 preface, that the sorrowful subject is compatible with aesthetic pleasure, whereas the morbid is not. Both "the gradual furnace of the world," which is Heine's Paris, and the "tyrannous single thought," which is Tristram's passion, destroy Joy; but the "melodious grave" of Merlin is a symbol that mere sorrow, such as Iseult suffers, can be transmuted by song into aesthetic experience. It is Arnold's belief that Iseult has done this by means of the tale of Merlin, and it is perhaps his hint that he himself has done it by means of the poem as a whole. For when we read, in the last few lines of the poem, that Merlin was immured by Vivian in a "daisied circle" and recall that the French word for daisy is *marguerite*, it is almost as if Arnold had left his personal signature in one corner of his painting.

Arnold makes this theme of the transmutation of sorrow through art more explicit in the closely related poem *The Church of Brou*. The poem was not published until 1853, but it is connected by many details both to *Tristram and Iseult* and to the other Marguerite poems: by the Alpine setting, the medieval story, the name of the Duchess Marguerite, the boar hunt resembling that on the arras, and the marble tomb of the dead lovers which recalls the lovers who seemed "of marble on a tomb" in *Tristram and Iseult*. Like *Tristram and Iseult* the poem is divided into three parts, of which the first tells, in ballad stanza, the death of the young Duke of Savoy while hunting the boar. His death "in the bright October morning" is the ultimate tragic fact, senseless and brutal. We are told that when the Duchess Marguerite looked upon his mangled body, all her life within her froze, and that she, who hitherto had never sorrowed, henceforth never smiled. She devoted all her life to the erection in the mountains of the Church of Brou, which would be her husband's shrine and her own. On completing it, she died, and the second part of the poem tells how this shrine, so beautiful amid the mountains, was a source of wonder to the common people. In the third part, which is conducted in the same meter as the third part of *Tristram and Iseult*, the poet attempts to elucidate this wonder by meditating on what the Duke and Duchess have done in thus exchanging life for marble form. Essentially, they have combined the timelessness of the Grecian Urn with the transcendence of the lovers in the *Eve of St. Agnes*. Being out of time, they cannot hunt in the crisp woods till eve, but neither will they be brought bloody home at night. And thus the benediction, "So sleep, for ever sleep, O marble Pair!" Or, if they are to wake, let it be at some moment of unusual beauty, when Nature is transfiguring the shrine into the very semblance of Heaven. Two such moments are then imagined, the one emphasizing the warm light of the setting sun suffusing the rosy pavements of the church, and the other the clear light of the moon and the rain, falling upon its leaden roof. The two scenes are as different as they well can be, and yet the second is as beautiful as the first. Indeed, it is perhaps more beautiful, for whereas the first causes the Duke and Duchess to look down and imagine that they are on the pavements of heaven, the latter causes them to look up and imagine that the "dim pillars high" are the columns of the courts of heaven. The former scene is encrusted with jewels, but it is on the lichen-crusted leads above that they hear "the rustle of the eternal rain of love." Clearly, the art that arises out of sorrow will come closer to the religious experience than the art created out of joy.

5 EMPEDOCLES ON ETNA

To be or not to be?
                    —Hamlet

In the summer of 1849 J. C. Shairp wrote to Clough, "I saw the said Hero—Matt—the day I left London. He goes in Autumn to the Tyrol with Slade. He was working at an 'Empedocles'—which seemed to be not much about the man who leapt in the crater— but his name & outward circumstances are used for the drapery of his own thoughts." How much they were so used Shairp would have realized if he could have followed Arnold to Switzerland (his actual destination rather than the Tyrol) and seen him act out his own drama in the Bernese Alps. For Arnold's ascent into the mountains in September 1849 to wrestle with his own soul was certainly analogous to Empedocles' ascent of Mt. Etna to wrestle with his soul and "poise his life at last." Indeed, on the day before Arnold went up into the mountains he penned to Clough a note which might almost have been written by Empedocles. "My dearest Clough," he said, "these are damned times —everything is against one—the height to which knowledge is come, the spread of luxury, our physical enervation, the absence of great *natures*, the unavoidable contact with millions of small

ones, newspapers, cities, light profligate friends, moral desper-
adoes like Carlyle, our own selves, and the sickening conscious-
ness of our difficulties: but for God's sake let us neither be fanat-
ics nor yet chalf blown by the wind but let us be ὡς ὁ φρονιμος
διαρισειεν and not as any one else διαρισειεν"—" 'as the prudent
man would define' and not as any one else would 'define.' "[1] So
Empedocles, according to his friend Pausanias, deplored "the
swelling evil of this time"—

> since all
> Clouds and grows daily worse in Sicily,
> Since broils tear us in twain, since this new swarm
> Of sophists has got empire in our schools. . . .

The significant difference, of course, is that when Arnold reached
the top of the mountain he did not, like Empedocles, throw him-
self into a volcano. Rather, in rejecting Obermann, he threw his
own personal Empedocles into the volcano and came back down,
a whole man, to lead a useful life in the cities of the plain. Thus,
although in one sense *Empedocles on Etna* dramatizes what Ar-
nold did, in another it dramatizes what he did not do. It drama-
tizes what he was saved from doing by the fact that he did it
vicariously in the realm of art.

Goethe has put the matter very well with respect to the *Sor-
rows of Werther*. Speaking of the morbid melancholy from
which he suffered in 1772, he says, "In my collection of weapons,
which was pretty considerable, I possessed a valuable and well-
sharpened dagger. I always laid it next to my bed, and before I
put out the light I tried whether I could not sink the sharp point
a couple of inches into my heart. As I was never able to do so, I
at last ridiculed myself, cast off all my hypochondriac caprices,
and decided to continue living. In order to be able to do this
calmly, however, I had to carry into effect some poetic task, in
which everything that I had felt, thought, and imagined about
this important matter should find verbal expression." The result

---

1. *Letters to Clough*, pp. 111, 112 n.; Tinker and Lowry, p. 287.

was *Werther*, written in four weeks. But if the work acted as a catharsis for the author, it had just the opposite effect upon his friends. "Just as I felt eased and clearer in mind at having transformed reality into poetry, my friends became bewildered, since they thought that they must transform poetry into reality, imitate a novel like this in real life and, in any case, shoot themselves; and what occurred at first among a few took place later among the general public, so that this book, which had done me so much good, was condemned as being highly dangerous."[2] The difference in Arnold's case was that he became bewildered and condemned his own work as highly dangerous. It was first published in 1852, and in 1853 he declined to reprint it in the new edition of his poems. This decision, elaborated in the Preface of 1853, may be regarded as a second public exorcism of the spirit of Empedocles.

Empedocles on Etna was written, then, while Arnold was in a state of transition with respect to the attitude which it represents, and this fact probably explains some of the ambiguities which the work contains. A clue to its understanding may be found in the poem *Courage*, which was also first published in 1852 and also was not reprinted in 1853—indeed, was never thereafter reprinted by Arnold. The poet begins by asserting that he well knows the truth of the lesson, man must renounce, must tame his rebel will. And yet, in the present age, when even the boldest are swept along by fate and circumstance,

> Those sterner spirits let me prize,
> Who, though the tendence of the whole
> They less than us might recognize,
> Kept, more than us, their strength of soul.

Let praise be given to the second Cato and to Lord Byron, not for what they did—for the fierce and turbid song of the one and the

---

2. *Autobiography*, trans. W. Rose in *The Sorrows of Young Werther* (London, 1929), pp. xxi, xxiv.

self-destruction of the other—but because what they did they did dauntlessly and with fiery courage.

> Our bane, disguise it as we may,
> Is weakness, is a faltering course,

and the poet asks that to the clearness of our age be added the "force" of theirs.

It was in this mood, one feels, that *Empedocles on Etna* was written. Though in the first Obermann poem the poet had learned to renounce, and though in *A Farewell* he had rejected the strong Byronic soul and had declared that what we call "force" is really "hardness" and that energy is "far less rare than love," still he must have felt uneasy at times lest all these wise words were merely euphemisms for knuckling under, for being conquered by the world. In the sonnet *The World's Triumphs*, also in the 1852 volume, he imagines the world sardonically remarking, "So many fiery spirits quite cool'd down!" and he could hardly forget that in *On the Rhine* he had compared himself to an extinct volcano. Well, perhaps he was not quite extinct. Perhaps he could fling out one final protest, could assert once again, in all its bitterness and integrity, the supreme Promethean defiance. And so this is what he did in *Empedocles on Etna*. It is the reaffirmation, in terms appropriate to his own day, of the spirit of Manfred or Faust, Prometheus or Obermann. It is the expression of "Man's unconquerable mind," of the "unconquerable Will . . . / And courage never to submit or yield."

And yet, even as Arnold composed the drama, he must have felt a little uneasy about it. Writing to Clough, he said, "You must tell me what Emerson says. Make him look at it. *You* in your heart are saying *mollis et exspes* [unstrung and hopeless] over again. But woe was upon me if I analysed not my situation: and Werther, Réné, and such like none of them analyse the modern situation in its true *blankness* and *barrenness*, and *unpoetry-lessness*."[3]

3. *Letters to Clough*, p. 126.

The theme of *Empedocles on Etna* centers around the contrast between three ways of life as represented by Callicles, Empedocles, and Pausanias. As usual, the contrast is developed partly by means of the natural scene. Lyell says in his *Principles of Geology* (1830–33):

> The cone [of Etna] is divided by nature into three distinct zones called the *fertile*, the *woody*, and the *desert* regions. The first of these, comprising the delightful country around the skirts of the mountain, is well cultivated, thickly inhabited, and covered with olives, vines, corn, fruit-trees, and aromatic herbs. Higher up, the woody region encircles the mountain—an extensive forest, six or seven miles in width, affording pasturage for numerous flocks. The trees are of various species, the chestnut, oak, and pine being most luxuriant; while in some tracts are groves of cork and beech. Above the forest is the desert region, a waste of black lava and scoriæ; where, on a kind of plain, rises the cone to the height of about eleven hundred feet, from which sulphureous vapours are continually evolved.[4]

Arnold collapses the fertile and woody regions into one and adds a third, the hot cities on the dusty plain below. Each of these he associates with one of his characters, Pausanias with the cities, Empedocles with the barren cone, and Callicles with the fertile and woody region of the lower slopes.

Callicles is a symbol of youthful Joy. By Pausanias he is twice called "boy" and once a "child," and though he is not actually that young, he so delights people by his innocence and beauty that they think of him in these terms. He has some elements of the Strayed Reveller in him, for we are told that he is "for ever coming on these hills . . . / With a gay revelling band," but that "he breaks from them / Sometimes, and wanders far among the glens." On this particular night he has "slipp'd out" from the feast of Peisianax to the portico to breathe, and there, taking off

4. Bk. II, chap. 12.

his soiled garland and seeing Empedocles about to depart, he "all night long / Through the cool lovely country follow'd [him]." Not the hot feast, then, but the cool lovely country is his natural habitat, and it is this country which he offers to Empedocles as a balm to his vexed and wounded spirit. "What mortal could be sick or sorry here?" he asks. "Pausanias . . . / Could scarce have lighted on a lovelier cure." The mules linger in the cool, wet turf; the goats munch the long grey tufts of moss; and the cattle gather knee-deep in the cool ford. It is here, in what Arnold calls The Last Glen—"the last / Of all the woody, high, well-water'd dells / On Etna—" that Callicles invites Empedocles to linger. For here, where "one sees one's footprints crush'd in the wet grass" and "one's breath curls in the air," man is in harmony with nature.

Callicles' music expresses this harmony. He is "the sweetest harp-player in Catana," and the music he sings, which is designed to assist nature with its soothing restorative power, is liquid, lovely, and unperplexed. It is the product of the mythical imagination, which sees the volcano as Typho pinioned under the mountain and peoples the glens with centaurs, mænads, and fauns. In the course of the drama he sings five lyrics, which tell the myths of Chiron the centaur, Cadmus and Harmonia, Typho and the Olympians, Marsyas and Apollo, and Apollo the Leader of the Muses.

The first lyric presents Chiron, in just such a glen as that in which Callicles is singing, teaching the young Achilles the things that it is needful for man to know. It goes without saying that these are very different from the things which Empedocles is soon to be teaching Pausanias in a different part of the mountain. They include the natural lore of the woods and the practical wisdom of men, and as Chiron was half man and half beast and was versed in the healing arts of music and medicine, it may be supposed that in Callicles' eyes this is the ideal education. It will appear to be so in the eyes of many readers, but Arnold will gradually make it clear what is wanting to Callicles' view. Here we may say that the Centaur was undoubtedly associated by Arnold with the prose poem of that name by Maurice de Guérin, which Arnold declaimed rhapsodically as a youth of twenty-five. Maurice de Guérin was to Arnold a kind of French Keats, and as Callicles is a Greek poet of the same type, we may apply to him what Arnold said of Guérin—that his poetry was a magical interpretress of the natural world, but not of the moral world. "To make magically near and real the life of Nature, and man's life only so far as it is part of that Nature, was his faculty; a faculty of naturalistic, not of moral interpretation."[5] Like Wordsworth in *Memorial Verses*, he did not attempt to solve Empedocles' problems, merely to "put them by." His name derives, of course, from the Greek word for beauty, and he would willingly take as his own the legend of the Grecian urn:

> "Beauty is truth, truth beauty,"—that is all
> Ye know on earth, and all ye need to know.

Empedocles, however, did not think so. Long ago, in his own youth, he too had been such a person as Callicles. Wandering through the warm Italian countryside with his friend Parmenides, he had enjoyed the sports of the country people, a flute note from the woods, sunset over the sea. "Then," he declared—and the accents of Wordsworth are unmistakable—

> Then we could still enjoy, then neither thought
> Nor outward things were closed and dead to us;
> But we received the shock of mighty thoughts
> On simple minds with a pure natural joy.

Since then, however, he has followed far the "Sun-born Virgins on the road of truth," and they have carried him beyond the world of pure natural joy. And so, though he had formerly loved the harp of Callicles and though he willingly pauses and listens to it now, he cannot linger in The Last Glen nor redescend the mountain. And as Callicles' lyrics sing of the cattle who gather

5. *Essays in Criticism: First Series* (1902), p. 107; Super, 3, 30.

in the cool ford and of the bright and aged snakes who bask by the sea-shore, we do not want him to, for we see that this would involve a descent to a lower form of existence, to man's life only so far as it is a part of nature. Therefore, despite Callicles' warning—

> glade,
> And stream, and sward, and chestnut-trees,
> End here; Etna beyond, in the broad glare
> Of the hot noon, without a shade,
> Slope beyond slope, up to the peak, lies bare—

Empedocles proceeds over the blazing slope to the lonely and turbulent peak which is his natural home.

But not before he has spoken to Pausanias. And who is Pausanias? He is a "good, learned, friendly, quiet man," who is described as Empedocles' physician. "Physician," however, in this drama of spiritual maladies is to be interpreted "physician of souls," and in this sense all the characters in the drama are physicians. The only question is, by what means do they heal? for Callicles heals by music, Empedocles by intellectual analysis, and Pausanias by "spells." This, indeed, is why he has followed Empedocles up the mountain. He has heard that Empedocles has recently performed a "miracle," calling back to life a woman, Pantheia, who had lain thirty long days in a cold trance of death, and he says that in these days, when the Gods visit us with sign and plague, to know the secret of that miracle were very well. "Bah!" replies Callicles,

> Thou a doctor! Thou art superstitious.
> Simple Pausanias, 'twas no miracle!
> Pantheia, for I know her kinsmen well,
> Was subject to these trances from a girl.
> Empedocles would say so, did he deign;
> But he still lets the people, whom he scorns,
> Gape and cry *wizard* at him, if they list.

Arnold's use of the word "miracle" in an otherwise classical play
is significant, for it points to the nineteenth-century parallel
which runs throughout the drama. Just as Callicles recalls the
Wordsworthian or Keatsian poet of nature and myth, and just as
the sophists who have won empire in the schools are analogous
to the triumphant Utilitarian or positivistic philosophers, so Pau-
sanias is the type of bewildered nineteenth-century clergyman
who sees in miracles the focal point in the conflict between sci-
ence and religion. Arnold admits in one of his letters that *Em-
pedocles on Etna* betrays an "impatience with the language and
assumptions of the popular theology of the day,"[6] and this im-
patience is centered on the figure of Pausanias. Empedocles, ac-
cording to one of Arnold's notebooks, represents "refusal of
limitation by the religious sentiment,"[7] that is to say, refusal to
limit one's intellect by the deep desire to believe which all men
have. Pausanias, then, would represent "limitation by the reli-
gious sentiment." Living as he does in one of the cities of the
plain, he is obviously a Slave, and that by which he is enslaved
is religion. He is one of an evil and adulterous generation who,
except they see signs and wonders, will not believe. And yet he
has to believe.

If Pausanias wrote poetry it would not be Romantic poetry
such as Callicles writes, or Arnoldian poetry such as Empedocles
writes, but Victorian poetry such as Tennyson and Browning
wrote. And one has the feeling that under the figure of Pausa-
nias Arnold may be making a sly allusion to his fellow poets. For
it is striking that the miracle in Christian story which is parallel
to the classical miracle of Pantheia is the raising of Lazarus, and
that both Tennyson and Browning made use of that miracle in
poems nearly contemporaneous with Arnold's. Tennyson used
it in *In Memoriam,* and since *In Memoriam,* published two years
before *Empedocles on Etna,* is the poem in which Tennyson
struggles with the same intellectual and spiritual problems as

6. Tinker and Lowry, p. 288.
7. Ibid., p. 11.

did Arnold, one suspects a covert allusion.[8] Of course, Tennyson's poem differs from Arnold's in that he won through to a kind of faith. But, as T. S. Eliot has said, the quality of Tennyson's faith is less high than the quality of his doubt, for it depends on a specious conception of evolution and a specious proof of immortality. Thus, despite the fact that *In Memoriam* is a beautiful poem and that Arnold admired its beauty, he might well have thought that intellectually it represents "limitation by the religious sentiment."

Or take the case of Browning. Browning's treatment of the Lazarus story is in the *Epistle of Karshish,* not published until 1855 and so not relevant here except as showing the importance of the Lazarus-Pantheia theme to the Victorian poet. But the poem of his which most closely resembles *Empedocles on Etna* is *Saul,* where a youthful harp-player very much like Callicles tries to relieve the gloom of an aged king very much like Empedocles. It is barely possible that Arnold was influenced by the first part of this poem, which was published in 1845. In that part David sang, as Callicles does, of the joy of mere living, and apparently in 1845 that was as far as Browning was able to go. But ten years later, under the influence of his wife and the writing of *Christmas-Eve and Easter-Day,* he had advanced in his faith to the point where he was able to add the humanistic argument and the argument from Christian revelation which make up the last part of the poem. By the Christian argument Saul is restored, whereas Empedocles dies in his volcano. It is very paradoxical that Browning should have been the person who persuaded Arnold to republish *Empedocles on Etna,* and one wonders what his motive was. Was it that the spectacle of what happened to Empedocles in 1852 led him to rescue Saul in 1855, or was it merely, as the letters to "dearest Isa" indicate, that he saw himself and Miss Blagden in the image of the "two bright and aged snakes"

8. *In Memoriam,* secs. 31–32. Cf. Kathleen Tillotson, "Rugby 1850: Arnold, Clough, Walrond, and In Memoriam," *Review of English Studies,* n.s., 4 (1953), 122–40.

basking in the glens?[9] If so, then he was really a follower of Callicles rather than Pausanias, and might have left his own poem where it was.

Pausanias, of course, does not receive from Empedocles the secret which he desires but instead is the recipient of a lengthy discourse which Empedocles believes will be more truly helpful to him. This discourse is couched in a harsh, crabbed style which deliberately contrasts with the musical qualities of Callicles' lyrics. It stands to the lyrics as the blackened waste of the volcano does to the wooded glens. It is generally disliked by readers because it is so aridly intellectual and uncouth, and once again, one may say that it is intended to be disliked. It is the statement of the unpleasant truths about the universe which a simple person like Pausanias needs to know if he is to live his life aright. It tells him that the universe was not made for his special benefit but existed long before he was born and doubtless will continue to exist after he dies. Neither beneficent nor malignant, it operates according to laws of its own which are perfectly regular and perfectly amoral. If Pausanias is unhappy, it is because he is unable to accept this fact but continually deludes himself with hopes or fears which are unfounded. In particular, he invents gods as the vehicle of these hopes and fears. If he could but put aside these illusions and see the world as it is, and if he could manage his own affairs with courage and decency, he would find enough pleasure by the way to make life reasonably acceptable. The advice is the sound advice of Carlyle, Spinoza, Epictetus, and Lucretius; it distinctly resembles the wan hopes of the later Mill. It is offered to Pausanias in the manner of an impatient adult lecturing a naughty child. In the beginning, the lecturer is harsh, and the exclamation "Fools!" appears frequently. Later on, there is a certain tender compassion for this bewildered friend. But throughout the discourse the tone is practical and the imagery

9. William Clyde DeVane, *A Browning Handbook* (2d ed. New York, 1955), p. 257; Tinker and Lowry, p. 286; *Dearest Isa: Robert Browning's Letters to Isabella Blagden*, ed. E. C. McAleer (Austin, 1951), p. 105 n.

humble. The examples used are those of the rude guest, the child who vents his rage upon the stones, the village churl who enjoys his simple pleasures, the soul of man as a toy mirror spinning in the wind, and the world itself as a toy new-made for our pleasure. In this simple and practical fashion does Empedocles keep his advice within the comprehension of his hearer.

This view of the discourse will perhaps rescue it from the misunderstanding to which it is sometimes subject. It is sometimes said that the discourse presents the "philosophy" of Empedocles and that, as such, it ought to bear a clear relation to the suicide which follows. Even Arnold has lent support to this view by suggesting that the discourse does explain the suicide. In a letter to a friend, Henry Dunn, in which he was concerned with denying that the discourse embodied his own personal views, he said, "No critic appears to remark that if Empedocles throws himself into Etna his creed can hardly be meant to be one to live by."[10] But the creed is meant to be one to live by, and it does not contain the reason why Empedocles throws himself into Etna. Indeed, it is not really Empedocles' "creed" at all. It is offered to Pausanias as a view of the world, better than what he has, by means of which he can, if he will, descend into the cities and live a life more satisfactory than that which he now knows. It is true that this life will not be very exalted, but at least it will be an honest life, not a deluded one, and that is what Pausanias primarily needs.

The practical, *ad hominem* character of the discourse, then, is its important feature. After it is over, Empedocles speaks of it as a "lesson" and says that by its means Pausanias "May bravelier front his life, and in himself / Find henceforth energy and heart. But I—" and he then indicates that for himself this advice is no cure. The reason why it is not is that it represents the exoteric, rather than the esoteric, side of his philosophy. True so far as it goes, it is purely practical in intent, like the Stoic and Epicurean thought from which it is derived, and it is not concerned with the speculative matters which have given rise to his own

10. Tinker and Lowry, p. 288.

problems. For Empedocles is the type of the lonely metaphysical thinker. He has looked upon the uttermost secrets of the world, and has seen them bare. Moreover, he has been blasted by what he saw. What these secrets are we are not told—any more than we are told what the curse was which Prometheus uttered, or the deed which Manfred did, or any other incommunicable absolute by means of which the Romantic hero is fulfilled and then destroyed. But we are made to understand that Empedocles has a direct, not a mythical, knowledge of reality. In the prose outline which Arnold drew up for the poem, he says, "He sees things as they are—the world as it is—God as he is: in their stern simplicity. The sight is a severe and mind-tasking one: to know the mysteries which are communicated to others by fragments, in parables."[11] When Callicles sings the myth of Typho, Empedocles comments, "He fables, yet speaks truth," and translates the fable into abstract moral terms. In his youth, when he first began the quest for truth, we are told that "if the sacred load oppress'd [his] brain," he would ease it in "the delightful commerce of the world." But now he can do so no longer. He has become the slave of his own intellect, of "the imperious lonely thinking-power." He apparently possesses the almost godlike capabilities which the pursuit of truth requires, but at the same time he discovers in himself emotional needs that cannot so be satisfied. The Romantic hero frequently unites in himself an element of the infinite with an element of the finite. This is the form which that incongruous union takes in Empedocles.

Arnold has discussed this problem of the disparity between intellectual and emotional needs in his essay of 1863, "Dr. Stanley's Lectures on the Jewish Church." The essay, which follows from Arnold's attack on Bishop Colenso's writings on the Pentateuch, distinguishes between the perfect freedom belonging to a purely speculative thinker and the obligation of a religious teacher to place his ideas in a proper relation with the religious life of his times. The distinction is analogous to that between

11. Ibid., p. 291.

Empedocles' thinking for himself and his ministering to the needs of Pausanias, and it clearly argues for an esoteric and an exoteric body of thought. Literary criticism, says Arnold, perceives

> that the ideal life—the *summum bonum* for a born thinker, for a philosopher like Parmenides, or Spinoza, or Hegel—is an eternal series of intellectual acts. It sees that this life treats all things, religion included, with entire freedom as subject-matter for thought, as elements in a vast movement of speculation. The few who live this life stand apart, and have an existence separate from that of the mass of mankind; they address an imaginary audience of their mates; the region which they inhabit is the laboratory wherein are fashioned the new intellectual ideas which, from time to time, take their place in the world. Are these few justified, in the sight of God, in so living? That is a question which literary criticism must not attempt to answer . . . No doubt, many boast of living this life, of inhabiting this purely intellectual region, who cannot really breathe its air: they vainly profess themselves able to live by thought alone, and to dispense with religion: the life of the many, and not the life of the few, would have been the right one for them. They follow the life of the few at their peril.[12]

When Empedocles, at the end of his solitary discourse, cries aloud for air—"The air is thin, the veins swell, / The temples tighten and throb there — / Air! Air!"—he is acknowledging that he does not really belong in this region, that he lives its life at his peril. In his essay, "The Modern Element in Literature," Arnold mentions other philosophers who were in the same situation. Lucretius, for example, withdrawing from the varied spectacle of Roman life, attempted to penetrate to the nature of things. "But," says Arnold, "there is no peace, no cheerfulness for him either in

12. Super, 3, 65–66.

the world from which he comes, or in the solitude to which he goes. With stern effort, with gloomy despair, he seems to rivet his eyes on the elementary reality, the naked framework of the world, because the world in its fulness and movement is too exciting a spectacle for his discomposed brain." So he is "overstrained, gloom-weighted, morbid . . ." So too with Epictetus and Marcus Aurelius. It is impossible, says Arnold, to rise from a reading of these philosophers "without feeling that the burden laid upon man is well-nigh greater than he can bear. Honour to the sages who have felt this, and yet have borne it! Yet, even for the sage, this sense of labour and sorrow in his march towards the goal constitutes a relative inferiority; the noblest souls of whatever creed, the pagan Empedocles as well as the Christian Paul, have insisted on the necessity of an inspiration, a joyful emotion, to make moral action perfect."[13]

In a modest way Arnold himself apparently bore this burden. Writing to Clough in February 1853, he declared, "Yes,—*congestion of the brain* is what we suffer from—I always feel it and say it—and cry for air like my own Empedocles." In his later years Arnold freely and engagingly admitted that he had no metaphysics—no "philosophy with coherent, interdependent, subordinate and derivative principles"—but in his youth he apparently attempted to acquire one. His reading lists for 1845–47 present a formidable array of technical philosophical talent. Starting with Victor Cousin's *Introduction à l'histoire de la philosophie*, they include several dialogues of Plato, Kant (the critique), Mill (the Logic), Berkeley, Augustine, Descartes on Method, Coleridge *passim*, Bacon (*De Augmentis*), Lucretius, Cudworth's *Intellectual System*, Humboldt on the *Bhagavad-Gita*, Stillingfleet, Schelling's *Bruno*, Plotinus, Herder's *Metakritik to Kant's Kritik*, and Creuzer's *Symbolik*. No wonder that in the letter to Clough about these "damned times" the first item which Arnold mentions is "the height to which knowledge is

13. Super, 1, 33–34; "Marcus Aurelius," *Essays in Criticism: First Series* (1902), p. 346; Super, 3, 134.

come;" and no wonder that in *The Second Best*, published in 1852, he declares,

> But so many books thou readest,
> But so many schemes thou breedest,
> But so many wishes feedest,
>   That thy poor head almost turns.

He is leading "A strain'd life, while overfeeding, / Like the rest, his wit with reading." Hence, on May 1, 1853, he writes to Clough, "I feel immensely—more and more clearly—what I *want*—what I have (I believe) lost and choked by my treatment of myself and the studies to which I have addicted myself. But what ought I to have done in preference to what I have done? there is the question."[14]

In these remarks we see developing the concept of the nineteenth- and twentieth-century "intellectual hero." Coleridge had foreshadowed it when by "abstruse research" he had tried to dull his sufferings and had dulled imagination instead. Mill became a pale, neurasthenic type of it in the famous chapter of his *Autobiography* in which he describes his "mental crisis." Under the education imposed upon him by his father he became so addicted to intellectual analysis that, by age twenty, he suddenly found himself indifferent to the ends which analysis was supposed to achieve. Ultimately, some degree of feeling returned, but in the meantime he had to adopt, as a solution to his difficulties, a kind of "as if" philosophy, whereby, although he knew with one half of his mind that one thing was true, he had to act, with the other half, as if it were not. This "dialogue of the mind with itself"[15]—Arnold's phrase for the malady of Hamlet, Faust, and Empedocles—became the characteristic of the post-Romantic introspective hero. George Sand quite properly distinguished be-

14. *Letters to Clough*, pp. 130, 136; Kenneth Allott, "Matthew Arnold's Early Reading-Lists in Three Early Diaries," *Victorian Studies*, 2 (1959), 254–66.

15. *Poetical Works*, p. xvii.

tween the early Romanticism of Werther, which involved simply the conflict of the individual against the world, and the more complex "modern" attitude of René and Obermann, which involved the individual against himself. In René it was superior abilities without will-power; in Obermann it was moral elevation without ability. In Empedocles it is intellectual power without emotional resource.

It is this that gives rise to Empedocles' dilemma, "Thou canst not live with men nor with thyself." That, in turn, determines the form of the second part of the drama, for in Act II Empedocles swings back and forth between the two poles of solitude and society until at last he ends in death. The oscillation begins mildly in the first act with Pausanias' and Callicles' discussion of the origin of Empedocles' malady. The former attributes it to external causes, the latter, more profoundly, to internal. The theme is then continued in the lyrics which Callicles sings at the beginning of Act II, for these lyrics are the occasion of Empedocles' dramatically re-enacting, first, his repudiation of the world and then of himself. The first lyric tells the story of Typho, the hundred-headed monster who made war on Zeus and who was pinioned under Etna, where his groans issue in the rumblings of the volcano. Empedocles not unnaturally identifies with him and sees in the petty, complacent Olympians a world of little men who throng about a philosopher, not for his wisdom, but for his arts of necromancy. And so in disgust he throws down his golden circlet and purple robe, "ensigns / Of my unloved preëminence / In an age like this," and repudiates the world.

The second lyric recounts the story of Marsyas and Apollo. Marsyas is the woodland faun who has presumptuously challenged Apollo to a musical contest, and since his flute is no match for the lyre of the god, he is defeated and now is to be flayed alive. Trembling and weeping, the mænads and other creatures of the woodland come flocking about the god, imploring mercy, but Apollo turns hautily away, young, arrogant, and cruel. What can Empedocles see in this but the flaying of his own joyous former self by his present cold, man-hating mood, and so he throws down his laurel bough—"Scornful Apollo's ensign, lie thou there!"—and repudiates himself.

In these two lyrics, then, Empedocles re-enacts his dilemma, "Thou canst not live with men nor with thyself." "O sage!" he cries, "Take then the one way left; / And turn thee to the elements, thy friends." With this speech the conflict changes its form, for whereas previously it has been between Empedocles and the social world of man, now it is between Empedocles and nature. Previously, the solitary vision of Empedocles had included nature, and it was merely that he was unable to endure this vision without human companionship. Now we wonder whether there is something in the vision itself which makes it intolerable. Is it nature that is so bleak and forbidding? the cosmos that is dead? Empedocles puts this question as he addresses the stars. "And you, ye stars . . . , / Have you, too, survived yourselves?" Are you no longer "the radiant, rejoicing, intelligent Sons of Heaven" which you were under the old dispensation, but have you become the "cold-shining lights" of modern science, who "renew, by necessity, / Night after night your courses?" No, the answer comes, neither stars, nor earth, nor cloud, nor sea are dead—

> I alone
> Am dead to life and joy, therefore I read
> In all things my own deadness.

Adopting, then, the answer which Coleridge had given in *Dejection: an Ode,* and which Arnold himself had given in *The Youth of Nature,* that the loss of Joy is the loss of a power in the individual, not of a quality in the world, Empedocles returns to himself as the source of his difficulties. But then, as he contemplates the death which will take the four elements in his body back to the elements in nature which are their home—body to earth, blood to water, heat to fire, and breath to air—he asks, "But mind? but thought?"

Where will *they* find their parent element?
What will receive *them*, who will call them home?

Wordsworth, meditating upon Mt. Snowdon, had sensed a Universal Mind in the workings of nature, but Empedocles, brooding upon Mt. Etna, found no such thing. Is the poem, then, becoming a critique of paganism, in that, unlike Christianity and Romanticism, it posited nothing in nature corresponding to mind in man? So it would appear for a moment, but then the poem swings back the other way, and we learn that the absence of mind in the universe is not a defect but a strength. For "mind" in this poem is not the Reason but the Understanding. Its effect upon man is to

> keep us prisoners of our consciousness,
> And never let us clasp and feel the All
> But through their [mind's and thought's] forms, and modes
> and stifling veils.

Mind or thought is then presented by the poet as the antithesis of "flesh" or "sense," and the mind-sense dilemma corresponds to that between the self and the world. The way to resolve this dilemma, then, is not through "mind" but through what Arnold calls "soul," and it turns out that "soul" is a synonym for the Buried Life. For if we would "poise our life at last," the way to do so is to be "true / To our own only true, deep-buried selves." Then, being one with that, "we are one with the whole world." For though there is no God or Universal Mind in Empedocles' world, there is an All, a "life of life," and the way to know this All is not by exaggerating one part of our nature at the expense of another, but by achieving a balance or harmony among them. For in accordance with the Platonic doctrine, soul is a harmony of all the elements, not anything distinct from them, and the All of the universe is likewise a harmony, the life-circulation of nature. If Arnold is thinking in terms of the *Bhagavad-Gita*, as he probably is, then what Empedocles comes to understand is that the Atman, or individual soul, is identical with the Brahman, or universal soul.

The answer, then, to the question whether Empedocles' malady has its source in his own nature or in the world is that, ultimately, it has its source in his own nature. This is the one great truth that he learns. Not, of course, that his world would ever be a cozy, anthropomorphic place in which to live. It is bleak, amoral, austere. And not that contemporary society affords much help. It is a world of little men, of uncongenial spirits. But Empedocles is well beyond complaining about that. His trouble is that he has not found it in him to live in this world with Joy. Had he balanced his own life, "lived ever in the light of [his] own soul," he might, perhaps, have "nursed an immortal vigour" such as he now perceives in nature. But he did not. He has exaggerated the thinking side and so has become

> A living man no more . . . !
> Nothing but a devouring flame of thought—
> But a naked, eternally restless mind!

This admission marks the lowest point in Empedocles' development. Once it is made, it immediately provokes a reaction. For even if he does not have it in him to be a joyous Nietzschean superman, neither does he wish to go to the other extreme and be "human, all too human." This is his greatest fear. He is afraid that under the pain of isolation he will break and become like Pausanias. In his prose outline for the drama Arnold says, "he desires to die; to be reunited with the universe, before by exaggerating his human side he had become utterly estranged from it." And so, in his last speech Empedocles firmly reasserts his own value. True, he had been a "slave of thought."

> But I have not grown easy in these bonds—
> But I have not denied what bonds these were.
> Yea, I take myself to witness,
> That I have loved no darkness,

Sophisticated no truth,
Nursed no delusion,
Allow'd no fear!

The meaning of this speech is made clear by a phrase from one of Arnold's notebooks: "Je ne me suis pas refugié avec un Dieu human, exclusif, antinaturel—no, I take myself to witness &c." Lacking, as Arnold says in his prose outline, "the religious consolation of other men, facile because adapted to their weaknesses,"[16] he nevertheless lives resolutely without it. He represents "refusal of limitation by the religious sentiment." His heroism is the heroism of pure intellectual integrity, of not believing what he would like to believe merely because it would be more comforting to do so. It may be that "the burden laid upon [him] is well-nigh greater than he can bear." But—"Honour to the sages who have felt this, and yet have borne it!" It may be that we should tame our will and submit, but—Honour to Byron and the second Cato, who did not submit! Honour to Obermann, who, in one of Arnold's essays, refused to become a *terrae filii* and go with the stream but cried, *Périssons en résistant!*[17] Honour to Empedocles, who in this final moment felt the old ardor glow within him, saw the living sea of fire rising to meet him, and knew that it had been granted him

Not to die wholly, not to be all enslaved.
I feel it in this hour.

Empedocles' suicide, then, is a complex act which cannot be interpreted wholly in one way or another. On the one hand, it is not, like the suicides of Werther and Manfred, the act whereby the Romantic hero transcends limitation and unites himself with the All. So much is indicated by the fact that Empedocles will not, after death, be received by the elements but, because he has lived by Strife, will be forced to go through a series of reincarna-

16. Tinker and Lowry, pp. 292, 291; Yale Manuscript, fol. 9r.
17. *Essays in Criticism: First Series* (1902), p. 28; Super, 3, 276.

tions for a period of 30,000 years. Like the damned in *Paradise Lost*, who are haled back and forth from ice to raging fire, Empedocles will be rejected by each of the four elements in turn. "For the mighty Air drives him into the Sea, and the Sea spews him forth on the dry Earth; Earth tosses him into the beams of the blazing Sun, and [Sun] flings him back to the eddies of Air. One takes him from the other, and all reject him."[18] So says a fragment from the writings of the historical Empedocles, which Arnold found in the edition of Simon Karsten and used in his poem. Empedocles' philosophy also provided, however, for certain purificatory rites whose purpose was to release the soul from the "wheel of birth," that is, from reincarnations, and return it to everlasting bliss. This idea Arnold is able to embody in his thought that ultimately Empedocles will abandon Strife and adopt that Love, or harmony of all the parts of the soul, which will give rise to the Buried Self. Until he does, however, he will be a slave of thought and tied to the "wheel."

On the other hand, Empedocles will not be wholly enslaved because of what he achieved in the last moment of his life. For Arnold found in the *Bhagavad-Gita*, whose thought is very closely related to the Orphic religion of Empedocles, the idea that the disposition of one's mind at the hour of death is very important in determining the soul's state after death. "Whatever condition of being one meditates on as he leaves the body at death, precisely to that condition he goes, his whole being infused therewith."[19] Therefore, since Empedocles meditates on fire, he goes to fire.

> —Ah, boil up, ye vapours!
> Leap and roar, thou sea of fire!

18. Simon Karsten, ed., *Philosophorum Graecorum veterum praesertim qui ante Platonem floruerunt operum reliquiae* (Amsterdam, 1830–38), 2, 85. The translation is from John Burnet, *Early Greek Philosophy* (New York, 1960), p. 222.

19. *Bhagavad-Gita*, VIII, 6 (tr. F. Edgerton).

My soul glows to meet you. . . .
Receive me, save me!

The volcanic element in Empedocles is received by the volcanic element in nature. Though in part his suicide is a destruction of a defiant self in hopes that a new harmonious self will be created, in part it is a reaffirmation of defiance as having its own validity in the modern world.

The total meaning of the drama, of course, does not lie in Empedocles alone, but in him in relation to Pausanias and especially to Callicles. And it is notable that Callicles undergoes a certain transformation throughout the poem. Beginning as a person, he ultimately becomes a voice, a disembodied song that drifts up the mountainside. Even these songs gradually change their character. The first two seem to speak in Callicles' own person, representing the green pastoral escapism that is the lower side of his philosophy. They invite to linger in the glen, as the cattle do, to bask in the sunshine, as do the bright and aged snakes. But the next two no longer seem to reflect his opinions. Instead, they rather lend themselves to the purposes of Empedocles. In the myth of Typho, for example, Callicles' intent is presumably to show Empedocles that everyone responds to the healing power of music except a perverse rebel like Typho. And in the first Pythian ode of Pindar, on which his lyric is modelled, he had a song which said just that. But in reinterpreting it he unluckily represented the gods, who did respond to the power of music, as so bland and complacent—so much "at ease in Zion"—as actually to confirm Empedocles in his preference for Typho. Similarly in the myth of Marsyas and Apollo. Here Callicles' purpose is again to demonstrate the therapeutic and persuasive power of music:

> The music of the lyre blows away
> The clouds which wrap the soul.

But strangely, he identifies himself with the music of Apollo:

> Oh! that Fate had let me see
> That triumph of the sweet persuasive lyre.

There is no reason why Callicles should consider the lyre of Apollo to be sweet or why he should wish to see what is essentially the triumph of Empedocles over himself. Neither is there any reason why he should want Empedocles to see it, for it can hardly have any effect upon him other than to fill him with self-disgust and drive him to suicide. But Callicles is blissfully ignorant of all this. He sings these songs simply because they are beautiful and because they are about music. He is the kind of artist who does not realize that poems have a content as well as a form. Empedocles, on the other hand, is the kind of artist who does not realize that poems have a form as well as a content. And so the one sings to the other songs whose form is designed to cure him, while the other listens to their content and is moved by them to the edge of destruction.

In the final lyric the process whereby Callicles becomes a kind of chorus or disembodied voice is carried to the point where his voice is indistinguishable from that of the author. For in the last lyric there is nothing said that is not also said in the Preface of 1853. This is what makes Arnold's rejection of the poem in the Preface so paradoxical—the fact that he had already rejected it in the poem itself. In the stanza,

> Not here, O Apollo!
> Are haunts meet for thee.
> But, where Helicon breaks down
> In cliff to the sea,

Callicles has said explicitly that Empedocles is not a proper subject for poetry. And although initially, as Apollo and the Muses stream up the moon-silvered inlets, the poem seems to be suggesting a renewed pastoralism, the essential similarity of this image to that in the third part of *The Forsaken Merman* and *To Marguerite—Continued* makes it clear that this is the third phase of Arnold's world, not the first. And the Apollo who leads the Muses is not the Apollo of the preceding lyric, nor is he Marsyas or Callicles. He is rather a new type of poet who will announce, as the proper subjects of poetry, those set forth in the Preface of 1853. "What are the eternal objects of Poetry?" asks Arnold in the Preface. "They are actions; human actions . . .; and what actions are the most excellent? Those, certainly, which most powerfully appeal to the great primary human affections: to those elementary feelings which subsist permanently in the race, and which are independent of time."[20] So of Apollo and the Muses:

> —Whose praise do they mention?
> Of what is it told?—
> What will be for ever;
> What was from of old.
>
> First hymn they the Father
> Of all things; and then,
> The rest of immortals,
> The action of men.
>
> The day in his hotness,
> The strife with the palm;
> The night in her silence,
> The stars in their calm.

20. *Poetical Works*, pp. xix–xx.

6 THE SCHOLAR-GIPSY

Was it a vision, or a waking dream?

—Keats

The story of *The Scholar-Gipsy* begins in 1844, when Arnold acquired a copy of Joseph Glanvill's *The Vanity of Dogmatizing* (1661). In the twentieth chapter of this work he found an account of a young Oxford lad of pregnant parts who, wanting the encouragement of preferment, left the university to live with the gipsies. Chancing, sometime after, to meet with a group of his former companions who expressed astonishment at his way of life, he told them that the gipsies were not such impostors as they were supposed, but that they had a traditional kind of learning among them of great value. To illustrate this learning, he placed his friends in one room of an inn while he went into another; then, returning among them, he told them what they had talked of in his absence, and he revealed that "what he did was by the power of *Imagination*, his Phancy *binding* theirs; and that himself had dictated to them the discourse, they held together, while he was from them."[1] He added that when he had fully mastered

1. P. 198. Arnold's copy, now in the Yale Library, is inscribed on the fly-leaf, "E Lib. M. Arnold 1844."

this art he intended to leave the gipsies and impart his knowledge to the world.

The art which the gipsies practised would be known today as hypnotism; among the Victorians it was known as animal magnetism or mesmerism. It is very possible that it was through this interest that Arnold was drawn to Glanvill's volume, for when the poem which resulted from it first appeared in the lists of his poetic projects, it was described as "The first mesmerist" (in 1849) and as "? the wandering Mesmerist" [in 1850–51].[2] Moreover, 1844 was the year in which England woke up to mesmerism.

Harriet Martineau, the friend of the Arnold's, was the means of this awakening. In that year, after a prolonged illness diagnosed as the result of uterine displacement and tumor, she experienced, or thought she experienced, a miraculous cure at the hands of the mesmerists Spencer Hall and Henry George Atkinson. Not being one to hide any new scientific miracle under her bushel, she immediately published her experience to the world in a series of five letters to the *Athenaeum*. These appeared in November–December 1844 and were later published as a pamphlet. *Zoist*, a periodical founded in 1843 for the discussion of cerebral physiology (phrenology) and mesmerism, noted that this had brought into the daily papers, and into general discussion, a doctrine which previously had been ignored. There was, indeed, a great controversy. In addition to relating her own case, Miss Martineau had given instances of clairvoyancy on the part of her landlady's niece, Jane. Unhappily, Dilke, the editor of the *Athenaeum*, published on December 28 "A Few Words by Way of Comment" which cast doubt on the credibility of Jane. Much discussion followed, and one may indicate its tenor by saying that Miss Barrett believed, Robert Browning did not. Jane Welsh Carlyle was caustic. Wordsworth, however, notes that Miss Fenwick is "strongly infected with the Mesmeric mania," and he is

2. Tinker and Lowry, pp. 12, 17. Glanvill appeared on Arnold's list of books to be read "From October 1845 to [blank]." Ibid., p. 205.

therefore pleased to tell her, in 1845, that "the Herald & Proclaimer of the Virtues of the Process"—namely Miss Martineau herself—"is desirous of obtaining a Lodging in these parts . . . She has dined with the Fletchers, with Doctor Davy, and drank tea with Mrs. Arnold—and they are all charmed with her."[3] Mrs. Arnold, indeed, was so charmed that she became a sort of convert to the doctrine, but there is no evidence that her son did. He had no interest, he said, in Miss Martineau's "cow-keeping miracles" or other miracles, and no respect for her veracity. "Is [Emerson] gone crazy as Miss Martineau says," he asked. "But this is probably one of her d——d lies." True, in the autumn of 1846 his expense account shows an item of five shillings for "Phrenologist," but there is no indication that this was spent seriously.[4] Surely, the title "The first mesmerist" was a joke. Indeed, one may suspect that Arnold was first drawn to Glanvill's book because he had heard that it contained the story of an Oxford youth who had anticipated Miss Martineau by learning about mesmerism from the gipsies. Certainly, when he read how this was done, "by the power of *Imagination*, his Phancy *binding* theirs," and that "there were warrantable wayes of heightening the *Imagination* to that pitch, as to bind anothers," he must have thought that the art was a very old one indeed. Orpheus certainly knew it and so did the Pied Piper of Hamelin. Clearly, the first mesmerist was not the gentleman who had given his name to the art, but the poet, and it must have been in some such spoofing sense that Arnold's title was intended.

Indeed, though Glanvill provided Arnold with materials for his poem, its real source lay in certain feelings that he had about Oxford, the Cumnor countryside, and his own youth. Writing to Tom in 1857, he said:

3. Theodora Bosanquet, *Harriet Martineau: An Essay in Comprehension* (London, 1927), pp. 131–53; Vera Wheatley, *The Life and Works of Harriet Martineau* (Fair Lawn, N.J., 1957), p. 245; *The Zoist*, 1 (1843–44), 60–61.

4. *Letters to Clough*, p. 131; Pocket Diary, September 1846 (Yale collection).

My thoughts . . . have turned to you more than ever during the last few days which I have been spending at Oxford. You alone of my brothers are associated with that life at Oxford, the *freest* and most delightful part, perhaps, of my life, when with you and Clough and Walrond I shook off all the bonds and formalities of the place, and enjoyed the spring of life and that unforgotten Oxfordshire and Berkshire country. Do you remember a poem of mine called 'The Scholar-Gipsy'? It was meant to fix the remembrance of those delightful wanderings of ours in the Cumner hills before they were quite effaced—and as such, Clough and Walrond accepted it, and it has had much success at Oxford, I am told, as was perhaps likely from its *couleur locale*. I am hardly ever at Oxford now, but the sentiment of the place is overpowering to me when I have leisure to feel it, and can shake off the interruptions which it is not so easy to shake off now as it was when we were young. But on Tuesday afternoon I smuggled myself away, and got up into one of our old coombs among the Cumner hills, and into a field waving deep with cowslips and grasses, and gathered such a bunch as you and I used to gather in the cowslip field on Lutterworth road long years ago.[5]

The period of which Arnold speaks is 1845–47, after he had taken his degree at Oxford and before he had left it to become secretary to Lord Lansdowne. As this was exactly the time when he was proposing to read Glanvill, it may be that he actually did take the book up into the Cumnor hills, as the poem says that he did. But one suspects that he more often took the idyls of Theocritus or the poems of Wordsworth and Keats, and that in reading the ode *To Autumn* or the lines about a "wise passiveness," he imbibed more of the spirit of the Scholar-Gipsy than he did from Glanvill. Perhaps, too, he brought the novels of George Sand which, with their wonderful sense of personal freedom,

5. Ward, *A Writer's Recollections*, pp. 53–54.

were a regnant influence in this hour. Certainly he took them with him when, in June 1846, he broke away from Oxford and wandered through the slumbering old provinces of central France, visiting the country and places of which her books are full. "I wandered," he says, "through a silent country of heathy and ferny *landes*, a region of granite boulders, holly, and broom, of copsewood and great chestnut trees; a region of broad light, and fresh breezes, and wide horizons." He impressed George Sand, whom he visited, as *un Milton jeune et voyageant*, and he was indeed enacting his Scholar-Gipsy.[6]

Under these influences the rather stiff and uninteresting figure of Glanvill becomes a myth of the Romantic imagination. In Glanvill the Scholar-Gipsy was not a wanderer, but Arnold's preliminary title, "? the wandering Mesmerist," shows that he had early seized upon this as a central characteristic. By wandering, the Scholar-Gipsy cannot merely seek the spark from heaven but he can also pass before our eyes the natural scenes with which he is associated. By far the greatest change which Arnold made in his hero is to combine him with the Cumnor countryside so that he becomes an emanation of that world, the mythical embodiment of quiet and sober woodlands. Like Lucy Gray, he is a kind of *genius loci*, or spirit of the countryside, and he is to be seen only by those who can apprehend this delicate and evanescent spirit. Needless to say, not everyone can do so. No don or proctor would ever see him, but countryfolk do, and children, and poets. Even these are most likely to see him in their most idle and unprofitable moments—boys when they are scaring rooks in the wheatfields, maidens when they are dancing about the elms, reapers when they have left their reaping to bathe in the abandoned lasher. Twilight and nightfall are the best times to see him, and the best places are those most secret and retired. Often he may be found close to water, that "Mediator between the inanimate and man," for Oxford riders coming home at eve see him

6. Pocket Diary, June–July 1846 (Yale collection); *Mixed Essays* (1883), pp. 236–38; *Letters*, 2, 151.

at the ferry, but "then they land, and thou art seen no more!" The reapers saw him on the way to bathe, but "when they came from bathing, thou wast gone!" If the poet wishes to see him, he lies in his boat "Moor'd to the cool bank in the summer-heats," for he knows that the Scholar-Gipsy also lies in his, "Trailing in the cool stream thy fingers wet." Indeed, seeing the Scholar-Gipsy and being the Scholar-Gipsy are a process imperfectly distinguished. One sees him by being him and in no other way. To set out deliberately to see him would be to frighten him away. Rather one idles in the wood without a thought of seeing him, looks up suddenly, and he is there!

In this way, the quest and the object of the quest are one and the same. Or, to put the matter differently, there are really two quests, and one is the object of the other. The poet is engaged upon a quest for the Scholar-Gipsy. But the Scholar-Gipsy is also engaged upon a quest to learn the secret of the gipsies' art. The gipsies' art represents any kind of divine or natural lore such as cannot be gathered from books but can be gathered intuitively from the world of nature. But the Scholar-Gipsy, as representing the shy and elusive spirit of nature, already embodies that secret. He is, then, the object of his own quest, and the poet is also the object of his own quest. In seeking the Scholar-Gipsy he seeks himself as poet, and he finds himself as poet in the course of writing his poem. It is by envisioning the Scholar-Gipsy as engaged upon an unending quest that the poet brings his quest to a successful, if temporary, conclusion.

For this poem, or the first part of it rather, is modelled upon the Romantic dream-vision, as exemplified in Coleridge's "conversation poems" and the great odes of Keats, especially the *Ode to a Nightingale*. The form of such a poem is as follows: the poet reposes in a natural scene and through some inciting cause, be it the flapping of a film of soot, the strains of an Aeolian harp, or the song of a bird, is led to meditate upon the scene until, dissolving as phenomenon, it is, by the power of imagination, re-created as a noumenal reality, with which the poet achieves creative union. Unfortunately, it is a union which cannot long endure, and so at the end of the poem there is a descent back to the level of ordinary reality but with the substance of the vision preserved forever in the work of art. In Arnold's poem the natural scene is presented in the opening three stanzas, especially in the third, where the poet has taken pains to distill, with almost pre-Raphaelite intensity, "all the live murmur of a summer's day." The poet's companion is dismissed to the workaday world which is his, and the poet is left alone to begin his quest. It is a quest which is conducted entirely in the imagination. The poet reads "the oft-read tale" again, and as he falls into reverie, the imagination fuses the tale with the natural scene about it into the poetic world we have just described. What he dreams is the substance of the ten scenes in which the Scholar-Gipsy appears—with the shepherds, the country boors, the poet himself, the hunters, the maidens, the bathers, the lone housewife, the children, the blackbird, and the poet once again. As a character in his own dream the poet is able to say, in the third scene, "And I myself seem half to know thy looks," but in the tenth scene the series culminates in the recognition between the poet and the Scholar-Gipsy as they pass upon the causeway chill. His sense that he has now seen the Scholar-Gipsy corresponds with our sense that indeed he has—that the poet, by the very process of imagining these episodes, has seen the Scholar-Gipsy in the only way that is necessary to man.

But just as Keats' vision ended with the fortuitous pronunciation of the word *forlorn* and he was brought back to reality with the rueful query, "Was it a vision, or a waking dream?" so Arnold, having followed his creation through a kind of shepherd's calendar to its death at the close of the year, suddenly cries, "But what—I dream!" and awakes to find himself on the cold hillside of a purely phenomenal slope in the Cumnor range. He is now in the state of mind in which the Scholar-Gipsy is merely a particular individual who died some two hundred years ago and who is now buried in some country churchyard. This state lasts for one stanza, and at the end of this stanza a poem by Keats or Shelley or Coleridge would have ended—with the myth asserted and left to stand in its own precarious fragility as possibly a vision and possibly a waking dream. But Arnold's poem does not end here —rather it goes on to complete the dialectic of its own more complicated situation.

The poem falls into five sections, though its essential structure is threefold. There is, first, the introductory section of three stanzas presenting the natural scene; then the imaginative vision of the Scholar-Gipsy which occupies the next ten stanzas; then the single stanza in which the vision is repudiated as a mere dream; then nine stanzas in which the essential validity of the vision, though not its mythical substance, is reasserted; and finally, the two concluding stanzas with their "end-symbol" of the Tyrian trader. One says that the structure is essentially threefold because its main movement is the vision, the loss of the vision, and its recreation in a different mode. It is the product, first, of the heart and imagination, then, of the senses and understanding, and finally, of the imaginative reason.

It is very difficult for critics to like all parts of this poem equally well or to believe that all parts are integral to its meaning. G. Wilson Knight and A. E. Dyson, for example, have written fine critiques which are diametrically opposed and of which one can only say that each is half right.[7] The reason for this is that Knight has emphasized the vision of the Scholar-Gipsy and the end-symbol of the Tyrian trader and has totally neglected the middle sections of the poem. Dyson, on the other hand, has neglected the Tyrian trader and the Scholar-Gipsy and has emphasized the central statement of the Gipsy's unfitness for the modern world. But actually the poem consists of all these parts—of the vision, the repudiation of the vision, and its recovery in a different mode.

7. G. Wilson Knight, "*The Scholar-Gipsy:* An Interpretation," *Review of English Studies,* n.s. 6 (1955), 53–62; A. E. Dyson, "The Last Enchantments," *Review of English Studies,* n.s. 8 (1957), 257–65.

To understand this we need to understand where the poet is situated in the poem. In the opening stanzas he is clearly not in the world. On the contrary, he is parting company with those shepherds, like Clough and his brother Tom, who are so agitated by the unrest of the late 1840's that they must engage in direct social action. For himself he will continue the quest for the ideal, and he does this, as we have already seen, by himself becoming a Scholar-Gipsy—a scholar with his book, a gipsy in his field. And just as Keats on the viewless wings of poesy can join the nightingale, so Arnold can say, "Already with thee!" and become a character in his own poetic dream. Thus, from the opening of the poem to line 131, the poet is not in the world but is with the Scholar-Gipsy.

But the descent which destroys the Gipsy changes the locus of the poet, and from line 131 on he is no longer with the Gipsy but is in the world. His repeated exhortations, "Fly *our* paths, *our* feverish contact fly," make this clear. And so, being in the world, he speaks as a representative of it, and this is what is responsible for the remarkable alteration in the language of the poem. For whereas before, the language was as beautifully imaginative as the best pastoral poetry of Milton or Keats, now it is starkly, almost bleakly abstract. It is, of course, appropriate that it should be. Why should we expect poetic language from one who has just fallen from the heights of the imagination onto the level of the phenomenal world? Why should we expect lush imagery of nature from one who has just been driven from the forest glade into the aridity of the burning plain? The language is as arid and barren as the world from which it comes. It speaks directly and abstractly of the complexity of the modern world. It does not venture elaborate metaphors or imagine scenes or create characters. Its only character is the historical one of Goethe, who, as the Stoic sage, is the king of this modern world, offering for our salvation analysis of its ills and patience to bear them. And yet, Goethe is an impressive figure. And his world, though it is not a product of the imagination, but of the senses and understanding, is an impressive world. It offers a strong, insistent urgency of tone, a vein of moral exhortation and indictment, which is very moving. All the best known and most quoted phrases from *The Scholar-Gipsy* come from this section—"this strange disease of modern life," "light half-believers of our casual creeds," and so on. Keats' *Ode to a Nightingale* gives only the meagerest glimpse of the real world of death and change, and so in a sense we hardly know what the supernal world is for. But Arnold gives a full and moving account of this world, and his account reacts upon the Scholar-Gipsy to modify our conception of him and of his relation to this world.

For though the Scholar-Gipsy died with the poet's awakening from his dream, he is reborn in the next stanza without the poet's beginning to dream again. When Keats said, "Thou wast not born for death, immortal Bird!" he was still in the midst of his imaginative vision. But when Arnold utters his equivalent statement, "—No, no, thou hast not felt the lapse of hours!" or "But thou possessest an immortal lot," he has emerged from his dream and is speaking in the sober light of day. He is saying that although the Scholar-Gipsy does not exist as a supernatural being created by seventeenth-century superstition, and although he does not have a really substantial existence as a mythical figure created by the Romantic imagination, he does exist as a moral truth which has a continuing validity in the modern world. And so Arnold applies this truth to the analysis of social and religious institutions. But in so doing he is thinking psychologically and morally, not mythically. His thinking is comparable to that at which he had arrived in his own Broad Church religious position. Though the myth of Christianity, as embodied in the Bible, certainly was not true, still it contained moral truths which were very necessary in the conduct of life. Therefore, these truths should be kept alive. The truth of the Scholar-Gipsy should also be kept alive, on the one hand by disengaging it from the flimsiness of seventeenth-century superstition and Romantic imagination and, on the other, by stubbornly preserving its integrity in the modern world.

This view suggests, however, that if the idea of the Scholar-Gipsy is to survive in the modern world, the image by which he is represented will have to be transformed. And so it is. In the lines which follow upon his death and resurrection he is presented in subtly different terms from those of the vision. In the vision he was a shy, romantic figure, elusive, diffident, and somewhat fey. He was a kind of odd fellow of the woods, dressed in antique hat, with "dark vague eyes, and soft abstracted air." He was a poetic idler, a dabbler in nooks and crannies, swinging on gates and trailing his fingers in the stream. But in the non-mythical statement of the fourth section he is made of sterner stuff. Here he has "*one* aim, *one* business, *one* desire," the italics conferring on him a single-minded purposiveness which has been quite foreign to him hitherto, as if he knew exactly where that spark from heaven was and was going straight for it! Whereas previously he was associated with multiplicity, appearing now here and now there, in the latter part of the poem he is associated with unity and is against the multiplicity of the world. And whereas previously he was a wanderer with the emphasis upon the wandering, now he is a wanderer with the emphasis upon the goal. Previously he wandered in nature, but nature has now disappeared from the poem and he is entirely associated with the spark from heaven. Morally, practically, religiously, this is a change for the better; poetically, it is a debasement. But it is part of the dialectic of the poem whereby Arnold gives to a poetic ideal the toughness it needs for survival in the real world.

And yet eventually this ideal is resurrected not merely in the moral but also in the poetic sense. By the end of the exhortation and indictment, and through its sanative power, the poet has been restored to some measure of the wholeness he had lost. Having fallen from imaginative vision into a lack of faith which altogether denied the Scholar-Gipsy, he has re-emerged into an understanding of his essential validity in an abstract, moral sense. By line 201 he is so far restored that he can actually invoke him again imaginatively, but this time it is in an image drawn, not from Glanvill, but from a sterner world of classical antiquity which will incorporate the new conception of the Gipsy developed in the moral discourse.

> O born in days when wits were fresh and clear,
>> And life ran gaily as the sparkling Thames;
>>> Before this strange disease of modern life,
>> With its sick hurry, its divided aims,
>>> Its heads o'ertax'd, its palsied hearts, was rife—
>>>> Fly hence, our contact fear!
>> Still fly, plunge deeper in the bowering wood!
>>> Averse, as Dido did with gesture stern
>>> From her false friend's approach in Hades turn,
>> Wave us away, and keep thy solitude!

The Dido image is appropriate because in her the ideal of love and personal faith was wronged by one whose errand was the practical founding of the most practical empire in the world. But it is also appropriate because the scene is Hades, the Hades in which the poet himself is located, and Dido is preserving her integrity *after* she has suffered, not before. And finally, her conflict with Aeneas represents the historic conflict between East and West, of which the Scholar-Gipsy's conflict with the world is a modern variant. And through her connection with Carthage, the colony of Tyre, she leads into the final symbol of the Tyrian trader, which is the culmination of the poem. One may say that the brief image of Dido is preparatory to the full restoration of poetic power which is exemplified by the elaborately developed symbol at the end of the poem.

The symbol of the Tyrian trader is one of Arnold's finest pieces:

> Then fly our greetings, fly our speech and smiles!
>> —As some grave Tyrian trader, from the sea,

Descried at sunrise an emerging prow
Lifting the cool-hair'd creepers stealthily,
   The fringes of a southward-facing brow
      Among the Ægæan isles;
And saw the merry Grecian coaster come,
   Freighted with amber grapes, and Chian wine,
   Green, bursting figs, and tunnies steep'd in brine—
And knew the intruders on his ancient home,

The young light-hearted masters of the waves—
   And snatch'd his rudder, and shook out more sail;
   And day and night held on indignantly
O'er the blue Midland waters with the gale,
   Betwixt the Syrtes and soft Sicily,
      To where the Atlantic raves
Outside the western straits; and unbent sails
   There, where down cloudy cliffs, through sheets of foam,
   Shy traffickers, the dark Iberians come;
And on the beach undid his corded bales.

This simile has caused difficulty for some readers because they are astonished to see Arnold using his favorite Greeks as a symbol for the world. But if one reads Alexander Kinglake's *Eothen* (1844)—as perhaps Arnold did—one will see in his chapter on "Greek Mariners" precisely the same picture of a debased, modern civilization, whose sailors timidly hug the shore, which Arnold exploits here. By contrast, the Tyrian trader is the grave representative of an ancient civilization which, finding itself superseded by low cunning, refuses to compete, but indignantly strikes out to a new world, harder but more pure. It is the same contrast that is made in *Empedocles on Etna* between Empedocles and the sophists:

The brave, impetuous heart yields everywhere
To the subtle, contriving head,

—except that here the heart does not yield. On the contrary, the main force of the simile is the sense it gives of heroic vitality and triumphant power. But if so, what a transformation of the Scholar-Gipsy! One may even say that the Gipsy, as we originally knew him, more closely resembles the Grecian coaster than the Tyrian trader. Certainly, the coaster's hide-away under "cool-hair'd creepers" among the Aegean isles is very similar to that of the poet in the high, half-reaped field where "pale pink convolvulus in tendrils creep." But there is an important difference, which is that the one is a true forest glade whereas the other is an imitation constructed by Revellers on the burning plain. Hence, when the Scholar-Gipsy emerges from his forest glade in the middle of the poem, he does not become like the Greeks, but like Dido in her Hell; and her "gesture stern" introduces the note of heroic vitality which is continued in the epithet "indignantly" of the Tyrian trader. But whereas Dido could not break out of her Hell, the trader not merely rejects the cool retreat of the Greeks but holds forth across the Mediterranean until he bursts through the "straits" which separate one realm from another and is rewarded with the fresh, invigorating air of the North Atlantic. If the figure of the Gipsy changes as he moves through the poem, it is because the poem itself is a dynamic one, which takes us through all three phases of Arnold's poetic world.

In the figure of the Tyrian trader Arnold has distilled a good bit of cultural history which he picked up from passages in Herodotus, Thucydides, Diodorus Siculus, and his father's *History of Rome*.[8] That he studied this matter carefully is evident from a late review of Curtius' *History of Greece*, where he speaks of the difficulty of gaining a clear view of these early cultural contacts between the Phoenicians and the Greeks. What he was interested

8. Matthew Arnold, *Essays, Letters, and Reviews*, ed. Fraser Neiman (Cambridge, Mass., 1960), pp. 126–27; Thucydides 6.2.6; Diodorus Siculus 5.20.1–2; Thomas Arnold, *History of Rome* (London, 1838), *1*, 484; R. H. Super, "Arnold's 'Tyrian Trader' in Thucydides," *N&Q*, 201 (1956), 397.

in, evidently, was the role of the Phoenicians as a transmitter of ancient culture, and he makes this point in the terms of his simile. For whereas the cargo of the Greeks was the Sybaritic one of "amber grapes and Chian wine, / Green, bursting figs, and tunnies steep'd in brine," that of the Tyrians was "corded bales," whose contents are wisely not specified but which our imagination fills with rich brocades, silks, and gold—and perhaps also with the alphabet and other instruments of learning. It is sometimes complained that Arnold's hero does not, as he promised to do, impart his knowledge to the world, but surely this is what is meant by the last line of the poem, where the trader "on the beach undid his corded bales." In Arnold's bale would have been the *Bhagavad-Gita*, his personal treasure from the East, which, though it was "foolishness to the Greeks" when he offered it to Clough, was to him a wisdom most deeply to be desired.

The transaction on the beach seems to reflect a passage in Herodotus:

> The Carthaginians also tell us that they trade with a race of men who live in a part of Libya beyond the Pillars of Heracles. On reaching this country, they unload their goods, arrange them tidily along the beach, and then, returning to their boats, raise a smoke. Seeing the smoke, the natives come down to the beach, place on the ground a certain quantity of gold in exchange for the goods, and go off again to a distance. The Carthaginians then come ashore and take a look at the gold; and if they think it represents a fair price for their wares, they collect it and go away; if, on the other hand, it seems too little, they go back aboard and wait, and the natives come and add to the gold until they are satisfied. There is perfect honesty on both sides; the Carthaginians never touch the gold until it equals in value what they have offered for sale, and the natives never touch the goods until the gold has been taken away.[9]

9. Herodotus 4.197, trans. Aubrey de Sélincourt (Penguin ed.), p. 307.

We are here dealing with the Carthaginians rather than the parent city of Tyre, and with Libya rather than Spain, but the situation is essentially the same as in Arnold. Thus, the smoke signals may explain the "cloudy cliffs," and the unusual manner of trading certainly explains why the dark Iberians are called "shy traffickers." But "shy" is the epithet of the Scholar-Gipsy, and since we certainly associate the dark Iberians with the Spanish gipsies, we feel we have come full circle, back to our original symbol once again. Dr. Arnold, in his *History of Rome*, speculates that colonies of the Iberians (not the gipsies but the aboriginal race) "crossed the Bay of Biscay, and established themselves on the coast of Cornwall," in which case "we ourselves have in some degree a national interest" in them.[10] A personal interest, he might have said, for Mrs. Arnold's family was of Cornish descent, and it is barely possible that our swarthy poet, who later lectured on the Celtic element in English culture, thought that he himself had some dark Iberian blood in his veins. In any case, in the 1840s George Borrow's books, *The Zincali; or, An Account of the Gypsies of Spain* and *The Bible in Spain*, had brought the Spanish gipsies into notice, and his *Lavengro* (1851), with its suggestive subtitle, *The Scholar—The Gypsy—The Priest*, tells the story of an English youth who went to live among the gipsies much in the manner of his seventeenth-century predecessor. In all these ways, then, we get the feeling of a traditional wisdom of the East transmitted to the West by poetic wanderers who were careful to preserve their integrity. At first they preserved it shyly, then sternly or even indignantly, but at last they emerged into a new world where shyness was possible once again.

The Scholar-Gipsy is Arnold's finest poem, and one feels that it is so because Arnold has here done, what Empedocles saw that he had to do but could not, "poise" his life at last. Probably he was enabled to do this partly because the poem was conceived and written so slowly, over a period that began in Arnold's hal-

10. Vol. 1, p. 486.

cyon days, extended through his crisis, and ended with his final adjustment to the world. As a result, the poem, almost uniquely among Arnold's major works, embodies his entire poetic myth, the forest glade, the burning plain, and the wide-glimmering sea. But also, the Scholar-Gipsy himself is a figure of perfect poise and balance. He is one of the few characters who can actually live in all these realms, or at least in the first realm and the third. As gipsy he looks backward to the realm of nature and as scholar he looks forward to the realm of culture. He is at once young and immeasurably old. He would be happy with the boy Callicles in *Empedocles on Etna* and also with Joubert in the critical prose. He is waiting for the spark to fall which has fallen in *Culture and Anarchy*, and the secret he would learn from the gipsies is not dissimilar from the method and secret of Jesus in *Literature and Dogma*. Like the Thames, with which he is associated, he seems to represent not any portion of man's life but its deeply spiritual nature wherever it flows. In the phrase which Arnold applied to George Sand's novels, he is "the sentiment of the ideal life, which is none other than man's normal life as we shall some day know it."[11]

This moment of balance, however, was not easily maintained, and in the poem itself we already see an indication of how it will end. For though the poem unites thought with feeling, poetic vision with social criticism, and ends with a symbol which synthesizes the two, still this symbol deliberately replaces a Romantic nature-figure with a stern, heroic figure drawn from classical antiquity. That Dido is from Virgil's epic is certainly one reason for her introduction into the poem, and that the Tyrian trader is grounded in Greek and Roman history adds to him the weight and actuality that Arnold desires. The origin of these figures foreshadows the direction of Arnold's interests. Just as Callicles' final lyric seems to anticipate the Preface of 1853, so too does the end-symbol of *The Scholar-Gipsy*. In that Preface Arnold will deprecate the influence of Keats, which is nowhere more appar-

11. *Mixed Essays* (1883), p. 240.

ent in his poetry than in this poem, and will urge the modern poet to write epics and tragedies on the model of the Greeks. "I am glad you like the Gipsy Scholar," he wrote to Clough on November 30, 1853, "—but what does it *do* for you? Homer *animates*—Shakespeare *animates*—in its poor way I think Sohrab and Rustum *animates*—the Gipsy Scholar at best awakens a pleasing melancholy. But this is not what we want.

> The complaining millions of men
> Darken in labour and pain—

what they want is something to *animate* and *ennoble* them—not merely to add zest to their melancholy or grace to their dreams. —I believe a feeling of this kind is the basis of my nature—and of my poetics."[12] Clearly, had *The Scholar-Gipsy* been finished in time to be published in the volume of 1852 along with *Empedocles on Etna*, it would have been rejected along with that poem in the Preface of 1853.

12. *Letters to Clough*, p. 146.

7 SOHRAB, BALDER, AND MEROPE

My father's spirit in arms! all is not well.

—Hamlet

In August 1853, in the course of making his rounds as Inspector of Schools, Arnold visited Froude at his Welsh home of Plas Gwynant. It will be recalled that Froude had not liked *The Strayed Reveller* because it was so insufferably calm and elegant, and he thought that Arnold had not earned the right to this calm through any actual experience of suffering. But when *Empedocles on Etna* appeared, Froude was pleased. He was, Arnold reported, "one of the very few people who much liked my last vein, or [thought me] to be other than the black villain my Maker made me." Nonetheless, though Froude liked the poem, he himself had already passed beyond the stage which it represented. "I should like you to see Froude," wrote Arnold to Clough, "—quantum mutatus! He goes to church, has family prayers—says the Nemesis ought never to have been published etc. etc.—his friends say that he is altogether changed and re-entered within the giron de l'Eglise—at any rate within the giron de la religion chrétienne: but I do not see the matter in this light and think that he conforms in the same sense in which Spinoza advised his mother to conform—and having purified his moral being, all that was mere fume and vanity and love of notoriety and opposition in his proceedings he has abandoned and regrets. This is my view. He is getting more and more literary, and vise au solide instead of beating the air. May we all follow his example." Arnold did follow Froude's example, for he went straight from Plas Gwynant to Fox How, where, in the month of September, he wrote the preface to *Poems* (1853) in which he repudiated *Empedocles on Etna* and formulated his new poetical creed.[1]

Actually, the more apparent motive of Arnold's preface was to express irritation with some of the young poets and critics of the day who were attracting more attention—and more favorable attention—than was Arnold himself. In the spring of the year Edwin Arnold—no relation but an annoying namesake—published *Poems Narrative and Lyrical*, which was reviewed along with *Empedocles on Etna* in the columns of the *Spectator*. The reviewer was R. S. Rintoul, the editor, and the passage which struck Arnold the most was the following: "The poet who would really fix the public attention must leave the exhausted past, and draw his subjects from matters of present import and therefore both of interest and novelty." Arnold was to quote this sentence in his preface, and he would italicize the word *therefore* to indicate what he considered the *non sequitur* of the argument.[2] Then, almost in the same month appeared the *Poems* of a Glasgow lace-pattern designer—now known as a "Spasmodic" poet—Alexander Smith, whose principal piece, *A Life-Drama*, quickly became the poem of the year. It too was reviewed along with Arnold's and was frequently given the nod. Arnold became conscious of it in March and asked Clough to look at it. On May 1 he declared that he had not read it—"I shrink from what is so intensely immature—but I think the extracts I have seen most remarkable—and I think at the same time he will not go far. I have not room or time for my reasons—but I think so. This kind

1. *Letters to Clough*, pp. 126, 136, 140, 144.
2. *Spectator*, 26 (1853), 325, quoted by Arnold in *Poetical Works*, p. xix.

does not go far: it dies like Keats or loses itself like Browning." Clough did look at the book and in the July number of the *North American Review* reviewed Smith and Arnold together, preferring Smith's modern subject and positive moral tone but praising Arnold's diction and manner over Smith's. The family at Fox How thought Clough's review "peu favorable," but Arnold gamely said that he did not think so.[3] Then, in August, in the *North British Review*, there appeared an article, now known to be by David Masson, which praised Smith's poem as "sublimated biography" and declared that "a true allegory of the state of one's own mind in a representative history . . . is perhaps the highest thing that one can attempt in the way of fictitious art."[4] It may have been this article which determined Arnold to add to his forthcoming collection of poems a preface. Froude advised against it, but Arnold thought he saw his way. Writing to his brother out in New Zealand, he expressed his fear that Tom would not like the preface from "not having much before your eyes the sins and offences at which it is directed: the first being that we have numbers of young gentlemen with really wonderful powers of perception and expression, but to whom there is wholly wanting a 'bedeutendes Individuum' [important subjectivity]—so that their productions are most unedifying and unsatisfactory."[5] The young gentlemen in question were Alexander Smith and Edwin Arnold and the critics of the *Spectator* and *North British Review*.

Smith in particular provided Arnold with an opportunity for saying something he had long been wanting to say. His *Life-Drama* was a kind of modern *Endymion*, and Clough pointed out that its faults, which were incoherence and the profusion of similes, were due primarily to the poet's choice of models—Shake-

3. *Letters to Clough*, pp. 133, 136, 140.
4. *North British Review*, *19* (1853), 338; this review has been identified as Masson's by Walter Houghton, editor of the Wellesley Index of Victorian Periodicals.
5. *Letters to Clough*, p. 141; Ward, *A Writer's Recollections*, p. 53.

speare, Keats, Tennyson, and Mrs. Browning. Arnold obviously could not attack his own contemporaries, but he could say something about the influence of Keats and Shakespeare on modern English poetry. In 1848–49, fresh from a reading of Monckton Milnes' *Life, Letters, and Literary Remains* of Keats, he wrote to Clough, "What a brute you were to tell me to read Keats' Letters. . . . What harm he has done in English Poetry," and he cited Browning's "multitudinousness" as an example. Gradually he developed the theory that it was perfectly proper in an earlier state of the world for poetry to be elaborate and involved, but that in the modern world, when life itself was so complex, great plainness and severity of language were required. "Keats and Shelley were on a false track when they set themselves to reproduce the exuberance of expression, the charm, the richness of images, and the felicity, of the Elizabethan poets. Yet critics cannot get to learn this, because the Elizabethan poets are our greatest, and our canons of poetry are founded on their works. They still think that the object of poetry is to produce exquisite bits and images."[6]

All this was brought home to Arnold while he was at Froude's. He found that he no longer enjoyed his old favorites. George Sand stuck in the throat, and as for Shakespeare, "How ill he often writes! but how often too how incomparably." Then in a postscript, "Read the details about poor Keats at the end of Haydon's first and the beginning of his second vol." [of the *Autobiography* (1853)]. It is not often realized to what an extent Arnold's attitude toward Keats was based on misinformation. The passage in question is an egregious piece of moralizing in which Haydon represents Keats as having "no decision of character" and "no object upon which to direct his great powers." He buckled under criticism and in his despondency flew to dissipation. "For six weeks he was scarcely sober, and—to show what a man does to gratify his appetites, when once they get the better of him—once covered his tongue and throat as far as he could

6. *Letters to Clough*, pp. 96–97, 124.

reach with Cayenne pepper, in order to appreciate the 'delicious coldness of claret in all its glory,'—his own expression."[7] No wonder that Arnold viewed Keats' illness as a kind of spiritual disease which also infected his poetry. And no wonder that he said of Smith, "This kind does not go far: it dies like Keats or loses itself like Browning."

The essential problem, then, was a moral one, and this means that it was a problem of the content of poetry rather than its form. But to say this is to point to a revolution which has occurred in Arnold's poetic theory since the days when he wrote *The Strayed Reveller, and Other Poems*. In that volume he had been concerned with developing an aesthetic distance between himself and his subject so that he could contemplate it without being affected by it. This is what he did in *The Strayed Reveller, Resignation, The Sick King in Bokhara, Mycerinus,* and *Shakespeare.* And his whole quarrel with Clough at this time was that Clough was so little interested in form, so much interested in content, that he used poetry for "depth-hunting," for "solving" the universe, rather than for making a representation of it. But around 1849 Arnold discovered that he also had problems to solve, and as a result, the volume *Empedocles on Etna* almost totally abandoned this formalistic view of poetry. Poetry was now very closely related to human life and was related to it by virtue of its contents. So, whereas in 1848 Arnold reminded Clough that "the Muse willingly *accompanies* life but that in no wise does she understand to *guide* it," in October 1852 he informed him that "modern poetry can only subsist by its *contents:* by becoming a complete magister vitae as the poetry of the ancients did." To this end it should "include" religion, instead of existing as poetry only. This was quite a new idea for Arnold. As early as March 1849 he had reluctantly conceded that in poetry the "rapturous Xtian" had an advantage over the "unintoxicated honest" like himself, but *Empedocles on Etna*, written between 1849 and

7. Ibid., p. 139; *The Life of Benjamin Robert Haydon, from His Autobiography and Journals*, ed. Tom Taylor (London, 1853), 2, 10.

1852, was clearly a product of the unintoxicated honest. It was seeing Froude, who had conformed in a purely external sense and merely for the sake of purifying his moral being, that led Arnold on even further. And when Clough evidently remonstrated at the idea, Arnold replied, "As to conformity I only recommend it so far as it frees from the unnatural and unhealthy attitude of contradiction and opposition—the *Qual der Negation* as Goethe calls it. Only positive convictions and feeling are worth anything —and the glow of these one can never feel so long as one is pugnacious and out of temper. This is my firm belief." He then goes on to say that "if one loved what was beautiful and interesting in itself *passionately* enough, one would produce what was excellent without troubling oneself with religious dogma at all. As it is, we are *warm* only when dealing with these last—and what is frigid is always bad."[8]

So saying, Arnold sat down and wrote the preface in which he rejected *Empedocles on Etna* from the new collection of his poems. The explanation which he gives for this action is curious. He says that the subject of the drama is morbid and that all art ought to be dedicated to Joy. It should "inspirit and rejoice the reader . . . , convey a charm, and infuse delight." Asking what are the situations from which no poetical enjoyment can be derived, he answers: "They are those in which the suffering finds no vent in action; in which a continuous state of mental distress is prolonged, unrelieved by incident, hope, or resistance; in which there is everything to be endured, nothing to be done. In such situations there is inevitably something morbid, in the description of them something monotonous. When they occur in actual life, they are painful, not tragic; the representation of them in poetry is painful also."[9] It is obvious that Arnold is dealing here with the same problem that Aristotle dealt with in the *Poetics*—why it is that tragedy gives pleasure. His use of the word "vent" recalls Aristotle's "catharsis." But it is equally obvious

8. *Letters to Clough*, pp. 84, 124, 103, 142–43.
9. *Poetical Works*, p. xviii.

that in attempting to refine upon Aristotle by suggesting that there are certain situations, painful in life, which will also be painful in art, he has totally perverted the Aristotelian doctrine. For one thing, he has focussed upon the hero rather than the spectator. What Aristotle says is that the spectator's passions find a vent in contemplating the sufferings of the hero, and that this release of tension through art is pleasurable. He nowhere says that the hero's passions should find a vent in action, nor is it imaginable that he would do so. Much depends, of course, upon the meaning of the word "action." In some places Arnold seems to use it in an inner, ideal sense, and if he means that his drama is not resolved, this is a good criticism. But here, equating it with "something to be done," he seems to be using it in a practical sense, and one may say that he has really combined Aristotle's *Poetics* with Carlyle's doctrine of work. The real, operative influence on this passage is not Aristotle but the chapter on the Everlasting Yea in *Sartor Resartus*. Under the guise of solving an aesthetic problem Arnold has solved a moral one: he has attempted to cure his hero—and himself—of Romantic morbidity by the advice of Carlyle to forget about oneself, turn outward upon the world, and engage in practical action.

Goethe had already applied this doctrine to the problems of the poet. In the *Conversations with Eckermann* he had declared, "The majority of our young poets have no fault but this, that their subjectivity is not important (*bedeutend*), and that they cannot find matter in the objective. At best, they only find a material which is similar to themselves, which corresponds to their own subjectivity." The passage is evidently the original of that in which Arnold had declared that "we have numbers of young gentlemen with really wonderful powers of perception and expression, but to whom there is wholly wanting a 'bedeutendes Individuum' "—an important subjectivity. The comments bring together the two strands in Arnold's preface, for whether the young gentlemen were of the Shakespeare-Keats-Tennyson school whose poetry consisted of exquisite bits and images, or whether they were of the Werther-René-Byron school whose poetry consisted of unrelieved distress, in either case their poetry was an allegory of the state of their own mind. But this, in Arnold's view, is precisely what poetry was not. "An allegory of the state of one's own mind, the highest problem of an art which imitates actions! No assuredly, it is not, it never can be so."[10]

As a result, in the latter part of his preface Arnold tries to help the young poet find matter in the objective. To this end he offers him three pieces of advice: first, that he should choose as his subject an action, not his own feelings; secondly, that he should concern himself with the over-all structure of the work of art rather than with details of expression; and thirdly, that he should find his plots and also his literary models among the ancients. By the first he will avoid subjectivity in his materials, by the second he will avoid it in his forms, and by the third in his literary tradition. Arnold was often criticized for his predilection for the ancients, and, when pressed, he had to admit that the main point was not whether an action was ancient or modern but whether it was excellent. But he really did believe that by subjecting oneself to a culture other than one's own—and the more alien the better —one could avoid the preoccupation with self which was the main malady of the age. "I know not how it is," he wrote, "but their commerce with the ancients appears to me to produce, in those who constantly practise it, a steadying and composing effect upon their judgment, not of literary works only, but of men and events in general. They are like persons who have had a very weighty and impressive experience: they are more truly than others under the empire of facts, and more independent of the language current among those with whom they live."[11]

The main significance, then, of Arnold's rejection of *Empedocles on Etna* and his writing the Preface of 1853 is that he was thereby moving from subjectivity into objectivity. Whether his

10. *Conversations with Eckermann*, tr. J. Oxenford, November 24, 1824; *Poetical Works*, p. xxiv.
11. *Poetical Works*, xxviii.

new objectivity was any more truly objective than his old subjectivity is, of course, a question, but in even thinking that it was he was making a move that had been made before by many of his countrymen. Wordsworth and Coleridge had made it in the poems which mark the end of their creative years, and Carlyle had made it in *Sartor Resartus*. Newman made it in turning from the private judgment of Anglicanism to the dogmatic principle of the Roman Catholic Church. Ruskin made it in turning from mountains and painting to architecture and society. To a certain extent it is simply the transition from youth to age, but it is also the transition from Romanticism to Victorianism. Indeed, it is the fact that in the first half of the nineteenth century, this normal personal development coincided with a larger cultural development which produced, when they reinforced one another, the remarkable conversions and crises which are a feature of these years. Wordsworth's and Coleridge's were associated with the period of reaction following the French Revolution, Carlyle's and Newman's with the agitation surrounding the first Reform Bill, and Arnold's and Ruskin's with the Revolution of 1848 and the conservative reaction which followed.

According to G. Kitson Clark, the change in the social temper of England between the late 1840s and the early 1850s was dramatic. The former period had brought to a head all the unrest, discontent, and misery which had been lingering over Europe ever since the French Revolution. In these years there was an economic crisis in England, famine in Ireland, agitation over the repeal of the Corn Laws, the collapse of Chartism, and finally revolution in Europe. But then, almost overnight, all this changed. With the years 1851–52 there was ushered in "what may be called the Victorian interlude, an era of peace, relative contentment and well-being."[12] Not that all problems were solved or that they would not become serious again, but just for the moment there was less unemployment, greater security, fewer and less menacing demon-

12. G. Kitson Clark, *The Making of Victorian England* (Cambridge, Mass., 1962), p. 31.

strations. In England all this was symbolized by the opening of the Great Exhibition in 1851, and in France by Louis Napoleon's *coup d'état* in December of the same year. It is remarkable to what an extent Arnold's development coincided with these changes. His period of *Sturm und Drang* with Marguerite was nearly contemporaneous with the Revolution of 1848 and his marriage with Miss Wightman (we imply no judgment upon it) with the establishment of the Second Empire. It is no wonder, then, that he was embarrassed by *Empedocles on Etna*. Right enough for 1848–49, what a thing to have appear in 1852! In 1852 Newman was publishing his serene and balanced lectures on the *Idea of a University,* and Ruskin was bringing out his most mature and luminous work, *The Stones of Venice*. In France, Leconte de Lisle was publishing his *Poèmes antiques,* with a preface which said very nearly the same thing as Arnold's, that in the hard impersonality of classical forms and subjects was to be found a bulwark against the febrile emotions of the present time. But while the rest of England was strolling through the Crystal Palace, Arnold was gnashing his teeth upon a mountain in Sicily. "I feel now," he wrote to Clough in December 1852, "where my poems (this set) are all wrong, which I did not feel a year ago," and we are told not only that he did not republish *Empedocles on Etna,* but that he withdrew it from circulation before fifty copies were sold.[13]

In his new volume *Sohrab and Rustum* replaced *Empedocles on Etna* as the principal piece, and there is no question that Arnold wished it to be considered Exhibit A of his new poetical creed. For it illustrates all three of the principles laid down in the preface. In the first place, its subject is an action, not his own feelings, and the action was "a thoroughly good one." "What a thing this is!" he wrote to Clough, "and how little do young writers feel what a thing it is—how it is *everything*." Then, too, he had taken great pains with the structure of the poem, and though, when he copied it out, he was less pleased with the composition

13. *Letters to Clough,* p. 126; *Poetical Works,* p. 502.

than he had been at first, he observed that English painters cannot compose either and therefore the deficiency was probably due to "the awkward incorrect Northern nature." Froude, on the other hand, thought "the working up of the situation . . . faultlessly beautiful."[14] Finally, he had gone to the ancients both for his story and his literary model. The story, of course, was not Greek but Persian. It derived from the legendary heroic materials embodied in the tenth-century epic of Firdausi, and though Arnold did not read Firdausi himself—rather depended on Sainte-Beuve's retelling of the story in a French review—still he had been at considerable pains to "orientalise" his similes. Homer, of course, was his model, and any school text will show how thickly strewn are the allusions and how faithfully the epic convention is followed. Hence, Arnold was a little annoyed when his friends suggested that the style was closer to that of Tennyson than of Homer. "Just read through Tennyson's Morte d'Arthur and Sohrab and Rustum one after the other," he counselled, "and you will see the difference in the *tissue* of the style of the two poems, and in its *movement*." "I think the poem has, if not the *rapidity*, at least the *fluidity* of Homer: and that it is in this respect that it is un-Tennysonian."[15]

Finally, *Sohrab and Rustum* satisfies the conditions of the Preface because it "animates." Arnold's faith that it did this seems to have been based upon the fact that it had animated him to compose it, for he had adopted at this time the idea, recently disseminated by Ruskin, that the happiness of the workman was a measure of the excellence of the work of art. Whether or not he was happy in composing the ungrammatical little quatrain,

> What Poets feel not, when they make,
> A pleasure in creating,
> The world, in *its* turn, will not take
> Pleasure in contemplating,

14. *Letters to Clough*, pp. 136, 139, 127 n.
15. Ibid., pp. 145, 146; *Letters*, 1, 37.

is unknown, but he sent it to Clough with the word that it was "terribly true,"[16] and he used it as a prefatory note to *Sohrab and Rustum*.

In all these ways, then, *Sohrab and Rustum* perfectly illustrates Arnold's new poetic creed. The only thing that he apparently never asked himself about was the meaning of the poem. In his comment upon it he discusses its structure, its style, its sources, its similes, the pleasure he had in composing it, and the probable pleasure it will give to others, but he never discusses its meaning. Yet the poem does have a meaning, and when one turns to consider what it is, he finds that it is not so far removed from Arnold's usual preoccupations as he apparently thought. One may even feel that the poem is as good as it is precisely because it does not take Arnold out of himself but is that very thing which he deplores, "a true allegory of the state of one's own mind."

Of course, if we consider the action of the poem alone, its meaning has to do with fate, and it is in this respect that Arnold's skill in composition is apparent. For he has devised a story in which two human hearts, longing for union, are thwarted in that longing and are finally brought together only in the moment of death. The irony of this action Arnold very well exploits. It is ironic that Sohrab should resist Peran-Wisa's advice to seek his father in peace and should persist in seeking him in the only way that will bring about his own death. It is ironic that Gudurz should take the very method of persuading Rustum to do battle which will lead him to do battle incognito and so prepare for the catastrophe. It is ironic that when Sohrab and Rustum feel in their hearts a prompting to drop their arms and embrace upon the sands, they do not do so, but allow these promptings to be stifled by anger and the warrior's pride. And finally, the recognition scene is supremely ironic. Thundering out the name "Rustum!" which he thinks will be a word of fear, the older warrior hurls his weapon, but Sohrab, hearing the name in surprise and joy,

16. *Letters to Clough*, p. 126.

drops his shield and is transfixed by his father's spear. Thus, Sohrab is defeated not by his father's prowess but by his own love, and the moment of recognition is the moment of death.

So far, then, the theme of *Sohrab and Rustum* is that of many a Greek tragedy or heroic poem, and if Arnold had written it in Greek some two thousand years ago, it would be a minor classic. But he has introduced into the poem elements of his symbolic world which were not present in the source and which make the poem, not different from *Empedocles on Etna*, but much the same. It is obvious, for example, that Rustum, as the grizzled man of war—stern, bitter, aloof—is a military version of Empedocles, and that Sohrab, the fresh, glancing youth, is closely akin to Callicles. Sohrab differs from Callicles chiefly in that he has left the gardens of his mother's palace, which are his peculiar forest glade, to venture into the desert and find his mature self in the ordeal of battle. Sohrab's need is to be recognized as the son of Rustum, and in order to do this he must not merely find Rustum but also disprove the rumor that Rustum had no son but only a puny daughter, who plies at home light female tasks with her mother. In other words, he must prove his manhood on the field of battle, and this is what the battle is really about. For Sohrab's technique of fighting is very different from his father's. He is David to his father's Goliath, the light English pinnace to the lumbering Spanish man-of-war. In this sense, he is partly a Strayed Reveller, and, as usual, his father misunderstands and thinks that he is a Reveller indeed. For when his father lunges heavily at him with his club and Sohrab lightly steps aside and sends his father sprawling in the dust, the latter cries out angrily, "Girl! nimble with thy feet, not with thy hands! / Curl'd minion, dancer, coiner of sweet words!" The taunt hurts, for it touches upon the central issue, and Sohrab responds with manly blows. Thus, he very soon proves to his father that although his technique of fighting involves agility rather than brute rage, he is as good a warrior as his father—could, indeed, have killed his father had he chose. But he also has the courtesy which his father lacks, and he does not take unfair advantage of his opportunities.

In *Empedocles on Etna* the two protagonists were characterized by the regions which they inhabited, and this is also true in *Sohrab and Rustum*. Rustum's world is the Oxus sands, Sohrab's the garden of his mother's palace in far-off Ader-baijan. This contrast is established through the initial formal similes by which each figure is introduced to the other. To Rustum, Sohrab seemed

> Like some young cypress, tall, and dark, and straight,
> Which in a queen's secluded garden throws
> Its slight dark shadow on the moonlit turf,
> By midnight, to a bubbling fountain's sound—
> So slender Sohrab seem'd, so softly rear'd.

But to Sohrab, Rustum's giant figure was

> planted on the sand,
> Sole, like some single tower, which a chief
> Hath builded on the waste in former years
> Against the robbers.

At the end of the poem the tower is fallen, and Rustum lies like a "black granite pillar" prone in the sand. But the garden is also desecrated, and Sohrab is like a white violet gathered by heedless children, or like a rich hyacinth cut by some unskillful gardener's hand. Where Sohrab is spring, Rustum is autumn and winter. His club was brought him by the winter storms, and his spear blazed bright and baleful like the autumn star. Hence, in the conflict between them he is in his element whereas Sohrab is not, for the season in which the conflict occurs is winter and the place the Oxus sands. Exultantly, Rustum reminds Sohrab:

> Thou art not in Afrasiab's gardens now
> With Tartar girls, with whom thou art wont to dance;

> But on the Oxus-sands, and in the dance
> Of battle, and with me, who make no play
> Of war.

Rustum speaks tauntingly because he knows that the terrain is on his side. How can a violet, a hyacinth, a cypress, survive in this arid scene? If Callicles had invaded the upper slopes of Etna and attempted to fight Empedocles with his own weapons, those of intellectual analysis, he too would have been worsted and destroyed. But he wisely lingered in his own habitat and contended by the lyric voice. Sohrab, however, in fighting with Rustum, is fighting with the very spirit of the desert.

> And you would say that sun and stars took part
> In that unnatural conflict; for a cloud
> Grew suddenly in Heaven, and dark'd the sun
> Over the fighters' heads; and a wind rose
> Under their feet, and moaning swept the plain,
> And in a sandy whirlwind wrapp'd the pair.
> In gloom they twain were wrapp'd, and they alone;
> For both the on-looking hosts on either hand
> Stood in broad daylight, and the sky was pure,
> And the sun sparkled on the Oxus stream.

The black cloud is the cloud of Rustum's anger. Swirling up out of the desert, it is to him what the volcano was to Empedocles; but whereas in the volcano only Empedocles was consumed, in the sandy whirlwind both men are enveloped and by it Sohrab is destroyed. As he is, nature through all her works suffers the same kind of convulsion as was suffered at the loss of the first garden: thunder rumbled in the air, lightning rent the cloud, Ruksh, the horse, uttered a dreadful cry, and Oxus curdled in its stream. This is the moment of crisis, the transition from Youth to Age, Spring to Winter, Joy to Gloom, and Life to Death, and as such Arnold symbolizes it by the image of the gorge. At least this must be the meaning of the very next formal simile, in which the breeding eagle, shot in spring by the hunter's arrow, lies dying "in some far stony gorge."

It is evident, then, that *Sohrab and Rustum* is not a radically different poem from *Empedocles on Etna*, but is essentially the same poem with a different ending. The one ends in fire, the other in water—in the river Oxus and the Aral Sea. Throughout the poem emphasis has been placed upon how low the Oxus is in the arid winter season. But at the end of the poem it flows majestically on, calm and full, and its fullness arises from the new source of feeling discovered in Rustum. For when Sohrab implores his father to come and sit beside him on the sand and call him son, we are told that Sohrab's voice "released the heart / Of Rustum," whose tears broke forth. "He cast / His arms round his son's neck, and wept aloud," and both the hosts fell silent at his grief. This release of pent-up human feeling is something that never happens to Empedocles, who maintains to the end the integrity of his defiant position. But Rustum acknowledges what had been wrong with his own life and corrects it, and so is released from the gloom in which he hitherto had lived. Both he and Sohrab "poise" their lives by incorporating their opposites within themselves. Sohrab finds in Rustum a father and discovers that that father is not harsh, but soft and tender. And Rustum finds in Sohrab a son and acknowledges that this son is not effeminate but a true warrior. In this discovery they exchange symbols. The dry, sterile thunder of Rustum's wrath has released itself in the rain of tears, and with this rain he waters the rich hyacinth which he has slain. But unlike the youth in the Greek legend, Sohrab is not reborn as a flower. Rather he asks Rustum to lay him in the lovely earth and heap a stately mound above his bones and "plant a far-seen pillar over all"—a pillar which will replace the "black granite pillar" of the now fallen Rustum and will confirm to the world that he is Rustum's son. The true self of Sohrab contains the pillar as well as the garden, the true self of Rustum the garden as well as the pillar.

The final reconciliation of the conflict is of course effected by the end-symbol of the river Oxus. Through this symbol our attention is turned away from the scene of death to one that signifies life, and we are told that life itself goes on despite this tragedy in which one life was extinguished. Critics have complained that the end-symbol does not really arise out of the poem that precedes it, but it is difficult to see how it could be more organically related either to the symbolic landscape or to the characters which that landscape represents. For the first reach of the river, in the high "mountain-cradle" of Pamere, where it flows "right for the polar star, . . . / Brimming, and bright, and large," has the clarity and fixity of purpose of Sohrab's youth; and the second, where "sands begin / To hem his watery march" and he becomes "a foil'd circuitous wanderer," takes us into Rustum's world, the world of the desert. Finally, the waters are released into the sea, which is their "luminous home" and from whose floor the "new-bathed stars emerge," just as Sohrab and Rustum find peace and a kind of new birth in their reconciliation upon the sand. The river comprehends and transcends all these things. It is neither Age nor Youth, Winter nor Spring, Life nor Death, Joy nor Gloom, but is the cyclical movement of them all. In this way it shows that the conflict we have just witnessed is but "an episode" (such is the subtitle of the poem) in the life-process, and that the river itself floats on, "rejoicing" under the stars.

If we now ask how successful the poem is, we find that discussion has often centered upon the similes, which are said to be inorganic and merely decorative. In a sense they are, but it is hoped that enough has been said to show that in their context they do function organically by completing the symbolic topography of the poem. They add to the desert, which is the sole scene of the poem's action, the garden, which is its necessary antithesis. Without the cypress, the hyacinth, and the violet, and the opposing symbols of lonely tower and black granite pillar, the story would not assume the status of a nature myth which it now has. The opening simile of the migrating cranes, for example, establishes the cyclical conception of the life-process which is the central theme of the poem. And most of the similes embody similar contrasts of seasons, times of day, qualities, and regions. The point, for example, of the two similes which contrast the reception of Sohrab's challenge in the two armies is not that the shiver of joy in the Tartar camp really is like a tremor running through a field of corn, or that the fear of the Persians really is like that of pedlars from Cabool in a high mountain pass, rather that their champions are denoted by these several scenes—Sohrab by the corn glistening with dew on a June morning, Rustum by the high mountain pass where birds are choked for want of air. A little later, when the two armies are drawn up opposite each other like "squares of standing corn," it has become autumn and reapers have cut a swath down the middle, and the men with their bristling spears are both the mowers and the mown. And still later, Sohrab is a "partridge in the corn" and Rustum is a hawk, and this leads into the eagle simile, where Sohrab in death lies, not among the corn, but in the "stony gorge" which recreates Rustum's stony mountain pass.

When the similes move beyond the natural world into the world of famous cities and rich men, their houses and possessions, we have the sense of an ordered, aristocratic civilization which is related not so much to any element in the poem as to the poem itself. For the poem also has this ordered, aristocratic character, which also arises out of a very ancient civilization. And the glimpses afforded us of this world make the same comment upon the struggle in the desert as is made by the poem itself. On the one hand, there is convulsion, on the other hand, calm. By their balanced form as by their lovely content the similes introduce into the poem the same element of repose as is introduced by the river Oxus. But they introduce it as art, not nature, and this is one aspect of their meaning. Sohrab first becomes a work of art when he is reduced, in the recognition scene, to the faint vermilion seal pricked upon his arm like that pricked in the clear porcelain vase by the cunning workman of Pekin. Curiously enough, we feel Sohrab's fragility primarily through the fragility of the workman, for when his studious forehead and thin hands are lighted by the evening lamp, he achieves the translucency of his own vase and so assists in the transformation of Sohrab. But this transformation is completed when, as we have already noted, there is erected over the grave of Sohrab the far-seen pillar which, though a kind of public "seal," indicating to the world that he is his father's son, is also, like the tomb built for the dead Moollah by the Sick King of Bokhara, a work of art. Of course, the true work of art erected over Sohrab's grave is the poem itself, a poem which Arnold originally entitled *The Death of Sohrab.*

In all these ways, then, the elements of the poem cohere into a unified work of art, and the poem is probably a much better piece than it is usually considered to be. But it is still not quite satisfactory, and the difficulty is that, like *Empedocles on Etna,* it is but half a poem. It is the second half of which *Empedocles on Etna* is the first. As the former is all conflict and no resolution, so the latter is all resolution and no conflict. Limpidity, placidity, complacency pervade it from the very beginning. The reason seems to be that Arnold wrote it in this spirit. He liked the story, he liked the similes, and he liked the structure—he also liked himself for producing it. He thought it was just what the "complaining millions" needed as a relief from their cares. It was his poetic Crystal Palace for the English people, a kind of showy pageant which he, as the Prince Albert of the literary world, would put on to distract the thoughts of the middle classes from the meager quality of their lives. This showy, self-conscious quality of the poem is its most unfortunate aspect. The similes preen themselves before the mirror of their style; the great, primary human affections pulsate audibly; and the river Oxus gurgles as it flows. Admirably as everything is done, one feels that it is all a little false. It is a poem produced in order to show the world what a poem should be, and as such, it inevitably fails. Tennyson produced something similar in the *Morte d'Arthur,* but his work has a haunting melancholy which is very real, and he also had the wisdom to surround his poem with a modern frame which adds an extra dimension of irony. Arnold's frame is the Preface of 1853, which urges us to read the poem straight and to take it seriously. This, with the best will in the world, it is somewhat difficult to do.

Arnold was to continue this line in *Balder Dead* and *Merope*, and as these do not even have the saving grace of *Sohrab and Rustum*, of being less objective than the author knew, we may treat them more briefly. *Balder Dead* was written during the year 1854 and was first published in the *Poems, Second Series*, of 1855. Its principal source was the prose *Edda* as given in Mallet's *Northern Antiquities*, with, of course, the usual echoes of Homer, Virgil, Dante, and Milton. In all likelihood, Arnold's attention was drawn to the subject by Froude, who in his review of the 1853 volume urged Arnold to consider themes from the northern mythology.[17] Arnold would already have known the story from Carlyle's retelling of it in the lecture on Odin in *Heroes and Hero-Worship*. To Carlyle it is an example of the "beautiful traits of pity" to be found in the Norse mythology.

Balder 'the white God' dies; the beautiful, benignant; he is the Sungod. They try all Nature for a remedy; but he is dead. Frigga, his mother, sends Hermoder to seek or see him: nine days and nine nights he rides through the gloomy deep valleys, a labyrinth of gloom; arrives at the Bridge with its gold roof: the Keeper says, 'Yes, Balder did pass here; but the Kingdom of the Dead is down yonder, far towards the North.' Hermoder rides on; leaps Hellgate, Hela's gate; does see Balder, and speaks with him; Balder cannot be delivered. Inexorable! Hela will not, for Odin or any God give him up. The beautiful and gentle has to remain there. His Wife had volunteered to go with him, to die with him. They shall for ever remain there. He sends his ring to Odin;

17. *Fraser's Magazine*, 49 (1854), 141; cf. *Westminster Review*, 61 (1854), 159.

215

Nanna his wife sends her *thimble* to Frigga, as a remembrance—Ah me!—

This passage gives the spirit of Arnold's poem much better than Mallet or the *Edda*, for in the original the emphasis is on the malign cunning whereby the forces of evil outwit the good and gain Balder for their own. Arnold omits most of this element but even so uses more of it than is really to his purpose, for his theme, as in so many of the early poems, is the loss of Joy in the modern world. Balder, who is a poet as well as a god, is a symbol of this Joy. Addressing him, Regner says:

> 'Balder, there yet are many Scalds in Heaven . . . ,
> But they harp ever on one string, and wake
> Remembrance in our soul of wars alone . . . .
> But when thou sangest, Balder, thou didst strike
> Another note, and, like a bird in spring,
> Thy voice of joyance minded us, and youth,
> And wife, and children, and our ancient home.'

Balder's death, then, is the death of Joy in Valhalla, and the journey of Hermod to Hela's realm, which makes up the principal action of the poem, is the effort, foredoomed to failure, to recover Joy. Thus, the poem once again treats Arnold's poetic myth, but we are now much further along in that myth than we were even in *Sohrab and Rustum*. For there we at least had as our principal subject the death of the hero, whereas here the poem opens with the hero already dead. "So on the floor lay Balder dead," is the opening line of the poem, and one should not say that this is merely a matter of beginning *in medias res*. We are far beyond that point, and the poem is really an elegy, though drawn out, by the insertion of inert matter, to epic proportions. Arnold recognized the difficulty and at one time thought of adding "a first book with an account of the circumstances of the death of Balder himself."[18] But he never did, and the reason is that he was not at

18. *Letters*, 1, 55.

this time interested in the loss of Joy or even in the burning plain. Having moved off the plain himself, he was only interested in the new world that was a-building. And so the one vivid passage in *Balder Dead*, the only thing that redeems it from utter flatness, is the speech at the end in which Balder envisions the final contest between good and evil and the New Heavens and the New Earth that will then arise.

> 'Far to the south, beyond the blue, there spreads
> Another Heaven, the boundless—no one yet
> Hath reach'd it; there hereafter shall arise
> The second Asgard, with another name.
> Thither, when o'er this present earth and Heavens
> The tempest of the latter days hath swept,
> And they from sight have disappear'd, and sunk,
> Shall a small remnant of the Gods repair;
> Hoder and I shall join them from the grave.
> There re-assembling we shall see emerge
> From the bright Ocean at our feet an earth
> More fresh, more verdant than the last, with fruits
> Self-springing, and a seed of man preserved,
> Who then shall live in peace, as now in war.'

This is the first time in Arnold's poetry that the third phase of his myth has been fully and distinctly stated. Obviously, it leads directly into his prose. Balder in his mildness is a type of Arnold's Jesus in *Literature and Dogma*, and the conception of the "remnant," derived from Isaiah, will reappear in *Rugby Chapel* and the late lecture "Numbers."

Arnold's next major work was *Merope*, but before he began this he renewed an attempt, initiated some years before, to do a drama on the subject of Lucretius. This project antedated even *Empedocles on Etna*. His notebooks and the register of the Oriel College Library show him reading Lucretius from 1845–47, and in 1866 he says that he had been at work on the subject "for

some twenty years."[19] The admonition "Chew Lucretius" heads
the list of literary projects for the year 1849, and in March of that
year, just after the appearance of *The Strayed Reveller, and
Other Poems,* Arnold wrote to his brother that he "had thoughts
of publishing another volume of short poems next spring, and a
tragedy I have long had in my head, the spring after." It is al-
most certain that this tragedy was "Lucretius."[20] We do not know
what kind of drama it was to be, whether of the type of *Empedo-
cles on Etna,* centering on a single gloom-weighted figure, or of
the type of refurbished Shakespearean drama with a variety of
character and incident, such as was being produced by Browning
and other of Arnold's contemporaries. But it is clear that Arnold
was diverted from it into *Empedocles on Etna,* probably because
he saw in the latter's suicide a much better vehicle for his theme
than anything afforded by the life of Lucretius. We know that
he actually used in *Empedocles on Etna* materials gathered for
"Lucretius," and Professors Tinker and Lowry are probably right
in suggesting that he was unable to get on with his play because
he had already said what he had to say in that vein in *Empedo-
cles on Etna.*

But in 1855, after finishing *Balder Dead,* he returned to "Lu-
cretius" again, and at this point we are able to be more specific
about the kind of work he intended. For photostats of about

19. See the discussion of "Lucretius" in Tinker and Lowry, pp. 340–47.
The MS "Register of Books taken out of the Oriel College Library by the
Provost and Fellows" shows that Arnold borrowed the first volume of
Havercamp's edition of Lucretius on October 19, 1846, and returned it on
March 2, 1847. He borrowed the second volume on July 8, 1847, but the
records do not show that he returned it.

20. Arnold's letter, as printed in Mrs. Humphry Ward's *A Writer's Rec-
ollections* (p. 43), continues: "At present I shall leave the short poems
to take their chance, only writing them when I cannot help it, and try to
get on with my Tragedy (Merope), which however will not be a very quick
affair." The original of this letter is not available, but one suspects that if it
were, it would show that the word "(Merope)" is Mrs. Humphry Ward's
interpolation, for she (not knowing about the Lucretius project) would nat-
urally have understood the letter in this way. There is no other evidence
that *Merope* was begun so early.

thirty pages of his working papers have survived, most of them in the form of a notebook bearing on its first page the lettered name "Mythologica."[21] The name is not quite appropriate because, although the notebook does contain genealogies of the gods, most of it is concerned with historical background for the play together with drafts of actual speeches and scenes. There are notes on the public careers of the various characters—Pompey, Clodius, Milo, Cicero, Scaurus, Caesar, and others—information on customs and institutions, chronologies of events, and notes on the vegetation and topography of the country around Rome. From these materials it is possible to gain a fairly good idea of what the drama was about. It was to deal with "the events at the end of 53 [B.C.]"—i.e. with the contest for power between the two political gangsters who represented the parties of Pompey and Caesar—T. Annius Milo and Publius Clodius. In 53 B.C., when Milo was a candidate for the consulship and Clodius for the praetorship, they met by chance on the Appian Way and Clodius was murdered. Milo was impeached, but his trial was conducted amidst such circumstances of violence and intimidation that Cicero, who was appointed to conduct the defence, was afraid to speak. His *Pro Milone* is an expanded form of the unspoken oration. Milo went into exile and was later killed in a rising against Caesar.

Two pages in Arnold's notebook which divide the characters into "Milonians" and "Clodians" suggest that this struggle was to be the main political backdrop to the play. Exactly how Lucretius was to be brought in is uncertain. Since Caius Memmius, to whom Lucretius addressed his poem, was a character on the Milonian side (he was the son-in-law of Sylla, from whose party the Milonians descended), Lucretius would presumably be associated with Milo, Cicero, and Pompey. And since his death, according to one tradition, occurred in the same year as Milo's trial,

21. Tinker and Lowry, p. 341. The "Mythologica" notebook itself was apparently destroyed during the war. I am indebted to Messrs. Howard F. Lowry and James E. Broderick for my knowledge of this material.

these two events would doubtless be dramatically associated. But it is likely that Lucretius was to be represented as the type of poet who showed himself inadequate to the political occasion, for all the references to him in Arnold's notes are unfavorable. One prose passage, drawn from Montaigne's essays but evidently to be used as an idea in the play, states, "All I aim at is to pass my time pleasantly & without any great reproach, & the recreations that most contribute to it, I take hold of: as to the rest, as little glorious & exemplary as you would desire." On which Caesar comments: "But Lucretius, with the same clearsightedness & Epicurean disillusionment, desires, in his own *personal* relations, a *romantic* character. —curiosity—feeling. the 2 motors. the 2nd dead the 1st survives." Another passage, which has also been cast into blank verse as a speech addressed to Oppius, states: "It is a sad thing to see a man who has been frittered away piecemeal by petty distractions, and who has never done his best. But it is still sadder to see a man who has done his best, who has reached his utmost limits—and finds his work a failure, and himself far less than he had imagined himself." That this refers to Lucretius is clear from another speech which reproves Lucretius for fretting against the weaknesses of his mental nature, which are as inalterable as physical disease. Also, it conforms with the picture of Lucretius in Arnold's 1857 lecture on "The Modern Element in Literature," where the philosopher is made an inadequate interpreter of his age because he is "overstrained, gloom-weighted, morbid." It is doubtful that Arnold would have had quite this view of Lucretius when he began the project in 1846. At that time he would have had at least as favorable a view of him as he had of Empedocles in 1852. But by the late 1850s the work was becoming a tragedy of the failure of Epicureanism in a time of political crisis, and doubtless one of Arnold's difficulties with the play was his increasing lack of sympathy with its main character.

But another difficulty must have been its form. For whatever may have been Arnold's original intention, it is clear that by the late 1850s he was planning a full-fledged historical drama comparable to nineteenth-century imitations of Shakespeare. In 1855–56 his reading lists show him studying, not merely Plutarch and Roman histories, but also *Coriolanus, Julius Caesar,* and *Anthony and Cleopatra.* In his working papers he noted, "—Ant. and Cleop. 443. The serious speaker speaks verse, the light one prose—" and this is exactly what they do in Arnold's existing drafts. There are half a dozen blank verse fragments of a brooding, philosophic sort and also two complete scenes in prose. These scenes, which may have been intended as the opening scenes of the tragedy, show Satyra, an elderly roué, leaving Athens to take possession of an estate which had been confiscated by Sylla and presented to him in exchange for the services of his aunt. Caius Memmius promises him letters of introduction, and in the next scene Satyra is urging the members of his household—Myrtilus, a cynic; Petta, a young girl; and Euphrosyne, an older woman— to hurry with the packing. The dialogue is brisk and lively and suggests that Arnold had a small talent in this way. One thinks of his translation of the fifteenth idyl of Theocritus in "Pagan and Mediæval Religious Sentiment" and of the more boisterous scenes in *Friendship's Garland.* But the work was not destined to be completed. In the first place, in the Preface of 1853 Arnold had discountenanced Shakespeare as a model for young writers and had recommended the Greeks. Yet here he was attempting a Shakespearean drama. And in the second place, he must have soon discovered that he did not have it in him to create a dozen different characters and launch them into truly dramatic action. And so, very suddenly, towards the end of 1856, he gave up "Lucretius" and began writing *Merope.*

Arnold says in his preface to *Merope* that he was led to that work through an admiration for the Greek tragic form. He wished to do for Greek tragedy what in *Sohrab and Rustum* and *Balder Dead* he had attempted to do for the epic. To this consideration the choice of subject was apparently secondary. Or rather, the subject would be determined by these formal considerations—by the need to find a story which was traditionally associated with the genre, which had all the requisites of excellent dramatic action, and which had not yet been treated in any surviving drama of the ancients. In the Preface of 1853 he had emphasized the importance of this and had appealed to Aristotle's *Poetics* as an authority. Now, in the fourteenth chapter of the *Poetics*, Arnold found what he wanted. There, Aristotle discusses the various situations which give rise to pity and fear. All of them involve a person's killing, or being about to kill, someone who is dear to him, and we are told that he may do this either knowingly or in ignorance. "Of all these ways," says Aristotle, "to be about to act knowing the persons, and then not to act, is the worst . . . The next and better way is that the deed should be perpetrated. Still better, that it should be perpetrated in ignorance, and the discovery made afterwards . . . The last case is the best, as when in the *Cresphontes* Merope is about to slay her son, but, recognising who he is, spares his life." The third case Arnold had used in *Sohrab and Rustum*. Now he could go that poem one better by using the fourth and superior kind in the particular example suggested by Aristotle.

The story of Merope, as Arnold develops it, is as follows: Twenty years before the opening of the play Cresphontes, king of Messenia, had been murdered by Polyphontes, who had usurped the kingdom. In the tumult which followed all the children of Cresphontes had been slain except one son, Æpytus, who escaped to Arcadia, where he was raised in the court of his uncle, Laias. In the meantime, Cresphontes' widow, Merope, has lived on in Messenia, wooed by Polyphontes but rejecting him and keeping alive her hope for vengeance through an annual messenger, Arcas, who brings her news of her son. On this twentieth anniversary of the murder, Æpytus and Laias secretly arrive in Messenia, the former attempting to divert suspicion by telling the story of his own death in a hunting accident, the latter circulating among the people to rally support. Meanwhile, Arcas arrives with news for Merope that her son and uncle have disappeared, and both suppose them to have been murdered by the youth who has just arrived. Merope is about to slay this youth as he sleeps, when Arcas recognizes him and intervenes. In a ceremony at the altar Æpytus slays Polyphontes and the people arise in his support.

This is Arnold's story, and if we are to believe his preface and his comments upon the play in his letters, he was interested in it solely as an excellent dramatic action. His preface dwells upon three things: the beauty of the Greek dramatic forms, the importance of choosing traditional stories and following the tradition as closely as possible, and the errors in dramaturgy made by his predecessors, Maffei, Voltaire, and Alfieri. Much of the preface, for example, is occupied with discussing whether Æpytus should or should not know of his own parentage, whether the recognition of Æpytus by Merope should be handled in a single scene or split in two, whether Merope should be wedded to Polyphontes or merely wooed by him, and so forth. At no point does Arnold comment on his interpretation of the story or even seem aware that he has used the story as the vehicle of a theme.

Yet this theme is certainly the chief source of the rather meager interest that the drama has for a modern reader. To the modern reader the recognition scene is, if anything, a foolish anticlimax, and the one respect in which the play is interesting is precisely that in which Arnold departed—and acknowledged that he departed—from tradition. Tradition, insofar as it stated anything about the character of Polyphontes, made him a villain, but Arnold made him a mixture of good and evil and, in so doing, gave to his work a totally un-Greek character. In a Greek tragedy the values are relatively clear, the issue is sharply defined, and the effect depends upon the inevitable and foreshadowed working out of the catastrophe. But here the values are not clear, and the interest rather depends upon the working out of the problem, which side is right, Polyphontes or Æpytus. The theme of the play is the complexity of the moral situation and the difficulty in politics of choosing between a pragmatic and an absolutistic ethic.

The issue is raised when Polyphontes proposes to Merope that they forget the feud which has divided them for the past twenty years, marry, and recognize her son as heir to the throne. He realizes that in proposing this his motives will be suspect, and he does not pretend to be better or more firmly entrenched than he is. But he thinks that there were good political reasons for what he did and that his twenty years' tolerance of Merope testifies to his good intentions. In any case, they should now look to the future, not the past, and should consider the arrangement that will be best for all concerned. In accents that would not be disowned by Bentham or the two Mills, Polyphontes states the liberal, pragmatic ethic of compromise.

Æpytus, on the other hand, embodies the older ethic of absolute values. In its primitive form this means the old Greek doctrine of natural vengeance, in its more refined form the doctrine of Justice. It asserts that a crime must be atoned for no matter how much further suffering its atonement begets. Murder is not a mere word, as Polyphontes almost asserts,[22] but is a sacrilege, a breach of the divine law, and the law must be satisfied. Ultimately, the position of Æpytus is religious, and this fact raises a problem which is lucidly stated by the second chorus. Though there is such a thing as the Good, says the Chorus, and it ought to rule, and though occasionally it can rule only through an appeal to force, who is to say where the Good lies? For the Good depends on motive, and even our own hearts are inscrutable—how much more, then, the hearts of others! For this reason Zeus and Justice have forbidden even the Good to employ force. John Stuart Mill, in his essay *On Liberty*, would agree, but Newman would say that the dogmatic principle involves as its corollary the principle of the visible church. If the Good exists, it must be embodied in some person or group of persons on earth; otherwise we are thrown back into relativism again.

Such, whether in nineteenth-century or Greek terms, is the issue of the play, and Merope is rightly called the protagonist be-

22. Lines 201, 276.

cause she is the torn swaying figure who stands at the center of the conflict and can see good in both sides. In the first half of the play she is chiefly opposed to Polyphontes and in the second half to Æpytus, and the revolution in her views comes in the recognition scene. That is, indeed, the true function of the scene, not that she here comes to know her son, but that she comes to know herself, and the nature of vengeance, more profoundly. Ultimately, she adopts a mediatorial view, which is that although in theory the relativistic ethic is wrong and the absolutistic ethic right—for there clearly is such a thing as the Good and perhaps occasionally it has to be established by force—still the person who appeals to force is then under a special obligation to validate his act by the purity and justice of his own life. This Polyphontes had not done. Musing on what manner of man he was, Merope says, "I find worth in thee, and badness too . . . a two-fold colour reigns in all."

> But thou, my son, study to make prevail
> One colour in thy life, the hue of truth;
> That justice, that sage order, not alone
> Natural vengeance, may maintain thine act,
> And make it stand indeed the will of Heaven.

The "two-fold colour" in the life of Polyphontes was the conflict between his best and his ordinary self. Æpytus, by making prevail "one colour" in his life, will eliminate the ordinary self and establish the best self. In "The Function of Criticism at the Present Time" Arnold says, "Force till right is ready."[23] Æpytus has exercised force: right must now be readied.

And yet, the reader has reason to believe that the transformation of Æpytus has already occurred within the play. When the Chorus, early in the drama, comforts Merope by reminding her that she rears "far 'mid Arcadian hills," a champion for vengeance, Merope laments that her son gives no thought to this task.

23. *Essays in Criticism: First Series* (1902), p. 12; Super, *3*, 265–66.

> For he, in the glens
> Of Lycæus afar,
> A gladsome hunter of deer,
> Basks in his morning of youth,
> Spares not a thought to his home.

This is the first appearance in the drama of Arnold's symbolic landscape, and it immediately associates Æpytus with those youthful lingerers in the forest glade who have not yet met their duties in the world. But the river of Æpytus' existence will not allow him long to linger, and when he arrives at the Messenian court, this is how he tells the story of his supposed death. The prince, he says, was pursuing a stag, which plunged into a lake, and he and the dogs plunged in after it.

> —There is a chasm rifted in the base
> Of that unfooted precipice, whose rock
> Walls on one side the deep Stymphalian Lake;
> There the lake-waters, which in ages gone
> Wash'd, as the marks upon the hills still show,
> All the Stymphalian plain, are now suck'd down.
> A headland, with one aged plane-tree crown'd,
> Parts from this cave-pierced cliff the shelving bay
> Where first the chase plunged in; the bay is smooth,
> But round the headland's point a current sets,
> Strong, black, tempestuous, to the cavern-mouth,
> Stoutly, under the headland's lee, they swam;
> But when they came abreast the point, the race
> Caught them as wind takes feathers, whirl'd them round
> Struggling in vain to cross it, swept them on,
> Stag, dogs, and hunter, to the yawning gulph.

All this, says the narrator, happened in "one flashing instant."

> A moment more—I saw the prince turn round
> Once in the black and arrowy race, and cast

An arm aloft for help; then sweep beneath
The low-brow'd cavern-arch, and disappear.

Arnold tells us in the preface to *Merope* that tradition is "an un-speakable support" to the poet: "It gives him the feeling that he is treading on solid ground. . . . Its importance I feel so strongly, that, where driven to invent in the false story told by Merope's son . . . of his own death, I could not satisfy myself until I discovered in Pausanias a tradition, which I took for my basis, of an Arcadian hunter drowned in the lake Stymphalus, down one of those singular Katabothra, or chasms in the limestone rock, so well known in Greece, in a manner similar to that in which Æpytus is represented to have perished."[24] It may be so, but, as Charles Lamb says, "the archetypes are in us, and eternal." We have met them before in Arnold's poem *A Dream* and in other poems where the youth is swept, in one flashing instant, over the cliff and onto the plain below. And one feels that this passage, almost alone in the drama, is vital and alive because in it Arnold is returning to the source of his true poetic feeling.

The meaning of the passage is clear. The false tale which Æpytus tells is actually a true tale. He has died as an idle youth hunting in the forest glade and has been reborn as a mature prince accepting his responsibilities. That he never was actually idle, but was only biding his time, is of course suggested by the image of the underground river. His true life was a "buried life," which comes to light in the recognition scene. Here he suffers a second symbolic death and rebirth, whereby he is recognized by his mother for what he truly is. "In word I died," he says, "that I in deed might live," and the word *deed* expresses the character of his transformation. Whereas the Duke of Savoy in the *Church of Brou* died in a hunting accident in order to be reborn into the world of art, Æpytus is reborn into political action.

Thus, one can say that although in form *Merope* follows

24. Super, 1, 53.

from the Preface of 1853, *Sohrab and Rustum,* and *Balder Dead,* in content it lies on a direct line between the *Sick King in Bokhara* and *Culture and Anarchy.* It is Arnold's first treatment of a political or social question since the poems of 1849, and it embodies a dramatically altered point of view. For although the Sick King was taught by the Vizier to believe in absolute values, he also learned that there was nothing he could do to realize these values in the world. The world was ruled by eternal laws of Nature or Fate, and man was best advised to take refuge in quietism, perhaps in art. This was the tenor of all the social poems of the 1849 volume. Even in *Balder Dead,* when Balder is told that he will be absent from the final conflict between good and evil, he replies that he is not sorry, for he is "long since weary of your storm" and finds in life "something too much of war and broils." Like Plato's philosopher, he would retire under the shelter of a wall and not emerge till the second Asgard. Not so Æpytus. He is the first of Arnold's heroes who actively imposes his will upon the world. With him, "Exit Hamlet, enter Fortinbras."

One puts the matter in these terms not merely because Arnold's youthful imagination was so deeply impregnated by *Hamlet,* but also because this play is a kind of classical version of the Shakespearean tragedy. Of course, as Arnold treats it, it is much changed. Claudius is not so surely a villain now, and Gertrude is not besmirched. But what is more, the son who comes home from foreign courts to revenge his father's murder is not introspective, but is a man of action. We have called him Fortinbras. Whereas in *Hamlet* the issue was clear and the hero delayed, here the issue is in doubt and the hero does not delay. Rather, after a scene in a bedchamber in which his mother nearly kills him, instead of he his mother, he cuts off his father's murderer in the very act of prayer. One does not know whether Æpytus was sensitive enough to suffer, but if he was, his sufferings found a vent in action.

It is significant that the publication of *Merope* preceded by just one year Arnold's own entrance into politics in the pamphlet

England and the Italian Question. It is also significant that Arnold connected this work with a new sense of identification which he felt with his father's spirit. Commenting on the pamphlet, he said, "I have often thought, since I published this on the Italian question, about dear papa's pamphlets. Whatever talent I have in this direction I certainly inherit from him, for his pamphleteering talent was one of his very strongest and most pronounced literary sides, if he had been in the way of developing it. It is the one literary side on which I feel myself in close contact with him, and that is a great pleasure. Even the positive style of statement I inherit."[25] Given this connection, it is natural to interpret *Merope* as a kind of allegory of the young Arnold's return, at his mother's behest, to reassume his rightful role as his father's son. Of course, something of this theme had already been started in *Sohrab and Rustum.* That poem is often interpreted as an expression of the Oedipus conflict, and certainly it would be wrong to deny that a sexual element is present. The redoubtable masculinity of Rustum, as witnessed by the vast club that he wields, the tower and pillar by which he is symbolized, together with the presumed effeminacy of the son, make it a conflict between the masculine and the feminine principles. And in the end, when the virility of the son has been established and that fact is recognized by planting a far-seen pillar over his grave, replacing the fallen pillar of his father, he is clearly the sexual victor. But on the level of the Super-Ego he has been conquered, and of course, it is his joy to be so conquered. One critic has said that the poem represents Arnold's *Vicisti, Galilæe!*—Galilean, thou hast conquered!—and this is also true. When Sohrab speaks of "My father, whom I seek through all the world," it is a spiritual father of whom he speaks, comparable to the spiritual authority which Arnold was seeking in the Preface of 1853. That Arnold found his father, both in the Preface and in the poem, is indicated by the fact that the volume containing these works is the first which he published under his full name. His first two

25. *Letters, 1, 125.*

volumes had appeared cryptically, as by "A," the single initial revealing about as much of the poet's name as the dandiacal stance did of his true self. But in the volume of 1853 his true self had come to the fore. Arnold wrote to Jane that in that volume there was only one poem *maladif*—only one "sickly" poem of which a son of Dr. Arnold should not be proud. Therefore, the name of Arnold could be allowed to appear on the titlepage, where it stands, a far-seen pillar over all, identifying the poet as his father's son.[26]

It is a striking coincidence, then, (though perhaps no more than that) that Arnold finished the writing of *Merope* in the very month, November 1857, which he chose to assign as the date of *Rugby Chapel*, the elegy in memory of his father. *Rugby Chapel* was probably not written until shortly before its publication in 1867, and so the date affixed to its title is something of a mystery. Possibly it represents the date of Arnold's reading Thomas Hughes' novel, *Tom Brown's School-Days* (1857), a magnificent tribute to his father which he might well have felt should have come from his hand rather than the hand of another. In a letter to his mother he says that the poem was occasioned by his reading of Fitzjames Stephen's attack upon his father in a review of the novel, but this review was not published until January 1858.[27] He chose, then, to antedate to the month when he finished *Merope* his decision to do for his father what Æpytus had done for his. This but once again illustrates to what an extent for Arnold the writing of a poem was an internal dramatic act.

The three poems which we have just discussed probably represent a necessary phase in Arnold's development, but they do

26. *Unpublished Letters*, p. 21. J. D. Coleridge, in a review of the 1853 volume, speaks of "the filial consideration for his father's name which has led him to publish two smaller volumes anonymously, and to reserve the avowal of his own authorship, till success, important in its nature if moderate in amount, had shown that he was not likely to discredit a name which any one might be proud to bear" (*The Christian Remembrancer*, 27, 1854, 310).

27. *Letters to Clough*, p. 164; *Edinburgh Review*, 107 (1858), 172–93.

not represent the best phase. They are an attempt to implement the theory of the Preface of 1853, which demands that the poet turn away from the self and make poems out of the not-self. In response to this theory Arnold turned to the matter of Persia, of Scandinavia, of Greece—to the most remote and alien in time and place that he could find. The theory also demands that the poet pour his thought into the mould provided by one of the great ancient genres, and in conformity with this Arnold produced two parts of an epic and a tragedy. By these means he did succeed in putting his own preoccupations behind him, for whereas *Sohrab and Rustum* is to some degree a personal poem, *Balder Dead* is not, and *Merope*, apart from its larger bearing, is almost purely an antiquarian exercise. But if the writing of the poems was productive of good for Arnold, the poems themselves are not good, and their method is certainly wrong. A better method was provided by the elegy. There, instead of turning from the self to the not-self, the poet turns from the ordinary self to the best self, and this is what Arnold attempted to do in his later years. Most of the elegies were written between 1855 and the publication of *New Poems* in 1867. They make up the bulk of the best poetry in that volume, and they constitute Arnold's major poetic vehicle in his last creative period.

8 THE USE OF ELEGY

> *Has this fellow no feeling of his business,*
> *that he sings at grave-making?*
>
> —Hamlet

It is a commonplace that Arnold is an elegiac poet, but not everyone would agree on what is meant by this phrase. Most people who use it mean that he has a vein of tender melancholy which leads him to lament, in beautiful but relaxing measure, the passing of an older and lovelier world. And there is, of course, this element in Arnold. We find it in *The Forsaken Merman*, in *Dover Beach*, and in *Stanzas from the Grande Chartreuse*. But it is not so important as its presence in these strikingly successful poems would suggest, and it is not at all characteristic of the elegies. The elegies, by and large, are positive poems which look to the future rather than lamenting the past. They are not tenderly elegiac, and they are not at all relaxing.

In order to see how this is true we need to see who are the subjects of Arnold's elegies. Arranged in the order in which the poems about them were composed (and ignoring the three late elegies on household pets), they are: Sénancour, the author of *Obermann* (1849), Wordsworth (1850), Wordsworth's son-in-law, Edward Quillinan (1851), Charlotte Brontë and Harriet

Martineau (1855), Heinrich Heine (1858–63), Arnold's brother, William Delafield Arnold (1859), Arthur Hugh Clough (1862–66), Arnold's father (1857–67), Sénancour again (1865–67), and Arthur P. Stanley (1881). The striking thing about this list is that so many of the subjects are public figures who represent intellectual and moral tendencies of the age. Even where they do not, as in the case of Arnold's brother, they are so treated in the poems that they come to represent such tendencies. In other words, they are symbolic figures who, quite as much as Arnold's fictional heroes, inhabit his imaginative world.

This being so, the order in which to read the elegies is the order in which their subjects lived and died in Arnold's imagination. This was not always the order in which they died in actuality or the order in which Arnold memorialized them, for he was sometimes slow in getting around to his elegies and they were sometimes slow in dying. Wordsworth, for example, in living on to 1850 was an obvious anachronism, and Arnold would have been ready to write his elegy at any time during the preceding decade. But if Wordsworth is placed at the head of the list, and if the unimportant elegy on Quillinan is neglected, then the poems that remain actually were written pretty much in the order of Arnold's myth. We may place them in four groups. There is, first of all, the inhabitants of the forest glade, and of this group Wordsworth is the sole representative. Then come Sénancour, Charlotte Brontë, Harriet Martineau, and Heine, who are all figures from the burning plain. William Delafield Arnold, Clough, and Arnold's father are transitional figures who begin on the burning plain but, to a greater or lesser degree, move on to the wide-glimmering sea. The reconstructed Sénancour and Arthur Stanley (perhaps also the three pets) are entirely figures from the third phase of the myth. It is obvious, then, that it will not do simply to group all the elegies together and call them "elegiac." Depending on who died and when, and on where Arnold imagined himself as standing in relation to that figure, the elegies have a great variety of tone and feeling. To give an account of them will not merely take us to the end of Arnold's poetic myth but it will also provide a kind of summary of his entire poetic method.

We begin, then, with *Memorial Verses*, the elegy on Wordsworth. As we have already noted, this is the only elegy which has as its subject an inhabitant of the forest glade. As a result, it is the only elegy which is elegiac in the conventional sense. It does lament the passing of an older and lovelier world. Wordsworth is seen as embodying the two values of poetry and nature, and we are told that with his death these values have been lost to the modern world. As to poetry, first Byron died, then Goethe, and now, with the passing of Wordsworth, "The last poetic voice is dumb." And as to nature, "few or none / Hears thy voice right, now he is gone." He was the very spirit of Joy, and with his death Joy has departed from the earth.

The abruptness of this statement is somewhat surprising because other men have died and yet the values which they represent have lived on. This, indeed, is the crux of the elegiac form. The elegy, especially in its pastoral version, has many conventions but none so necessary to its structure as that whereby the poet, toward the end of his lament, suddenly discovers that the person whom he is mourning is not dead but in some sense lives on. This discovery is of course attended by a sharp reversal of feeling. So Bion in his *Lament for Adonis* suddenly calls upon Cypris to weep no more, for Adonis is lovely in death and must be wept again another year. So Milton in *Lycidas* stills the refrain, "Lycidas is dead, dead ere his prime," with the new voice,

> Weep no more, woeful shepherds, weep no more,
> For Lycidas your sorrow is not dead.

And Shelley in *Adonais* reverses the main movement of his poem with the cry,

> Peace, peace! he is not dead, he doth not sleep—
> He hath awakened from the dream of life.

Whether based upon the pagan conception of the dying god or on the Christian faith in immortality, this convention affords to the elegist the essential means of both artistic and philosophic reconciliation. Arnold with his classical education understood this, and in *Memorial Verses* he is writing an elegy. But there is no reversal in that poem. Wordsworth is dead and he will not return—a finalism which is the more glaring because in the case of Goethe and Byron, who are associated with Wordsworth in the poem, there is a possibility of their return.

> Time may restore us in his course
> Goethe's sage mind and Byron's force;
> But where will Europe's latter hour
> Again find Wordsworth's healing power?

The answer is that it will not find it again, and the reason is clear. The speaker in the poem is located on the burning plain ("this iron time"), and Byron and Goethe are figures from that plain. The former is the type of the Promethean rebel, the latter of the Stoic sage, and so there may well be other Byrons and other Goethes again. But there will not be other Wordsworths. He is the last survivor of an idyllic age which has long since passed away.

Memorial Verses is the only one of Arnold's elegies in which there is no reversal. All the others are marked by a sharp break, a kind of lyric peripeteia, in which the poet's attitude towards his subject is dramatically changed. But Arnold puts this break to a very different use from that found in the conventional elegy. For whereas normally the elegy asserts that what has been lost here on earth will be recovered in another sphere, Arnold asserts that what has been lost here on earth will be replaced—also on earth —by something different. In other words, his elegy is an instrument of change rather than of permanence. It is purely naturalistic in its assumptions, and it is related to his philosophy of history.

The use Arnold makes of the elegy may be observed most easily in a poem which we have already examined, the *Stanzas in Memory of the Author of 'Obermann.'* The poem begins, we recall, by praising Obermann as one of three in the modern world who have known to see their way. "To thee we come, then!" cries the poet, and he is about to give himself wholly to Obermann when suddenly, in line 128, there is a sharp break in the thought—the elegiac reversal—and he calls out, "—Away!"

> Away the dreams that but deceive
> And thou, sad guide, adieu!
> I go, fate drives me; but I leave
> Half of my life with you.

In the stanzas which follow the poet declares that he "in the world must live," and though he hopes that Obermann will not disapprove, he ends the poem with "a last, a last farewell." It is only in this sense that Obermann "dies" within the poem: he dies in the world of Arnold's estimation, and thus the elegiac reversal is really a reversal in reverse. That is to say, instead of lamenting, "Lycidas is dead," and then discovering that in some sense he lives on, Arnold says, "Lycidas is alive (alive as an influence in me)," and then contrives to kill him off in the course of the poem. In the second Obermann poem he speaks of his subject as "Thou master of my wandering youth, / But left this many a year." The *Stanzas in Memory*—or, more properly, *in Forgetfulness*—of *the Author of 'Obermann'* is the place where this leaving is recorded. In a letter to his tutor, Herbert Hill, he says, "My separation of myself, finally, from him and his influence, is related in a poem in my Second Series."[1]

In this poem, then, we see Arnold using the elegy as a device of spiritual repudiation, and the point is that for a figure on the burning plain he could hardly do otherwise. Morbid and unwholesome as these figures are, he wants to put them behind him, and the elegy is an instrument for doing so. Hence the fact that

1. Tinker and Lowry, p. 271.

the dates of the elegies so often do not correspond with the dates of the subjects' death. Arnold simply had to wait to write the poems until he could spiritually enter into the events of which they spoke. For Sénancour he waited three years, for Clough he waited five, for Heine he waited seven, and for his father he waited from fifteen to twenty-five. An elegy is supposed to be an occasional poem, but it is obvious that the occasion of these poems is something that happened to Arnold rather than something that happened to his subject. Their theme is not the death or rebirth of their subjects but the death or rebirth in Arnold of something corresponding to their subjects.

We may see the process again in *Haworth Churchyard*, an elegy on Charlotte Brontë written six years after the Obermann poem in 1855. It is a little curious that Arnold should have written this elegy at all, for he did not really like Miss Brontë or particularly admire her novels. Just two years before, he had found *Villette* disagreeable. "The writer's mind," he wrote, "contains nothing but hunger, rebellion, and rage, and therefore that is all that she can, in fact, put into her book." And as for Harriet Martineau, whose name he coupled with that of Miss Brontë, when his mother chided him for showing such respect to one who had recently caused a scandal by her open avowal of atheism, he became alarmed lest he had committed an indiscretion. He replied that he "knew absolutely nothing of Harriet Martineau's works or debated matters—had not even seen them, that I know of, nor do I ever mention her creed with the slightest applause, but only her boldness in avowing it." Nevertheless, even this boldness he did not really admire, not in 1855. He had chosen to couple her name with Miss Brontë's, partly because he had met both ladies on the same evening some five years before and partly because at the moment of Miss Brontë's death Miss Martineau was also lying dangerously ill. Presumably he thought he could kill two birds with one stone. If so, he was mistaken, for Miss Martineau proved a singularly tough old bird and survived another twenty years. This, of course, was an acutely embarrassing circumstance for Arnold. Not only did it indicate that he was prepared to bear her death with equanimity twenty years before that degree of stoicism was necessary, but it also prevented him from republishing his very fine elegy until the event which it so confidently predicted had occurred. When it did occur, he republished immediately and added an Epilogue which (I am afraid we shall have to say) was his poetical revenge. For it too reverses the reversal. In the elegy itself there had been only a very tenuous kind of reawakening promised to the dead in the final adjuration,

> Sleep, O cluster of friends,
> Sleep!—or only when May,
> Brought by the west-wind, returns . . .

only then awaken, to view the summer, the sky, the heather in bloom. But by 1877 this cluster of friends had beccme so repugnant to Arnold that he was actually afraid lest, by republishing the poem, he should "overpraise a personage so antipathetic to me as H. M. My first impression of her is, in spite of her undeniable talent, energy and merit—what an unpleasant life and unpleasant nature!"[2] And so, his Epilogue is really a recantation. Referring to his hope of their reawakening, he declares,

> So I sang; but the Muse,
> Shaking her head, took the harp—
> Stern interrupted my strain,
> Angrily smote on the chords,

and demanded that "unquiet souls" such as these should find themselves again only in "the dark fermentation of earth, / In the never idle workshop of nature." By this Arnold seems to mean that they should enjoy no spiritual resurrection but, like Empedocles, should mingle with earth, air, fire, and water through all eternity. As purely natural forces they should return to the world of nature from which they came.

2. *Letters*, 1, 34, 51; 2, 158.

If this seems a somewhat ungracious poem by way of elegy, we ought to suspend our judgment until we see what Arnold did to Heine in the elegy entitled *Heine's Grave*. Arnold first read Heine in 1848, and initially he was "disgusted." "The Byronism of a German, of a man trying to be gloomy, cynical, impassioned, *moqueur*, etc., all *à la fois* . . . is the most ridiculous thing in the world. . . . I see the French call this Heine a 'Voltaire au claire de lune,' which is very happy." It so happened, however, that the English generally were experiencing a fit of sanctimonious horror about Heine, Carlyle calling him a "filthy, foetid sausage of spoiled victuals," and Kingsley replying to his daughter's question, "Who is Heine?" with the words, "A very wicked man, my dear." Obviously, rather than agree with such persons, Arnold would be the champion of Heine, and in 1861 he assured Clough that he was a "far more profitable" study than Tennyson. He was impressed by the picture of the poet lying for the last eight years of his life on a sick-bed in Paris and sending forth from his "mattress-grave" arrowy shafts of irony and satire.[3] In this sense he was a very symbol of the modern spirit—the spirit which, undaunted by evil but unable to reply any longer with the true Byronic thunder, replied with mockery and laughter. And it is in this way, as a kind of bitter, continental version of Mycerinus and the Strayed Reveller, that he is presented in the poem.

The trouble is that by 1862–63, when the poem was written, Arnold no longer admired Promethean defiance as he once had, and in the poem he can hardly wait to tell us so. For the elegiac reversal occurs very early, in line 37 of a 230-line poem, and once again it is a reversal in reverse. After only a few words of praise the poet is interrupted by harsh, mocking laughter, the laughter of the "Bitter Spirits" (apparently Muses) who claim

3. Ibid., 1, 11; Sol Liptzin, *The English Legend of Heinrich Heine* (New York, 1954), and his "The English Reception of Heine," *Victorian Newsletter*, 11 (1957), 14–16; Walter Houghton, *The Victorian Frame of Mind* (New Haven, 1957), pp. 172–73; *Letters to Clough*, p. 154; Tinker and Lowry, pp. 242–48.

Heine as their own. Arnold, I am afraid, does not contest this claim very strongly. "I knew he was yours," he says, and then proceeds to the main question of the poem, which is,

> What, then, so harsh and malign,
> Heine! distils from thy life?
> Poisons the peace of thy grave?

The answer is that Heine had every other gift but Love and, wanting that, also wanted Charm. Charm, we are now told, is what "makes [the] song of the poet divine." Well, it may be so. We can, of course, remember a time in Arnold's youth when it was Joy which made the song of the poet divine, and we may suspect that Charm is simply the watered-down, mid-Victorian equivalent of Joy. We may also think that Arnold has offended more people by his Charm, which is now known as "smiling insolence," than by any other quality he possesses. Nevertheless, it is true that just at this time he was very much interested in acquiring Charm. He was eager to *get at* the English public. "Such a public as it is," he wrote to his mother, "and such a work as one wants to do with it! Partly nature, partly time and study have also by this time taught me thoroughly the precious truth that everything turns upon one's exercising the power of *persuasion, of charm*; that without this all fury, energy, reasoning power, acquirement, are thrown away and only render their owner more miserable. Even in one's ridicule one must preserve a sweetness and good-humour."[4] Heine did not preserve this sweetness and good-humour, and therefore Heine must be rejected, and this is exactly what Arnold did, in words of one syllable, at the end of the poem. "Bitter and strange, was the life / Of Heine . . . may a life / Other and milder be mine!"

Indeed, Arnold felt that he could put his finger on the precise moment in his life when he and Heine had parted company, and it was the same moment when he had parted from Obermann.

---

4. *Letters, 1, 234.*

For Heine's dilemma is presented in the same terms as Obermann's—solitude vs. the world—the world being represented by the Paris drawing rooms in which he had been forced to live out his later years, and solitude by the Hartz mountains in which he had wandered in his youth. Indeed, there is some suggestion that Heine was a Callicles at heart and that his bitterness was due to his not having been able to fulfill himself in a free life of nature. But then, when the matter is considered more closely, we learn that it was not that—there was some defect in himself, and Goethe, who had pointed out the defect, had also exemplified the remedy. For Goethe too had visited the Hartz in his youth, "passionate, eager, . . . all in ferment,"

> —but he
> Destined to work and to live
> Left it, and thou, alas!
> Only to laugh and to die.[5]

Like Goethe, Arnold too had descended the mountains to work and to live. For him the moment had been that day in September 1849 when he had come down out of the Bernese Alps to put Marguerite and Obermann behind him. On that occasion he had chosen Goethe rather than Heine as his guide, and now, in 1862, his elegy is a kind of prayer of thanksgiving that he had not done otherwise. For Heine's reward was to be buried in a curiously ambiguous grave in Montmartre cemetery which Arnold visited in September 1858. It was Arnold's habit to see in graves a symbol of the true, inner life of the man, and as he looked at Heine's grave he thought he saw such a symbol. It had enough of "shadow, and verdure, and cool" so that initially it appeared a refuge from the uproar of the Paris streets. But as Arnold meditated the matter more closely, he saw that the grave was really an extension of the sick-room, as the sick-room was an extension

5. Heine's account of his youthful wanderings in the Hartz (the source of *Heine's Grave*, 152–90) is found in *Reisebilder*, Book 1 (1826). Arnold's own note refers to Goethe's *Harzreise im Winter*.

of the city, and that in the black tombstone and yellow limes, the artificial flowers "yellow and black," the trim alleys, and the hot September sun, there was evidence of something harsh and malign which had distilled from Heine's life to poison the peace of his grave. And so he rejected Heine, almost taunting him with the fact that his grave was not near still water or cool shade, as would clearly be the case with a poet who possessed love. He had "no sepulchre built / In the laurell'd rock, o'er the blue / Naples bay," as had Virgil; "no tomb / On Ravenna sands, in the shade / Of Ravenna pines," as had Dante; "no grave / By the Avon side, in the bright / Stratford meadows," as had Shakespeare. *Heine's Grave* is the title of the poem because the grave is the symbol of everything Arnold had to say about the man.

Indeed, in his elegies Arnold habitually uses graves, tombs, and sepulchres in this way. Poetically, they are a part of his symbolic landscape, and when they come at the end of a poem, as they frequently do, they also relate to his use of the end-symbol. They provide an image upon which the mind of the reader can rest and which gathers up in itself much of the meaning of the poem. They also correspond to Arnold's conception of the life after death. In the sonnet *Immortality* Arnold urges that "the energy of life may be / Kept on after the grave, but not begun," and generally, in accord with his naturalistic assumptions, he considers that the life after death will not be different from this life but will be a continuation and confirmation of it. Thus he always puts his heroes in "heavens" that are appropriate to the life they led on earth. His father, who was so active in this life, he conceives as going "to the sounding labour-house vast / Of being," and the Brontës, who were purely natural forces, are returned to the world of nature from which they came. Empedocles' grave is the element of fire in which he lived, and Wordsworth's is Grasmere churchyard, kept fresh by Rotha's stream. In Arnold's fictional poems he had no difficulty in accommodating the tomb to the symbolic role which it was intended to play. The daisied circle of Merlin, the marble "mattress-grave" of Tristram, the far-seen pillar of Sohrab, and the brick-work tomb of the dead Moollah are all entirely appropriate to the meaning of their lives. But when he came to historical figures, the recalcitrant nature of reality sometimes gave him trouble. In *The Church of Brou*, for example, the tomb among the mountains was the perfect expression of a love which transcended death. It so happened, however, that the real church of Brou was not among the mountains but on the flat plains of La Bresse, and that the tombs of the lovers were not at all such as Arnold had described them. When these facts were pointed out to him, he was so chagrined by his errors that he first suppressed the historical parts of the poem and then relegated the whole to Early Poems as though to apologize for his inaccuracy.

He made a similar error at the end of *Stanzas in Memory of the Author of 'Obermann,'* but here it was deliberate. Speculating on whether his hero was buried by Lake Leman in Switzerland or among the "swarms of men" on the "granite terraces" of Paris, he described both alternatives, remaining *in utrumque paratus*. The reason for this is obvious. Having presented Obermann as one who felt the call both to solitude and the world, he wished to continue this theme even in the description of the grave. Sainte-Beuve, however, thought that Arnold actually was in uncertainty on the point, and so he wrote him to say that Sénancour was buried at Sèvres near Paris and that his tomb bore the words, "Éternité, deviens mon asyle."[6] Whether or not Arnold was grateful for this information we do not know, but he certainly had no intention of resolving Obermann's conflict either by eternity or by a village on the outskirts of Paris.

Arnold's trouble with the church of Brou and the village of Sèvres, however, was as nothing compared with his trouble with the Haworth churchyard in the elegy devoted to the Brontës. In that poem he had utilized the bleak Yorkshire moors as the perfect symbol of the angry young women who were his subject.

6. Tinker and Lowry, p. 254 n.

True, he had never visited Haworth churchyard and did not know much about the Brontës, but then he had "pumped" Mrs. Gaskell at dinner and had the benefit of information from his sister Jane. In the autumn of 1850, shortly after Miss Brontë's first visit to Fox How, Jane and her husband had driven over to Haworth for the afternoon, and Jane had described the occasion in a letter. As the letter contains practically all the information which appears in the poem—even to the rainy weather—it is probable that it was Arnold's source.

Though the weather was drizzly, we resolved to make our long-planned excursion to Haworth; so we packed ourselves into the buffalo-skin, and that into the gig, and set off about eleven. The rain ceased, and the day was just suited to the scenery,—wild and chill,—with great masses of cloud glooming over the moors, and here and there a ray of sunshine covertly stealing through, and resting with a dim magical light upon some high bleak village; or darting down into some deep glen, lighting up the tall chimney, or glistening on the windows and wet roof of the mill which lies couching in the bottom. The country got wilder and wilder as we approached Haworth; for the last four miles we were ascending a huge moor, at the very top of which lies the dreary black-looking village of Haworth. The village-street itself is one of the steepest hills I have ever seen, and the stones are so horribly jolting that I should have got out and walked with W——, if possible, but, having once begun the ascent, to stop was out of the question. At the top was the inn where we put up, close by the church; & the clergyman's house, we were told, was at the top of the churchyard. So through that we went,—a dreary, dreary place, literally *paved* with rain-blackened tombstones, and all on the slope, for at Haworth there is on the highest height a higher still, and Mr. Brontë's house stands considerably above the church. There was the house before us, a small, oblong stone house, with not a tree to screen it from the cutting wind; but how we were to get at it from the churchyard, we could not see! There was an old man in the churchyard, brooding like a Ghoul over the graves, with a sort of grim hilarity on his face. I thought he looked hardly human; however, he was human enough to tell us the way; and presently we found ourselves in the little bare parlour.[7]

How could one doubt, after reading this, that the Brontës were buried in the churchyard? Arnold assumed that they were and made the churchyard the title and the symbol of his poem. But no sooner had he published it than he learned from Mrs. Gaskell that it was all wrong. The graves were inside the church, and Anne's was miles away at Scarborough. Arnold's reply is characteristic: "I am almost sorry you told me about the place of their burial. It really seems to put the finishing touch to the strange cross-grained character of the fortunes of that ill-fated family that they should even be placed after death in the wrong, uncongenial spot." On this sentence the editor of the letter comments, "What does this mean? They were buried in the Brontë tomb in Haworth Church." It means, Mr. Editor, that they carried their perversity so far as not to be buried where Matthew Arnold thought they ought to be. However, the poet overcame his resentment and graciously concluded his letter: "Farewell, my dear

7. E. C. Gaskell, *The Life of Charlotte Brontë* (New York, 1857), 2, 155–56. The writer of the letter is not identified either here or in Clement Shorter, *The Brontës, Life and Letters* (London, 1908), 2, 176–78, but Mrs. Humphry Ward (*A Writer's Recollections*, p. 38) says it was Jane. Charlotte Brontë first came to the Lake District in August 1850, at which time she met Mrs. Gaskell and Mrs. Arnold and her daughters, but not Matthew. Miss Martineau was away from home but wrote to express regret and invite her back. Jane and William Forster then visited Miss Brontë at Haworth from their new home at Rawdon, Yorkshire, in late September or early October (her letter is dated October 3, 1850). Finally, Miss Brontë returned to the Lake District in December as the guest of Miss Martineau, and this was the occasion of the dinner at Edward Quillinan's to which Arnold refers in the opening lines of his poem.

Mrs. Gaskell, with renewed thanks. May *you*, at any rate, long continue living and working, and delighting us all."[8]

Haworth Churchyard is certainly the most inept poem that Arnold ever wrote, and one of the worst. One is especially astonished at his employing, as a circumlocution for saying that Miss Martineau was not yet dead, the phrase, "The Muse / Gains,not an earth-deafen'd ear." In view of the fact that Miss Martineau was stone deaf and always carried a large ear-trumpet, this pastoralism seems especially inappropriate, but Arnold repeats it a few lines later with reference to Miss Brontë: "Console we cannot, her ear / Is deaf." One is inclined to cry with humpbacked Richard,

> Was ever woman in this humour woo'd?
> Was ever woman in this humour won?

but the fact is that Arnold was not attempting to woo them. Indeed, this whole series of poems—the Obermann poem, *Heine's Grave*, and *Haworth Churchyard*—form a kind of *Retro Satana*, or "Get thee behind me, Satan," and they are not so much elegies as attempts on Arnold's part to exorcise an evil spirit which had formerly dwelt within him. It would perhaps be undignified to cite the words of the popular song, "I'll be glad when you're dead, you rascal you," but it would not be inappropriate to quote Antony, "I come to bury Caesar, not to praise him." For this is clearly what Arnold's elegies attempt to do.

Arnold had stood at Heine's grave in Montmartre cemetery in September 1858. The following April he was again in Paris when he received the news of the death of his brother, William Delafield Arnold, at San Roque, near the Rock of Gibraltar. Willy had gone out to India in 1848 as an ensign in the native army, had written a successful novel, *Oakfield, or Fellowship in the*

8. *Letters Addressed to Mrs. Gaskell by Celebrated Contemporaries, Now in the Possession of the John Rylands Library*, ed. R. D. Waller (Manchester, 1935), p. 37 and note.

East, and had become Director of Public Instruction in the Punjab. In 1858 his wife Fanny had died and had been buried at Dharmsala, at the foot of the Himalayas. Now, his own health broken, he was returning home when he fell seriously ill at Cairo, struggled on across the Mediterranean, and finally was put ashore at Gibraltar, where, on April 9, he died. Arnold did not know in time to reach him and so was filled with a sense of being so near and yet so far. A few weeks later his business took him to Auray on the coast of Brittany, and from there he went to Carnac for the sake of the great druidical monument.

It is a very wild country [he wrote to his wife]—broom and furze, broom and furze everywhere—and a few patches of pine forest. The sea runs into the land everywhere, and beautiful church towers rise on all sides of you, for this is a land of churches. The stones of Carnac are very singular, but the chapel of St. Michel, on a hill between the stones and the village of Carnac, I liked better still; the view over the stones and the strange country of Morbihan (the little sea), on the spur of Carnac by the sea, and beyond the bay and peninsula of Quiberon, where the emigrants landed, and beyond that the Atlantic. All this at between six and seven on a perfectly still, cloudless evening in May, with the sea like glass, and the solitude all round entire. I got back to Auray at eight.[9]

As Arnold looked out over this scene and saw sails passing in the distance—where William would have passed had he lived—he thought,

> Oh, could he once have reach'd this air
> Freshen'd by plunging tides, by showers!
> Have felt this breath he loved, of fair
> Cool Northern fields, and grass, and flowers!

9. *Letters*, 1, 95.

Could he once have reached it—as I have reached it—he would have been restored, as I have been restored. No triumphant feeling is expressed in the poem, but the whole opening section, which describes the scene as Arnold viewed it from the chapel, is filled with a sense of vitality, beauty, health, and faith— the open sky, the coast of Brittany bright and wide below, the sheep grazing in the daisied fields, the mild May evening, the cuckoo flying from bush to bush, the red orchis gleaming, the golden furze, the beaches glistening in the fading light. But it is not simply the natural beauty of the scene that strikes him, it is also the fact that all its associations are religious and vital. The coast is "weird and still," as though "the wizard Merlin's will / Yet charm'd it from his forest-grave." Behind are the giant stones of Carnac, bearded with lichens, scrawled and grey, which, though no priestly stern procession moves through their pillared aisles, yet, like the Runic stones of *The Grande Chartreuse*, testify to a faith once living. And today there "rise up, all round, the Christian spires," for this is a land of churches. Thus we are given the sense of a continuous religious tradition—paganism, medieval magic, Christian faith—and all in perfect harmony with the beauty and vitality of the land. It is this state which Arnold, both in his physical travels and in his religious evolution, has now reached. Ah! if William could have reached it too!

> He long'd for it—press'd on.—In vain!
> At the Straits fail'd that spirit brave.
> The south was parent of his pain,
> The south is mistress of his grave.

Employing the same symbol that he had used in *The Scholar-Gipsy*, Arnold visualized the Straits of Gibraltar as a kind of spiritual narrows which William had to negotiate in order to move off the burning plain. The Tyrian trader had done it, and Arnold had done it, but William had not. It was a part of the strange pathos of his life that he had come so near and yet remained so far.

With these thoughts in his mind Arnold travelled to the south of France and came, on May 19, to the town of Cette on the Gulf of Lions. From the beach there he could look across in imagination to where his brother was buried, and he discovered to his astonishment that he had been wrong about his brother's grave. The south may have been the parent of his pain, but it was not the mistress of his grave. On the contrary, as *A Southern Night* asserts, both William's grave, by this "gracious Midland sea," and that of his wife, by those "hoary Indian hills," were lovely, mystic, cool. In a sense they were too good for them. These persons were "jaded Englishmen" whose "dusty lives" had been spent wholly in the world's service, and yet they had achieved the most beautiful and romantic resting-place on earth. Surely they ought to have been buried in the heart of some great city, and spots such as these should have been reserved for some Hindu sage or grey crusading knight, some youthful troubadour or romantic maiden, stealing by moonlight to her pirate lover. "But you," says Arnold—

> a grave for knight or sage,
> Romantic, solitary, still,
> O spent ones of a work-day age!
> Befits you ill.

"So sang I," but then—and this is the elegiac reversal—the poet "checks his strain" and is reminded by the midnight breeze that there is no one more worthy of this lovely sepulture than an English lady and an English gentleman.

Parallel to this reversal in his conception of his brother is another in the feelings of the poet himself, for as Arnold gazes out across the Mediterranean, he is reminded of a similar moonlit evening years before. It is the second of the two evenings described in *A Summer Night*, and although historically we do not know what that evening was, it was apparently sometime in the late 1840s. For then the poet was eating out his own heart with restless yearning, whereas now his troubles are forgot in the troubles of others. Thus the perception that through a life of service his brother had transcended both the dusty Englishman he was thought to be and the Romantic solitary who was admired in his stead was the means of a similar transformation on the part of the poet. He was born as Christian gentleman by giving birth to that conception of his brother.

We come now to *Thyrsis*, the elegy on Clough, which was written between 1862 and its publication in 1866. It is usually treated along with *The Scholar-Gipsy*, as a companion to that poem, and of course, there is every reason for doing so. The two poems employ the same locale, they are written in the same stanza and the same pastoral mode, and they were placed one after another in all of Arnold's collections. Still, they were written fifteen years apart, and with Arnold fifteen years—especially when they extend from the early 'fifties to the mid 'sixties—is a long time. Much has happened in that time, and indeed, this "much" is essentially what the poem is about. By separating *Thyrsis* from *The Scholar-Gipsy*, then, and considering it in the context of the elegies, one not only avoids the elementary mistake of saying that Clough "is" the Scholar-Gipsy but he also sees how different the two poems are. For the one is primarily a Romantic dream-vision which creates an ideal figure who lives outside of time, whereas the other is an elegy about a human figure who lived in time and was thereby destroyed.

When Clough died in Florence on November 13, 1861, it was generally agreed that he had not lived up to the brilliant promise of his Rugby years. At Oxford he had "failed" in his examination, and although he had partially redeemed this failure by a fellowship at Oriel, he had perversely resigned his fellowship after a few years, partly out of irritation with the Thirty-Nine Articles and partly out of a restless desire to help in the work of social betterment. He went over to Paris to watch the Revolution of 1848 and to Rome to see Garibaldi fight the French, but he found no sense of commitment, and his new job at University

Hall was not better, but rather worse, than the old one at Oriel. Nothing opened up in Australia or America, and so he settled down in the Education Office in a routine task which, unlike his friend, he did not dignify by literary employment. In 1849 he had published the delightful, if unregenerate, *Bothie of Tober-na-Vuolich*, but his next poem, *Amours de Voyage*, rather perplexed and pained even his most sympathetic admirers. And so, on his death, it was an open question whether he had failed merely in the eyes of the world or whether, in some deeper sense, he had actually been a failure.

Arnold's letters show that his mind hovered around this question and also that he was led back in meditation to those early days when Clough was the senior and most brilliant member of that "little interior company" at Oxford in 1845–47.[10] What had happened to make his life go wrong? Surely at that date anyone would have prophesied greater things of Clough than of the dandy Arnold, and yet here was Arnold, increasingly acknowledged as one of the authentic poets of the day, elected Professor of Poetry at the University of Oxford and delivering at that moment the lectures on translating Homer which would lay the basis of a distinguished critical reputation. Comparisons are odious, but one does not have to be a La Rochefoucauld to say that on the death of an old college chum they are inevitable. Even in the elegies which we have already examined there is, without any triumphant feeling, an unexpressed vein of thought that goes somewhat like this: "This person, with whom I was once associated, or whom I admired, is now dead and I am alive. Had I gone on as he did, I too might be dead, but I turned aside from sickness into health and so stand here, at Carnac, or before Heine's grave, or meditating on the strange fate of the two ladies with whom I once had dinner. And so, paying tribute to what was great in them, I also pass judgment on their errors and draw from their lives the profound moral lesson, 'There but for

10. Ibid., pp. 176–77.

the grace of God go I!' " In the case of Heine and Obermann, Arnold thought that he could put his finger on the exact moment when he and they had parted company: for Heine it was in the Hartz mountains, for himself and Obermann in the Bernese Alps, when he had descended to work and live, they to languish and die. Similarly, Arnold thought that he could put his finger on the exact moment when he and Clough had parted company, but in this case the scene was not the Swiss Alps but the Cumnor hills, and the date was about a year earlier, in November 1848. Clough had just taken his dramatic departure from Oriel and had published his irrepressible *Bothie of Tober-na-Vuolich*, and so, for the anti-Establishment set, he was the hero of the hour. "—I have been at Oxford the last two days," wrote Arnold, "and hearing Sellar and the rest of that clique who know neither life nor themselves rave about your poem gave me a strong almost bitter feeling with respect to them, the age, the poem, even you. Yes I said to myself something tells me I can, if need be, at last dispense with them all, even with him: better that, than be sucked for an hour even into the Time Stream in which they and he plunge and bellow." Of course, Arnold was being mockstern, and there was no open rupture; a few years later he and Clough were breakfasting together frequently again, and much of the old intimacy was re-established. Still, something had come between them which could not be ignored, and in February 1853, when Arnold, in answer to his friend's complaint, was writing a long "historical" letter about their relationship, he admitted that "there was one time indeed—shortly after you had published the Bothie—that I felt a strong disposition to intellectual seclusion, and to the barring out all influences that I felt troubled without advancing me." He assured Clough that this estrangement was "merely a contemplated one and it never took place." Indeed, such was the charm of Clough's company and his mode of being that "I could not have forgone these on a mere theory of intellectual diatetics." "I am and always shall be, whatever I do or say, powerfully attracted towards you, and vitally connected with you . . . , for ever linked with you by intellectual bonds—the strongest of all." Still, if "you ask me in what I think or have thought you going wrong," it is in this: that you never would "resolve to be thyself," but were always worrying whether you shouldn't be something different from what you were. "You have I am convinced lost infinite time in this way: it is what I call your morbid conscientiousness—you are the most conscientious man I ever knew: but on some lines morbidly so, and it spoils your action." A few months later he repudiated the idea that he was merely using his friend "as food for speculation": that was a "morbid suspicion" and should be put aside. Still, the discussion of this matter continued through the summer and into the fall, for on October 10, nine days after finishing the Preface of 1853, Arnold wrote: "Forgive my scold the other day—when one is trying to emerge to hard land it is irritating to find your friend not only persisting in 'weltering to the parching wind' himself, but doing his best to pull you back into the Sea also."[11] The allusion to *Lycidas* is significant. By George Sand, Arnold had been called *un Milton jeune et voyageant*. Now that he was reaching the end of his voyage, he was apparently thinking of Clough as his prospective Edward King.

In Arnold's view the moment when Clough had "died" was the moment when he had thrown himself into the Time Stream and made himself subject to change and death. And that was the moment, in 1848, when "Thyrsis of his own will went away." Thus, though the death of Clough in 1861 provided the occasion for the poem, its subject, insofar as it is about Clough, is not his death but his going away. It is about his abandoning the ideal of the Scholar-Gipsy. The Scholar-Gipsy lived in a world outside of Time and so was not subject to death. Thyrsis too could have lived in that world if he had wished, but he would not. "Some life of men unblest / He knew, which made him droop, and fill'd his head." And so, in the earlier poem, he was allowed

11. *Letters to Clough*, pp. 95, 129–30, 136, 144.

by the poet to depart, and was only adjured, when once the fields were still and the dogs and men all gone to rest, to return and once "again begin the quest." Meanwhile, in a nook of the high, half-reaped field, the poet would wait for him—would wait till sun-down. Actually, it was just one year that Arnold waited. In the *Stanzas in Memory of the Author of 'Obermann,'* dated November 1849, the poet declared that he too "in the world must live," and we recall that in *The Scholar-Gipsy* this shift of locus was acknowledged by the poet's awakening from his dream and finding himself, in mid-poem, no longer with the Gipsy but in the world. But in both poems he drew two distinctions between himself and Clough. One was that whereas Thyrsis "of his own will went away," Arnold was driven by fate. And the other was that Arnold intended so to live in the world as to remain essentially unspotted by it. It is true, when he was writing the *Stanzas in Memory of the Author of 'Obermann,'* he included Clough among those "Children of the Second Birth, / Whom the world could not tame."[12] But the question now was, whether, and in what degree, either he or Clough had been faithful to the ideal since their parting in the high half-reaped field some fifteen years before.

In order to find out, Arnold needed to revisit the fields. In January 1862, in thanking Mrs. Clough for some of her husband's poems which she had sent him, he wrote, "I shall take them with me to Oxford, where I shall go alone after Easter;— and there, among the Cumner hills where we have so often rambled, I shall be able to think him over as I could wish."[13] There can hardly be any doubt that Arnold actually did take something like the walk described in *Thyrsis* and that in so doing he found the structure of his poem. It is the structure of the "place revisited," the device employed in Wordsworth's *Brothers*, in *Tintern Abbey*, and in Arnold's own *Resignation*. Its advantage is that it begets self-consciousness. One becomes conscious of

12. Ibid., p. 110.
13. Ibid., p. 160.

self by being conscious of a place that was formerly associated with the self. In this way too one becomes conscious of time. Place is the medium on which the passing of time is recorded, and so in this place, which is at once recognizably the same and yet bewilderingly different, the poet has an indicator of all that has happened in the intervening years. Simply by traversing the fields he can develop the theme, which is central to the poem, of the contest between permanence and change.

At the beginning of the poem change is triumphant everywhere. "How changed is here each spot man makes or fills." In the spot which man makes, the two Hinkseys, "nothing keeps the same." The examples given, however, show that we are here on the level of mere popular folkways and superstition—things dear to the human heart but whose loss is relatively light and trivial. More serious is the question, "Are ye too changed, ye hills?" for this evokes Wordsworthian and Biblical echoes of the "everlasting hills," from whence cometh our help. If they are changed, then change is triumphant indeed. But as the poet begins his walk he is confident that they are not changed. With only the slightest hesitation ("Runs it not here?") about the track by Childsworth Farm, in thought he follows that track to his very goal, the signal-elm, and from that vantage turns and looks out over the familiar scene to the well-known Vale, the weirs, the youthful Thames, and to Oxford, unchanged in its loveliness. She is lovely at "all times," now in winter as formerly in spring. Indeed, on this winter eve cold is overcome by spring warmth, and the poet finds himself, in imagination, safe in his forest glade. But then, in line 22, with the word *Only*, the same word which introduced the discordant note in *Dover Beach*, the poet falters and perceives that he himself is subject to change and that the signal-elm which he so confidently expected to see—"I miss it! is it gone?" And with this third question the poet is prepared to enter seriously upon the exploration of his theme.

For if the answer to this question is affirmative, then change does indeed rule all, not merely the social world of man and the natural world of the hills, but also the world of spiritual values. For the tree, though in a sense a part of the natural landscape, has become a private symbol between Thyrsis and the poet of the enduring validity of their youthful ideal:

> while it stood, we said,
> Our friend, the Gipsy-Scholar, was not dead;
> While the tree lived, he in these fields lived on.

He was a symbol of that abiding inward life which all men desire, and thus, with the question about the tree the poet is no longer exploring the Cumnor hills but is exploring a region of the mind. When he says, in the next line, "Too rare, too rare, grow now my visits here," he is not speaking of the natural scene, for he is not a Wordsworthian poet. He is speaking of the depths of his own soul, with which he has been too infrequently in communion. The line echoes another line in the contemporary poem *Palladium:* "We visit it by moments, ah, too rare!" There the reference is explicitly to the soul, which is compared to the image of Pallas Athene, on which the safety of Troy depended. Like the signal-elm, it was placed on high, far above the city, and we are told that "while this stood, Troy could not fall."

> So, in its lovely moonlight, lives the soul.
> Mountains surround it, and sweet virgin air;
> Cold plashing, past it, crystal waters roll;
> We visit it by moments, ah, too rare!

The essential question is one of *power.* It is "some loss of habit's power" which first makes the poet falter, and when he renews the attempt, it is with the cry, "Who, if not I, for questing here hath power?" The word has almost Lawrentian overtones of a vital, procreative force, a joyous union with nature and with oneself, which would enable him to recreate the vision of the Scholar-Gipsy once again. Can he do it? As in *Dejection: an Ode,* it is not so much a question of whether the tree is there as of whether he can see it. Essentially, it is a question of poetry.

Has he been so long in the world that his poetic powers have been completely dissipated, or do they still survive? If they do, he ought to be able, like his predecessors from of old, to "flute his friend, like Orpheus, from the dead." Wordsworth, however, is the only one in Arnold's poetic pantheon whose "healing power" is ever compared to that of Orpheus, and Wordsworth, we know, is dead. And so the poet launches into that lovely stanza,

> O easy access to the hearer's grace
> When Dorian shepherds sang to Proserpine!

which expresses the relative difficulty of writing poetry in a modern, unpoetic age. In ancient times the muses walked the earth, and poets spoke directly to them as to a friend. But now, in a later age, and a northern land, and to an aging poet, what chance that poetry would have this magic power?

Nonetheless, the poet will try:—

> Well! wind-dispersed and vain the words will be,
> Yet, Thyrsis, let me give my grief its hour
> In the old haunt, and find our tree-topp'd hill!
> Who, if not I, for questing here hath power?

What these lines indicate is that Arnold's quest for the tree will be accomplished by giving his grief its hour, that is, by writing an elegy. And so, a hundred lines after the beginning of the poem we get an elegy within an elegy which has as its purpose to determine whether the elegist can sing. If he can, if he proves the vitality of his poetic powers, then, whatever he accomplishes for his friend, he will at least have fluted himself from the dead. As Coleridge said of the damsel with a dulcimer, "Could I revive within me / Her symphony and song," and did so in the act of the poem, so Arnold, referring to the vision of the Scholar-Gipsy, revives it within him and becomes the poet once again. In this way he solves a problem which is central to the other great Romantic poems about the failure of poetic power. The paradox in Wordsworth's *Immortality Ode,* Coleridge's *Dejection: an Ode,* and Hopkins' sonnet to Robert Bridges is that the poems themselves belie the event of which they speak. But Arnold has included within his poem, as its central episode, the act of imagination by which that poem was restored. "A timely utterance gave that thought relief," says Wordsworth, but the utterance is outside the poem. In *Thyrsis* it occupies approximately lines 101–71.

As the poem within the poem is an elegy, its structure necessarily repeats that of the larger poem, and that is why, in lines 101–50, we get a reintroduction of themes already stated in lines 1–40. The theme of the poet's intimate knowledge of the countryside, already stated in the opening stanzas, is now more confidently repeated in lines 105–11, but with this difference, that the poet now understands that his power derives from this knowledge. Then, just as his confidence had been checked before by the word *Only,* so now the word *But* reintroduces the theme of change, which once again floods across the poem. It encompasses the dingle, the green bank, the girl, and the mowers. "They all are gone, and thou art gone as well!" And once again it also encompasses the poet.

> Yes! thou art gone! and round me too the night
> In ever-nearing circle weaves her shade.

The effect of this descent of night is to transform the forest glade into a darkling plain. The soft, spring warmth becomes chill, the flowers are replaced by brambles, and the luxuriant Thames valley becomes an "upland dim" in which the fog creeps from bush to bush. But the more startling effect is upon the poet's imagination. For as he feels this chill descend, he simultaneously falters in his grasp upon imaginative reality. The language and conceptions of the poem coarsen. The images are too quickly translated into their moral equivalent, and they are distorted into something altogether out of keeping with the poem. The descending night with its darkness and its chill becomes Death, and the poet so far forgets where he is (or rather *when* he is) as to make his foot "less prompt to meet the *morning* dew." His way becomes the Way of Life, the hill becomes the Citadel of Truth, and it is not a low Cumnor hill with an elm atop, but a mountain towering high in the clouds and bearing upon its summit the "throne of Truth." In *The Scholar-Gipsy* Goethe "dejectedly" took his seat upon the "intellectual throne," but the Scholar-Gipsy never did. Had he been invited to, he certainly would have done so dejectedly, but he fled such places rather than sought them. And when we learn that this same mountain is apparently "the fort / Of the long-batter'd world," we wonder whether the poet is coming or going. If he is seeking the Scholar-Gipsy, he is seeking him in the wrong place, and in truth, the whole conception of this stanza is not idyllic and poetic, but moral and heroic. It derives not from Romantic poetry but from ancient Stoicism and evangelical Christianity. Probably its actual source is Hesiod's *Works and Days:* "Full across the way of Virtue the immortal gods have set the sweat of the brow; long and steep is the path that reaches to her, and rough at the beginning; but when you reach the highest point, hard though it is, in the end it becomes easy."[14] For the poet it has not yet become easy, and his stanza bears the marks of strain and effort. It is one of the passages most frequently quoted from the poem, as seeming to contain its moral message, but imaginatively it is the nadir of the poem. The poet, bewildered and lost, is about to lie down and give himself to death, when suddenly, by ceasing to try, he is miraculously saved.

This is the elegiac reversal, and it is accomplished by the poet's "hushing" his false poetic voice and assuming his true. By so doing, he is once again placed in his imaginative landscape and achieves his poetic vision.

> Look, adown the dusk hill-side,
> A troop of Oxford hunters going home,
> As in old days, jovial and talking, ride!

14. Lines 288–92. Donne's third Satire has also been cited.

From hunting with the Berkshire hounds they come.
Quick! let me fly, and cross
Into yon farther field!—'Tis done; and see,
Back'd by the sunset, which doth glorify
The orange and pale violet evening-sky,
Bare on its lonely ridge, the Tree! the Tree!

Why does Arnold have his protagonist see the tree in this way? Part of the answer is that the tree is not to be seen by scaling a mountain-top or battering down a fortress, but in the same way that the Scholar-Gipsy was seen by boys, blackbirds, mowers, and poets. You turn around and he is there! Part of it is that hunters are for Arnold a symbol of joyous vitality, and they stir up the landscape and make it vibrate a little. Moreover, they are an element of permanence, riding out of *The Scholar-Gipsy* "as in old days" and indicating that all is essentially the same. And finally, they precipitate the poet into that instinctive movement which is the right one. Where effort had failed, he now "flies"— that is, he does what the Scholar-Gipsy did, and so, acting like the Scholar-Gipsy, he becomes the Gipsy and sees his tree again. Of course, he cannot reach the tree that night, but this too is proper, for the tree (unlike the throne and the fort) is not something to be reached. As a "signal" elm, it operates from afar, and the quest itself, not the achievement of the quest, is the essence of its meaning. So Arnold, in the exactly contemporaneous preface to the *Essays in Criticism*, berates the *Saturday Review* for falling victim to the "beautiful but deluding idea" that the British nation has "found the last word of its philosophy." "No," he says, "we are seekers still!" and he gives to Oxford, "so venerable, so lovely, so unravaged by the fierce intellectual life of our century," the function of "ever calling us near to the true goal of all of us, to the ideal, to perfection,—to beauty, in a word, which is only truth seen from another side."[15] This, too, is the function of the tree; and so, in recovering his vision of the tree, Arnold

15. *Essays in Criticism: First Series* (1902), pp. x–xi; Super, *3*, 289–90.

has not reached the end of his road but has merely renewed his power to continue a seeker still.

But what of Thyrsis? The elegiac reversal of line 157 is not merely the peripeteia of the elegy within the elegy but is also the major turn in the elegy as a whole. It is significant, then, that it involves not the death and rebirth of Thyrsis but the loss and recovery of the tree, and that the tree, in some sense, is the central figure of the poem. Arnold conceded to his friend Shairp that "if one reads the poem as a memorial poem, . . . not enough is said about Clough in it; I feel this so much that I do not send the poem to Mrs. Clough."[16] It is not merely, however, that not enough is said about Clough in it, but rather that so much of what is said is critical. In the early stanzas Clough is compared to the cuckoo, that "too quick despairer" who petulantly flies away when the first bloom is off the spring, not realizing that summer and autumn "have their music too" and that the cycle of nature will bring a new spring in another year. So, in the cycle of history, if Clough could have waited the passing of storms which a more far-sighted person would have known were transitory, he would have survived into the better times which are already in prospect. But "he could not wait their passing, he is dead." In this way his death becomes slightly ludicrous, the unnecessary destruction of a witless and flighty person who could have been saved by a little forethought. Where the ordinary elegy contains a section in which the poet accuses various powers of negligence in permitting the death of the beloved, Arnold's poem does not employ this convention, for "Thyrsis of his own will went away." His death was really a kind of suicide.

Still, by asserting, with respect to the cuckoo, that rebirth is the law of nature, the poet has opened the way to assert this of Clough too, and the elegy within the elegy is the proposed means of doing this. Unfortunately, when the elegy is accomplished and the poet turns to include his friend in its discovery

16. *Letters*, 1, 380.

—"Hear it, O Thyrsis, still our tree is there!"—he finds that his friend cannot hear it and that his death in Florence is a second symbolic desertion of the Cumnor fields.

> Ah, vain! These English fields, this upland dim,
>   These brambles pale with mist engarlanded,
> That lone, sky-pointing tree, are not for him;
>   To a boon southern country he is fled. . . .

The poet, then, is left alone on the darkling plain. But though he is alone, he will not despair, for the sight of the tree against the western sky is a sign that the Scholar-Gipsy still haunts these hills, "outliving thee." And, if he is "a wanderer still, then why not me?" Together with the Scholar-Gipsy the poet will pursue the "fugitive and gracious light" which is their ideal, and the final vision we have is of the two of them going off together, outliving Clough.

If the poem ended at this point (and in some ways it would be a better poem if it did) we would have to say that *Thyrsis* belongs with those elegies like *Heine's Grave, Haworth Churchyard*, and *Stanzas in Memory of the Author of 'Obermann'* which come to bury their subject not to praise him. Its theme is how Thyrsis abandoned the ideal of the Scholar-Gipsy and so subjected himself to Time and Death, and how the poet, though visiting too rarely this country of the soul, revisits it now and rededicates himself to poetry. However, the poem does not end here, and, whatever may have been the motives, poetic or personal, for Arnold's adding the last three stanzas, these stanzas reinclude Thyrsis within the old ideal. We are now told that although he did go away and lived for a time with "men of care," yet essentially he never abandoned the vision of the Scholar-Gipsy and was a wanderer until he died. Indeed, at the very end of the poem it is his voice which is to come, " 'mid city-noise," and remind the poet, "Our tree yet crowns the hill, / Our Scholar travels yet the loved hill-side."

Poetically, it is awkward to have Thyrsis voice the very words which in the poem he could not hear, and one has the feeling that Arnold, in his desire, perhaps, to do right by his friend, was led to do wrong by his poem. Of course, one recognizes that the "boon southern country" to which Clough fled was not merely Italy but was also a version of that country "far to the south, beyond the blue," where Balder envisioned the rise of the second Asgard. There, wandering in the great Mother's train divine, Thyrsis could easily have achieved any kind of knowledge, and we should have to suppose that he learned about the tree through the "immortal chants of old," which we are told he could hear though he could not hear Arnold's. These chants are particularly the Lityerses songs sung by the Phrygian reapers in worship of the vegetation deity Daphnis. All over the ancient world, under the various names of Maneros songs in Egypt, Linus songs in Phoenicia, and Lityerses songs in Phrygia, these popular chants celebrated the death and rebirth of the harvest gods. More sophisticatedly, they survived in the Greek and Latin classical elegies, and Arnold's stanza alludes especially to the fifth and eighth of Virgil's *Eclogues*. From these *Eclogues* came most of the quotations, including lines alluding to Thyrsis and Daphnis, which form the epigraphs of Clough's "Long-Vacation Pastoral," *The Bothie of Tober-na-Vuolich*. Clough may be supposed, then, to have rejoined in death a better version of the world which he lived in in his life and to have gained an "easy access" to those values from which Arnold, alone in the Cumnor hills, was still debarred.

Such one may suppose to be Arnold's meaning. The only difficulty is that when one compares the "boon southern country" to which Clough has fled with the "upland dim" in which Arnold still wanders, one finds the latter more chaste and more convincing. There is something coarse and flamboyant about the "broad lucent Arno-vale" with its flowery oleanders, when set against the misty English upland with brambles and a "lone sky-pointing tree." The contrast is the same as that which Ruskin drew in *The Stones of Venice* between St. Mark's as a "long low pyramid of colored light," and the gaunt, aspiring height of an English cathedral, or that which Browning drew in *Home-Thoughts from Abroad* between the English buttercup and "this gaudy melon-flower," which symbolized the beauty of Italy. So Arnold is content to be " 'neath the mild canopy of English air" with his tree rather than to enjoy "all the marvel of the golden skies" with a translated Daphnis. And the reader too persists in admiring, more than the subject of the poem, the one who remained behind, faithful to the quiet, austere, and difficult ideal of the Scholar-Gipsy.

If we now pause and consider what we have learned about Arnold's elegies, the first thing we would have to say is that they are the poetic counterpart of his imaginative world. We have perhaps obscured this fact by saying that the elegy is divided into two parts by means of the elegiac reversal. So it is in its actual structure, but the complete world which the elegy presupposes is divided into three parts by means of two elegiac reversals. The first of these is simply the death of the subject, and therefore the first part of the world occurs before the poem opens. To use again the example of *Lycidas*, the first part consists of the happy days when

> we were nursed upon the self-same hill,
> Fed the same flock by fountain, shade, and rill.

This part is terminated by the first elegiac reversal, "But O the heavy change now thou art gone." The second part, then, consists of the body of lamentation and is terminated by the more usual reversal,

> Weep no more, woeful shepherds, weep no more,
> For Lycidas your sorrow is not dead.

The third part is the final phase of recovery and reconciliation. It is obvious that Arnold's poetic myth corresponds exactly with this structure: his forest glade is the happy times together, his burning plain the body of lamentation, and his wide-glimmering sea the period of reconciliation. Moreover, his image of the gorge or strait which connects one part of his world with another corresponds to the structural device of the elegiac reversal, and the River of Life corresponds to the current of thought or feeling which sweeps him through his song. This last device is of great value to Arnold, for it not only gives a strong compulsive movement to his thought, but it also enables him to attribute his views to some power larger than himself. Just as in his essays he will attribute to History or the Zeitgeist the unfavorable judgments which he passes upon his countrymen, so in the elegies he will attribute them to muses, breezes, or fate. In *A Summer Night* it is the midnight breeze which "checks his strain" and reminds him that no one is more worthy of a romantic resting-place than an English gentleman of noble feeling. In *Heine's Grave* it is the Bitter Spirits of Heine's own poetry which mock his efforts to claim the bard as his own and remind him that Heine wanted love and so also wanted charm. And in *Haworth Churchyard* it is again the Muse which interrupts him and angrily denies to the Brontës the reawakening which the poet had promised. In this way Arnold is able to give weight and objectivity to value judgments which are his own.

This correspondence of the elegy to the myth explains the different forms which the elegy takes in Arnold's work. If the subject is an inhabitant of the forest glade, as in the case of Wordsworth, then we get the first elegiac reversal but not the second, for in 1850 Arnold did not believe that the forest glade could ever be recreated again. But if the subject is an inhabitant of the burning plain, then we do not get a first reversal, since his death is not a "heavy change," and the second reversal is a reversal in reverse. This is the form of the elegies on Obermann, Charlotte Brontë, and Heine. Then, when Arnold is a little further along in his own myth, he discovers that persons whom he had thought to be on the burning plain actually were not, and this revisal of opinion constitutes a conventional elegiac reversal in which the subject dies in Arnold's estimation as one thing and is reborn as another. *Thyrsis* is an ambiguous example, *A Southern Night* a much clearer one. It is notable, however, that in the latter case Arnold required two poems in which to make the discovery. In *Stanzas from Carnac*, though he himself was placed by the wide-glimmering sea, he was under the impression that his brother was not. But in *A Southern Night* he found that he was wrong, and so the two poems together constitute a single elegiac form. The one is the "elegiac reversal" of the other. Finally, in the very late elegies, such as *Rugby Chapel*, the second Obermann poem, and *Westminster Abbey*, Arnold hardly bothers with either the forest glade or the burning plain but proceeds directly to the wide-glimmering sea. This means that there is no first elegiac reversal (except perhaps in *Westminster Abbey*) and that the second is a conventional one and comes very early in the poem. In the case of *Obermann Once More* it comes so early that one may consider that poem to be the second part of an elegy of which the *Stanzas in Memory of the Author of 'Obermann'* is the first part. The fact that Arnold wrote his elegies in fragments and that these fragments are distributed over his entire poetic career is simply an indication that he spiritually enacted his myth as he went along.

Indeed, taking this larger view of the elegies, we can now see that a great deal of Arnold's poetic production is elegiac in character. *Balder Dead*, as we have already indicated, is essentially an elegy drawn out, by the insertion of inert matter, into epic proportions. *Sohrab and Rustum*, initially entitled *The Death of Sohrab*, is an elegy for lost youth. *The Church of Brou* is an elegy for the Duke of Savoy in which the poet reproduces in words the elegy which the Duchess has carved in stone. The *Sick King in Bokhara* is a double elegy, both for the King, who becomes well, and for the Moollah, who is redeemed through punishment and understanding. *Tristram and Iseult* is another double elegy, Tristram dying as himself to be reborn in the form of his own children, Iseult dying as Ireland to be reborn as Brittany. All the love poems taken together constitute one large elegy in which woman dies as Marguerite and is reborn as Mrs. Arnold. Likewise, the poet dies as passionate lover and is reborn as son or brother. *Empedocles on Etna* is a truncated elegy in which Empedocles dies with only the promise of rebirth when he shall poise his life at last. But more largely, the drama *Empedocles on Etna* "dies" as morbid art through the "elegiac reversal" of the Preface of 1853 in order to be reborn as wholesome art in *Sohrab and Rustum*. Indeed, in this sense both of Arnold's first two volumes die in order to be reborn as their successor. Of *The Strayed Reveller, and Other Poems* Arnold wrote that he was impatient at having been "faussé" in it, and to Jane he said, "My last volume I have got absolutely to dislike." But *Empedocles on Etna* was no better. "I feel now," he wrote to Clough, "where my poems (this set) are all wrong," and so he withdrew them from circulation before fifty copies were sold.[17] Not until his third volume did Arnold produce a work which he did not immediately dislike on publication, and this attitude toward his poetry was but symptomatic of his attitude toward life in general. Speaking of Béranger, he wrote, "I am glad to be tired of an author: one link in the immense series of cognoscenda et indagenda despatched."[18] In this respect, he is strongly to be contrasted with Newman. Newman was a person who was deeply attached to his own past and who loved to feel it accumulating behind him. As a result, he kept every scrap of paper that ever passed through his hands, and writing his *Apologia* was not only an easy task but was also deeply moving and of great delight. Arnold, on the other hand, requested that no biography of him should ever be written, and he undoubtedly destroyed many of

17. *Letters to Clough*, pp. 109, 126; *Unpublished Letters*, p. 14; *Poetical Works*, p. 502. The letter in which Arnold criticizes his poems as "fragments" (*Unpublished Letters*, p. 18) should be dated 1849, not "1853?" as the reference to the French expedition against Rome makes clear. Thus the allusion is to *The Strayed Reveller, and Other Poems*.

18. *Letters to Clough*, p. 93.

the materials which would have made it possible. The ultimate reason for this difference is that Newman believed in "two and two only absolute and luminously self-evident beings, myself and my Creator," whereas Arnold believed in two and two only luminously self-evident beings, his Best Self and his Ordinary Self. Newman's task, then, was to strengthen the links between himself and his Creator, Arnold's to repudiate the Ordinary Self and strengthen the Best Self. Arnold agreed with Goethe, as paraphrased by Tennyson,

> I held it truth, with him who sings
> To one clear harp in divers tones,
> That men may rise on stepping-stones
> Of their dead selves to higher things.[19]

With Arnold the elegies were these stepping-stones.

The psychological basis, then, of the elegies, and so of Arnold's whole imaginative myth, is the doctrine of the Two Selves. Once again, of course, one has the problem of reconciling a dualistic terminology with a tripartite system, but the key to the reconciliation is the shift in language which Arnold made between his early and his later years. In later years, especially in the prose, Arnold speaks of the Best Self and the Ordinary Self, and these obviously correspond to the last two phases of his myth. By one's Ordinary Self he lives on the burning plain, by his Best Self on the wide-glimmering sea. But in the poetry he speaks of the True or Buried Self, and the opposite of this is not the Ordinary Self but the various masks and disguises which we wear in the world. The True Self dwells in the forest glade, and it becomes the Buried Self when, as a result of the traumatic experience of the gorge, it is forced underground in the burning plain. Later it will come to the surface again, but at this point it is called the Best Self rather than the True Self, and this shift in terminology reveals a shift in attitude. It indicates, in the first

19. *In Memoriam*, i.

place, that the conflict is now between the Good and the Bad rather than the False and the True and, in the second place, that the onus of evil is now on the self rather than the world. We have moved from a romantic conception of things, where reality lies deep within the center and the outside is false, to a more religious conception, where the good is placed on high and the lower parts of nature are bad. Of course, from the very first Arnold had been prepared for either alternative. We see this in *In Utrumque Paratus* and in the two poems of his thirteenth year. But generally speaking, in the early poetry the "real" is located in subterranean rivers, in coral islands underneath the sea, and in hidden volcanic fires, and it is only in the late 1850s and early 1860s that we exchange the real for the good, which begins to be placed on high. "Sink, O youth, in thy soul! . . . / Rally the good in the depths of thyself!" so says Arnold in the 1852 poem *The Youth of Man*. But in 1867 in *East London* the soul sets up "a mark of everlasting light, / Above the howling senses' ebb and flow," and in *Palladium* the soul is compared to an image of the god placed far above the city. The most striking example of this is the tree in *Thyrsis*.

For this reason it is important to realize that the tree does not appear in *The Scholar-Gipsy*. Many readers are vague on this point, and some even confuse the Fyfield elm in *The Scholar-Gipsy* with the signal-elm in *Thyrsis*, but of course they are not the same. True, we are told in *Thyrsis* that the tree formed a part of the original mythology which the two friends wove about the Scholar-Gipsy:

> while it stood, we said
> Our friend, the Gipsy-Scholar, was not dead;
> While the tree lived, he in these fields lived on—

but there is no trace of this idea in the earlier poem. Indeed, though the Scholar-Gipsy is once seen making for the Hinksey ridge, he is characteristically located in the valleys. He is associated with the river, not the tree, and this shift from the depths to the heights is one of the most significant changes which Arnold makes in his myth. It associates the Gipsy, not with the subterranean river of our Buried Life, but with the Palladium of our Best Self. Where in the former poem he passively "waits" for the "spark from heaven" to fall, in the latter he actively "seeks" a "fugitive and gracious light." The light in *Thyrsis* replaces the spark in *The Scholar-Gipsy*, and in the final stanzas it becomes associated with the tree. In this way the signal-elm becomes a kind of beacon set upon a hill and guiding the traveller through the dark. We have seen, of course, that the crisis of the poem came when this "Excelsior" ideal presented itself to the poet in its crudest and most moralistic form, and that the poem was successful because the poet rejected that and reverted to passivity again. But the lure has not altogether been resisted. To a certain extent the questers have been transformed from vagabond gipsies who idle about the valleys to Galahad types who "follow the gleam," upward and onward, "on, to the City of God."

Of course, Dr. Arnold would have approved this change, and there is some evidence that it is his tree. We know that he loved the Cumnor hills long before they were discovered by his son, and that he introduced them to Clough. Clough, going up to Oxford, had the poor judgment to write back to the Doctor that he did not admire the country around about Oxford so much as that around Rugby, and the Doctor, who regarded Warwickshire as a dull, barren plain, hastened to set him right. "I delight in your enjoyment of Oxford, and in what you say of the union amongst our Rugby men there. But I cannot think that you are yet thoroughly aquainted with the country about Oxford, as you prefer the Rugby fields to it. Not to mention Bagley Wood, do you know the little valleys that debouche on the Valley of the Thames behind the Hinkseys; do you know Horspath, nestling under Shotover; or Elsfield, on its green slope, or all the variety of Cumnor Hill, or the wider skirmishing ground by Beckley, Stanton St. John's, and Foresthill, which we used to expatiate over on whole holidays?" "I know these slopes," said Arnold, "who knows them if not I?" but his father had known them before. Indeed, his father had also known a tree. "I wonder," he wrote to George Cornish, just a year before his letter to Clough, "whether I could find your tree in Bagley Wood, on which you once sat exalted?"[20] Evidently, in Dr. Arnold's youth there were also trees which were the object of a walk and which it might be difficult to find again. Could it be that he had introduced the two young men to this form of questing and also taught them to attach a symbolic significance to it? We are told by the daughter of one of Matthew Arnold's closest friends, George G. Bradley, that the field in which the signal-elm was probably located was called by old Oxford men "Arnold's Field, because it had been a favorite haunt of Dr. Arnold's."[21]

It is not the historical connection, however, but the symbolic one that is important, and for this there is considerable evidence. In *Lines written on first leaving home for a public school* Arnold had associated his father with the idea of toiling up a hill toward some goal, and in *Stanzas from the Grande Chartreuse* his father was certainly among the "rigorous teachers" who "seized my youth, / . . . Show'd me the high, white star of Truth, / There bade me gaze, and there aspire." When his father died, Arnold told a friend that the first thing that struck him was that the family had lost the sole source of its information,[22] and in *Rugby Chapel* he expressed this thought under the image of a tree.

> We who till then in thy shade
> Rested as under the boughs
> Of a mighty oak, have endured
> Sunshine and rain as we might,
> Bare, unshaded, alone,
> Lacking the shelter of thee.

20. Stanley, *Life* (1845), 1, 241, 109, 76–77.
21. Margaret Woods, "Matthew Arnold," *Essays and Studies by Members of the English Association*, 15 (Oxford, 1929), 19.
22. R. E. Prothero, *The Life and Correspondence of Arthur Penrhyn Stanley* (London, 1893), 1, 74.

It is of no importance that the original of Arnold's tree actually was an oak,[23] for Arnold was not enough of a dendrologist even to make a fortunate error. But it is important that Arnold associated his father with objects of towering strength which were placed on high and were identified with Truth, for in *Thyrsis* it is this, as much as the Scholar-Gipsy, that the poet is seeking. Thus, one has the feeling that when, in the Easter of 1862, Arnold revisited the Cumnor hills to "think [Clough] over as I could wish," his mind went back beyond Clough to an earlier roamer of those fields and he not only confirmed his departure from Clough but also renewed his solidarity with his father. One would not call *Thyrsis* an act of sibling rivalry, but in it the brilliant pupil of his father is displaced, and Arnold, through the transformation of the imagery, finds his father once again.

This event is finally consummated in *Rugby Chapel*. Arnold's brother notes that in 1842, when their father died, Arnold "could not have written of his father's great qualities with the profound and yearning appreciation which is shown in 'Rugby Chapel,' composed fourteen years later."[24] Actually, though the poem is dated 1857, it was probably not completed much before its publication in 1867, so that in point of fact Arnold waited some fifteen to twenty-five years to compose it. By that time, far from feeling any imperfect sympathy with his father, he had developed a strong sense that in his school work and his religious and social essays he was continuing the work that his father had begun. The beginning of this appreciation may be seen in a letter which Arnold wrote to his mother in 1855. He is thanking her for sending him an early letter of his father's which she had just found, in which the Doctor was making plans for the education and welfare of his then eight-year-old son, and Arnold was touched

23. A. F. Pollard, "Matthew Arnold's Elm," *Times Literary Supplement*, 38 (March 25, 1939), 175, (April 15, 1939), pp. 217–18; E. B. Poulton, ibid. (April 22, 1939), pp. 233–34; E. A. Greening Lamborn, "Matthew Arnold's Tree," *N&Q*, 188 (1945), 71–74.

24. *Manchester Guardian* (May 18, 1888), p. 8.

by the thought of this silent parental love, exercising itself even when he was least aware. "This is just what makes him great," he declared, "that he was not only a good man saving his own soul by righteousness, but that he carried so many others with him in his hand, and saved them, if they would let him, along with himself." This idea—the central conception of the poem—was then reinforced two years later when he read Thomas Hughes' novel, *Tom Brown's School-Days* (1857). For the high point of this work comes on the last day of school when Tom, hitherto a careless fellow and not much an admirer of the Doctor, learns that the Doctor had arranged that he, East, and Arthur should be together in the same study so that Tom would have someone to concern himself about and get into less mischief. It came as a "new light" to Tom to find that, "besides teaching the sixth, and governing and guiding the whole School, editing classics, and writing histories, the great Head-master had found time in those busy years to watch over the career, even of him, Tom Brown. . . ." The novel ends, of course, with Tom on his knees in Rugby Chapel before the Doctor's tomb and being led by "hero-worship" of him to the possibility of the worship of One higher than him, "the King and Lord of heroes."[25]

It is at this point that Arnold's poem begins, and that is one reason why it was dated November 1857. It was dated from the time when Arnold's father, through the aid of this somewhat athletic but moving book, was reborn in the imagination of the son. As a result, the poem is concerned almost exclusively with the third phase of the myth. Admittedly, an elegy published twenty-five years after the event cannot very well say, "O the heavy change now thou art gone!" It can only say, "Lycidas your sorrow is not dead." Still, the poem makes this statement rather early (at line 15 of a 208-line poem), and the form of the statement is curious. It was determined by a review of *Tom Brown's School-Days* written by the positivist critic Fitzjames Stephen.

25. *Letters*, 1, 48; *Tom Brown's School-Days* (2d ed., London, 1857), pp. 407, 425.

"It was Fitzjames Stephen's thesis," wrote Arnold, "maintained in the Edinburgh Review, of Papa's being a narrow bustling fanatic, which moved me first to the poem." The function of the poem was to refute this thesis—"to fix," as Arnold said in strangely hagiographic language, "the true legend about Papa, as those who knew him best feel it ought to run."[26] As a result, the elegiac reversal took the form of rescuing the Doctor, not from death, but from misconception, and once again, this was done through the agency of the tomb. In most of the elegies the tomb is placed at the end of the poem as a symbol of what the subject was. Here it is placed at the beginning as a symbol of what he was not. "Gloom" is what characterizes the tomb and what was attributed to Dr. Arnold by Fitzjames Stephen. "But ah!" says the poet, "that word, *gloom*, to my mind / Brings thee back, in the light / of thy radiant vigour," and through this curious method —a kind of *lucus a non lucendo!*—the elegiac reversal is accomplished.

In the rest of the poem affirmation proceeds unchecked, and it involves a considerable revision of Arnold's previous poetic equipment. For though we are once again on the burning plain, it is now uncomfortably recognizable as the wilderness through which the children of Israel wandered. And the mountain is no longer Etna or an Alp but Mt. Horeb or Mt. Sinai. Moreover, the protagonists are not lonely figures brooding upon some mountain height but a band of pilgrims in the valley struggling to reach the mountain. And on top of the mountain is not a tree or a Palladium or a throne, but an inn, whose gaunt and taciturn host holds his lantern in our faces and asks such questions as we expect to be asked only at the gates of Heaven. "Whom in our party we bring? / Whom we have left in the snow?" And at this point the Romantic hero falls back abashed, and there steps forward a new hero, the Servant or Son of God, who "would not *alone* be saved" but saved others along with himself. It is predicted that under his guidance the company will proceed,

26. *Letters to Clough*, p. 164.

THE USE OF ELEGY

"On, to the bound of the waste, / On, to the City of God"—a place which has not hitherto been mentioned in Arnold's poetry, except as the second Asgard.

The last part of the poem may be best understood as a kind of palinode to *Resignation*, the one other poem associated with the death of Arnold's father. It will be recalled that the occasion of that poem was a walk which Arnold took with Jane, probably in 1843, just ten years after the children had taken the same walk on the Wythburn Fells with their father and Captain Hamilton. The difference now was that their father was dead and Jane had suffered a shattering blow in the breaking off of her engagement just three weeks before the wedding. Hence, the theme of resignation. The theme is developed by means of a contrast among three groups of figures representing three different ways of life: first, the daemonic questers who felt that salvation consisted in reaching some Mecca, some Jerusalem, some Rome—some City of God! But the poet sees that these are really thralls to their own passion and that reaching their goal will not really bring them repose. Secondly, there are the gipsies, who ramble aimlessly about the countryside with no idea of a fixed goal until at last death ends their lot. And finally, there is the poet, who sits quietly on the mountain-top and contemplates the whole of life but does not take part in it. He is not unsympathetic to the people —he does not say, "I am alone"—but he does not share their aspirations. And to Fausta's impatience that they are today retracing their steps instead of making furiously for some goal, the poet replies:

> Not milder is the general lot
> Because our spirits have forgot,
> In action's dizzying eddy whirl'd,
> The something that infects the world.

He has rejected Byronism and muddling through, but he does not seem aware that there is any other alternative.

Yet he had overlooked one character in his own poem, and

that was his father. In the earlier walk his father had served as leader.

> High on a bank our leader stands,
> Reviews and ranks his motley bands,
> Makes clear our goal to every eye—
> The valley's western boundary.

As they mount up,

> There climbing hangs, a far-seen sign,
> Our wavering, many-colour'd line;

until at last they reach the cool-shaded farms, the "noisy town" of Keswick, and ultimately the "wide-glimmering sea." This role of the Doctor had also been emphasized by Arthur Stanley in his pious *Life*, published in 1845. "Most of all, perhaps, was to be observed his delight in those long mountain walks, when they would start with their provisions for the day, himself the guide and life of the party, always on the look out how best to break the ascent by gentle stages, comforting the little ones in their falls, and helping forward those who were tired, himself always keeping with the laggers, that none might strain their strength by trying to be in front with him—and then, when his assistance was not wanted, the liveliest of all; his step so light, his eye so quick in finding flowers to take home to those who were not of the party."[27] Operating, perhaps, a little too much like Pippa in *Pippa Passes*, this is the same Doctor who reappears in *Rugby Chapel*, but now shepherding, not a band of little children, but the "host of mankind."

> See! in the rocks of the world
> Marches the host of mankind,
> A feeble, wavering line.
> Where are they tending?—A God
> Marshall'd them, gave them their goal.

27. Stanley, *Life* (1845), 1, 243.

Though the way is long and the marchers faint, the Servants or Sons of God give them courage.

> Langour is not in your heart,
> Weakness is not in your word,
> Weariness not on your brow. . . .
> Ye move through the ranks, recall
> The stragglers, refresh the outworn,
> Praise, re-inspire the brave!

So, strengthening the wavering line, they continue their march, "On, to the City of God," which replaces both the noisy town and the wide-glimmering sea of *Resignation*.

"I always think," Dr. Arnold used to say, "of that magnificent sentence of Bacon, 'In this world, God only and the angels may be spectators.' "[28] In *Resignation* Arnold was a spectator, but in *Rugby Chapel* he has adopted his father's and Lord Bacon's opinion. Once again he has distinguished among three ways of life: the majority of men, who "eddy about / Here and there" (like the gipsies); the few, who make for some clear-purposed goal (like the questers); and then, not the poet sitting removed from it all on the mountain-top, but the Servant or Son of God, who saves others along with himself.

The alternatives of the City of God and the sea as the final goal of Arnold's myth correspond to the alternatives of the Best and the Buried Self, and so to the two major characters in the last phase of the myth, the Servants or Sons of God and the Children of the Second Birth. The latter, as their name implies, are simply the Children of the Forest reborn after their experience on the burning plain. They have all the mildness, gentleness, and purity of the first group but without their innocence. Also, as they have been chastened and subdued by suffering, their Joy often approaches Calm. The ideal is first announced in *Stanzas in Memory of the Author of 'Obermann,'* where they make up a

---

28. Ibid., p. 195.

small, transfigured band who live in the world but are not of it. It is continued in the Marguerite poems, where the poet discovers that the true bent of both their natures is to be gentle, tranquil, true. It is more fully developed in Iseult of Brittany and the poet Balder, and is perhaps most dramatically recognized in the tribute to William Delafield Arnold and his wife Fanny. Finally, it is claimed for the poet himself in the poem on Heine: "May a life / Other and milder be mine!" In the prose it is exemplified in the phrase "sweetness and light" and in the mildness and sweet reasonableness of Arnold's conception of Jesus. In its mingling of Hellenism and the New Testament it is the very epitome of the Victorian ideal.

The Servants or Sons of God, on the other hand, are Old Testament figures and so are distinctly Hebraic. Unlike the Children, they are not simply themselves reborn but are related to something outside of themselves, namely, God. Arnold hesitates how to call them:

> Servants of God!—or sons
> Shall I not call you? because
> Not as servants ye knew
> Your Father's innermost mind . . .

The term Servants implies a relationship to the Slave, but with the suggestion that they differ from the Slave in that the work they do is God's work, not the world's, and that they do it willingly. So willingly, indeed, that they are more properly called Sons, and this term relates them again to the Children. Indeed, they could be considered simply the Children of the Second Birth at a slightly later stage of their development, when they have not merely emerged from repression but have actually strengthened the ego to the point where they are now willing to repress others. They now feel confident that their True Self is, objectively, the Best Self; for, as Servants who do their Father's will, their will is the will of God. The Hellenic Children have discovered what reason and the will of God are; now they, as the Hebraic Sons, will make these qualities prevail.

As a result, along with the emergence of this character in Arnold's poetry, there is a great increase in the imagery of warfare and contention. Examples are *The Last Word, The Lord's Messengers, Bacchanalia,* and *Palladium.* Where in Arnold's earlier poems the burning plain was a place where individuals wandered in their isolation, now it is a place where armies clash in combat. And they are not "ignorant armies," either, who are unsure which side they are on. The issues are perfectly clear, and the only question is whether one fights the good fight or not. The final stage is perhaps observable in *Culture and Anarchy,* where, asking how one should deal with rioting, Arnold quotes with approval his father's view. "As for rioting, the old Roman way of dealing with *that* is always the right one; flog the rank and file, and fling the ring-leaders from the Tarpeian Rock!"[29] Though Dr. Arnold often employed the former method at Rugby, the latter clearly represents a new use to which mountains may be put in Arnold. In the early volumes poets brooded upon mountains and occasionally threw themselves into volcanoes. Later, the Servants of God helped others up the mountains. Now they are throwing those down who did not behave. Fortunately, this was not Arnold's final view. The offending passage was removed from the second edition of *Culture and Anarchy,* and in Arnold's other works the Servant of God adopts the milder methods of the Children of the Second Birth.

One may see this in the last of Arnold's major elegies, *Obermann Once More.* We have called this poem the second half of an elegy of which *Stanzas in Memory of the Author of 'Obermann'* is the first half, and in respect to substance that is true. But in method the poem is a dream-vision and so is better associated with *The Scholar-Gipsy.* As in that work, the poet lies down in a high Alpine field, presumably with Obermann's book

29. *Culture and Anarchy,* ed. J. Dover Wilson (Cambridge, 1954), p. 203.

beside him, and there "muses" upon his author until, as night falls, the figure of Obermann suddenly stands before him on the grass. Recognizing his former follower, Obermann begins to speak, and his speech, which extends to 250 lines, occupies the same position in this poem as the discourse of Empedocles does in *Empedocles on Etna*. Indeed, had it been given on Etna, it would have provided hope for the dejected Pausanias without involving him in superstition, and it might have saved Empedocles himself where the myths of Callicles could not help. For what it offers is not a dry rationalism which denies what it cannot feel or a poetic fancy which asserts what it does not know, but a moving vision of human history over the past two thousand years. This vision, which Arnold will draw out more fully in *Literature and Dogma*, distinguishes four different historical epochs: the pagan world in the first century B.C., the new age of faith initiated by Christianity, the gradual withdrawal of faith during the modern period, and the new order that is now about to be. Obviously, this is the Goethean philosophy of history which postulates alternating epochs of skepticism and faith, and Arnold's point is to emphasize the parallel between the first age and the third and between the second and the fourth. For just as the emptiness of paganism could be followed by an age of faith, so the emptiness of our age can also be followed by faith, and this not because of any historical determinism but simply through the understanding afforded by human history. For in retelling the Christian story Arnold emphasizes the subjectivity of religious events. "He lived while we believed," and his death occurred, not on the cross but in the hearts of men. So, in the same manner that he first was born, he can be born again. He was first born when the brooding East so well "mused" upon her problems that "a morning broke / Across her spirit grey." In this poem Arnold too has so well "mused" that a morning breaks across his spirit grey. For him it is the Easter morn of Christ's rising from the dead. Not in the conventional sense, of course. Arnold has been too well schooled in the Higher Criticism for that. For him Jerusalem is merely a "lorn Syrian town" set amid "sun, and arid stone, / And crumbling wall, and sultry sand," and those who wait outside Christ's empty tomb await in vain. The only word that comes from that tomb is that man, "unduped of fancy," must henceforth resign his "all too human creeds, and scan / Simply the way divine." He must learn that the values of religion, which were hitherto thought to be objective and divine, are really subjective and human, and that only by recognizing this fact can we distinguish the essence of Christianity from the *Aberglaube*, or superfluous belief, with which it has been encrusted.

Thus, what started out as an elegy for the author of *Obermann* has become a vision of the risen Christ. Even the tomb, which is a central symbol in the poem, is not that by Lake Leman or the granite terraces of Paris, but is the tomb of Christ. And, though Christ is not risen in any literal sense, the Obermann who is risen bears so little resemblance to his predecessor in the other poem, is so mild and gentle, so deeply inward and spiritually serene, that he seems rather to embody Jesus than merely to announce him. The book which he carries in his breast is wisely not named. Presumably we are to take it as his own. But if we were to open it and read, it would surely sound like the New Testament or the *Imitatio Christi*. For the message of this poem is, Close thy *Obermann* and open thy *Imitatio Christi*.

With this vision Arnold recovers the Joy which he had lost when he left the forest glade and descended to the burning plain. But it is not precisely the same Joy. It is, in the first place, a "joy whose grounds are true" and, in the second, "joy that should all hearts employ." By these two conditions it transcends both the first phase of human existence and the second, and is a synthesis of the two. For on the burning plain, whatever kind of solution the Sage or Strayed Reveller might achieve—not of Joy but at least of Calm—it always involved some removal from his fellow men into an aristocratic seclusion. But Thomas Arnold "would not *alone* / Be saved," and Obermann asks, "Who can be *alone* elate, / While the world lies forlorn?" No, the new Joy must be "joy in widest commonalty spread"—it must be "*one common wave of thought and joy*," as it was in the first age. But then, it must also be true. The Joy of the Romantic poets, and of childhood, and of the childhood of the world had some element of illusion about it, of a divine illusion, which is unsatisfactory to modern man. "He fables, yet speaks truth," says Empedocles of the myth-making Callicles, and though Callicles had Joy and Empedocles had not, we now need a recovered Joy which will be acceptable to the adult as well as to the youth. The faculty through which we are to find this, according to Arnold, is the "imaginative reason."

We have already observed that imaginative reason is that synthesis of intellect and feeling which is characteristic of the modern spirit. It does not deny the evidence of the senses and understanding, but neither does it deny that of the heart and imagination. It is at once profoundly satisfying and profoundly true. As such, it combines the best elements of science and religion and yet transcends these by remaining poetry. In the late essays "Literature and Science" and "The Study of Poetry" Arnold explores the interrelationships of science, poetry, and religion in such a way as to make religion analogous to the forest glade, science to the burning plain, and poetry to the wide-glimmering sea. Science, for example, tells us things which are acceptable to the senses and understanding but not to the heart and imagination. It makes such statements as Mr. Darwin's that "our ancestor was a hairy quadruped furnished with a tail and pointed ears, probably arboreal in his habits."[30] Objectively, this may have been true, but subjectively it is not. It does not correspond to anything that we know about ourselves or to the powers by which we would build up our life. Religion, on the other hand, says that our ancestors were "two of far nobler shape erect and tall," and this does correspond to what we know about

---

30. "Literature and Science," *Discourses in America* (1896), p. 110.

ourselves and to the powers by which we would build up our life. The only trouble is that the statement of religion, which is a beautiful myth about the nature of man, has been taken to be a scientific truth about the origin of man. "Our religion has materialised itself in the fact, in the supposed fact; it has attached its emotion to the fact, and now the fact is failing it." Poetry does not make this mistake. Poetry makes the same statement as religion (the quotation is actually from *Paradise Lost*), but it does not assert that this statement is objectively true. "For poetry the idea is everything; the rest is a world of illusion, of divine illusion. Poetry attaches its emotion to the idea; the idea *is* the fact."[31]

Modern readers, interpreting this passage in terms of their own theories of poetry as an autonomous art, tend to overlook the fact that Arnold distinguishes between "the idea," which *is* the fact, and "the rest," which is a world of illusion. And they also overlook that Arnold is here speaking not of all poetry but only of that which is "worthy of its high destinies," the poetry of the imaginative reason. For some poetry does attach its emotion to the illusion, the divine illusion, and the illusion can fail it. In Arnold's view this is what had happened to the poetry of the English Romantic movement. It was too exclusively a product of the imagination. It was too personal and private, too transitory and unenduring. It "did not know enough" in the sense simply of knowing the great, substantial ideas which had operated in human history. It was very beautiful, but it was essentially a dream. Keats says of Adam that he awoke and found his dream was true, but the Romantic poets awoke and found their dreams were false. One after another they awoke upon the "cold hillside" of a purely phenomenal world. Arnold himself began life upon that cold hillside and was forced to write the greater part of his poetry from that situation. For a long time he wrote it in terms of the senses and understanding. But the late paganism of Epictetus

31. *Essays in Criticism: Second Series* (1900), pp. 1–2.

and Lucretius and even Marcus Aurelius was not enough. Religion was morality "touched with emotion," and poetry, if it was not pure imagination, was not pure reason either—it was the imaginative reason. And so, in *Obermann Once More*, Arnold dreamed a dream whose substance was neither the dry rationalism of Empedocles nor the sensuous myth of Callicles but was his own personal myth embodied in human history. And he awoke and found it true. The morning which broke in his dreams actually was breaking when he emerged from his dream. Whereas in *The Scholar-Gipsy* he awoke and found himself back in the phenomenal world, here he awoke and found himself forward in his dream. He had actually dreamed himself off the burning plain into the next phase of human history.

Arnold did this in the same way that Adam did it, by realizing his dream in himself. His elegies repudiate a lower nature and create a higher nature, and insofar as his whole poetry had an elegiac character, this was its larger function. It did not hang nostalgically over the past, lamenting a lost paradise, but tried with honesty and integrity to create a "paradise within thee, happier far." "It might have been thought," wrote Arnold's brother, "that this mood [of mild pessimism in *The Strayed Reveller*] would grow upon him . . . But there was nothing more remarkable in Matthew Arnold's unique personality than his power of recovery and self-correction. Several qualities contributed to this—first, the strength of his intellect . . . ; secondly, that cool, shrewd good sense which never deserted him; thirdly, the affectionateness and kindliness of his nature; . . . [and finally] a clear perception, which was perhaps hereditary, of the necessity and dignity of work."[32] Though in 1849 Arnold felt that he had never yet succeeded on any one great occasion in consciously mastering himself, yet he speaks of the necessity of continually making war on depression and low spirits, and he has the faith that "our spirits retain their conquests: that from the height they

32. *Manchester Guardian* (May 18, 1888), p. 8.

succeed in raising themselves to, they can never fall." About this he was not quite right. He did fall, and he had to raise himself again and again, but on each successive occasion the attempt was easier. Auden has said of Arnold that he "thrust his gift in prison till it died," but with this Arnold would not have agreed. It was not his gift that he thrust in prison; rather it was an element of darkness which long had troubled that gift. "No one," wrote Arnold in 1865, "has a stronger and more abiding sense than I have of the 'daemonic' element—as Goethe called it— which underlies and encompasses our life; but I think, as Goethe thought, that the right thing is, while conscious of this element, and of all that there is inexplicable round one, to keep pushing on one's posts into the darkness, and to establish no post that is not perfectly in light and firm."[33] In *Obermann Once More* he had reached the light. The dawn breaking over the Valais-depth was now his imaginative present. But having reached it, he must help others to reach it too, for the new Joy must be one that could "all hearts employ." Therefore, in the final moments of his vision he is adjured by Obermann—

> Though more than half thy years be past,
> And spent thy youthful prime—

to use the time and strength that are left him communicating this Joy to others. He has saved himself—now he must save others along with himself, and for this the instrument is prose. It has always been something of a problem why Arnold turned from poetry to prose, and the answer may be given in various ways. But one way of stating it is simply to say that the task of the poetry was done. It told the story of a river which descended from the hills, all but lost itself in the sands of the desert, and finally emptied into the sea. Once it reached the sea its story was done. Milton did not continue *Lycidas* after saying, "Tomorrow to fresh woods and pastures new," nor *Paradise Lost* after saying,

---

33. *Letters to Clough*, pp. 110, 93; *Letters*, 1, 289.

"The world was all before them where to choose." Newman did not continue the *Apologia* after he had come into the haven of the Catholic Church. Neither did Arnold continue writing poetry after he had reached the new dawn of *Obermann Once More*.

BIBLIOGRAPHY

I. ARNOLD'S WORKS AND LETTERS

Complete Prose Works, ed. R. H. Super, Ann Arbor, University of Michigan Press, 1961– .

Essays, Letters, and Reviews, ed. Fraser Neiman, Cambridge, Harvard University Press, 1960.

Letters to Arthur Hugh Clough, ed. H. F. Lowry, London and New York, Oxford University Press, 1932.

Letters, 1848–1888, ed. G. W. E. Russell, 2 vols. New York, 1895.

"Diaries, the Unpublished Items: A Transcription and Commentary," by William B. Guthrie, Ph.D. dissertation, University of Virginia, 1957, 4 vols. University Microfilms, Inc., Ann Arbor, Mich.

Note-books, ed. H. F. Lowry, K. Young, and W. H. Dunn, London and New York, Oxford University Press, 1952.

Poems, ed. Kenneth Allott, New York, Barnes and Noble, Inc., 1965.

Poetical Works, ed. C. B. Tinker and H. F. Lowry, London and New York, Oxford University Press, 1950.

Unpublished Letters, ed. Arnold Whitridge, New Haven, 1923.

Works, Edition de Luxe, 15 vols. London, 1903–04. Volume 15 contains the *Bibliography of Matthew Arnold* by T. B. Smart.

II. BOOKS

Allott, Kenneth, *Matthew Arnold*, Writers and their Work, 60, London, Longmans Green, [1955].

Arnold, Thomas, [Jr.], *Passages in a Wandering Life*, London, 1900.

Bamford, T. W., *Thomas Arnold*, London, The Cresset Press, 1960.

Baum, Paull F., *Ten Studies in the Poetry of Matthew Arnold*, Durham, Duke University Press, 1958.

Bonnerot, Louis, *Matthew Arnold, poète: Essai de biographie psychologique*, Paris, 1947.
——, ed. and trans., *Matthew Arnold: Empedocle sur l'Etna, étude critique et traduction*, Paris, [1947].
Buckler, William E., *Matthew Arnold's Books: Toward a Publishing Diary*, Geneva and Paris, Librairie E. Droz and Librairie Minard, 1958.
Butler, A. G., *The Three Friends: A Story of Rugby in the Forties*, London, 1900.
Chambers, E. K., *Matthew Arnold: A Study*, Oxford, 1947.
Chorley, Katherine, *Arthur Hugh Clough: The Uncommitted Mind*, Oxford, Clarendon Press, 1962.
Clough, A. H., *The Correspondence of Arthur Hugh Clough*, ed. F. L. Mulhauser, 2 vols. Oxford, Clarendon Press, 1957.
Dunn, Waldo H., *James Anthony Froude: A Biography*, 2 vols. Oxford, Clarendon Press, 1961–63.
Fletcher, Mrs. Eliza Dawson, *The Autobiography of Mrs. Fletcher, with Letters and Other Family Memorials*, [ed. Mary Richardson], privately printed, Carlisle, 1874.
Gottfried, Leon, *Matthew Arnold and the Romantics*, Lincoln, University of Nebraska Press, [1963].
Houghton, Ralph E. C., *The Influence of the Classics on the Poetry of Matthew Arnold*, Oxford, 1923.
Houghton, Walter E., *The Poetry of Clough: An Essay in Revaluation*, New Haven, Yale University Press, 1963.
——, *The Victorian Frame of Mind, 1830–1870*, New Haven, Yale University Press, 1957.
James, D. J., *Matthew Arnold and the Decline of English Romanticism*, Oxford, Clarendon Press, 1961.
Jamison, William A., *Arnold and the Romantics*, Copenhagen, Rosenkilde and Bagger, 1958.
Johnson, E. D. H., *The Alien Vision of Victorian Poetry*, Princeton, Princeton University Press, 1952.
Johnson, W. Stacy, *The Voices of Matthew Arnold*, New Haven, Yale University Press, 1961.
Jump, J. D., *Matthew Arnold*, London, Longmans Green, 1955.
Kermode, Frank, *Romantic Image*, London, Routledge and Kegan Paul, 1957.
Kingsmill, Hugh [pseud. of H. K. Lunn], *Matthew Arnold*, London, 1928.
Knight, William, *Principal Shairp and His Friends*, London, 1888.

MacDonald, Isobel, *The Buried Self: A Background to the Poems of Matthew Arnold, 1848–1851,* London, 1949.

Miller, J. Hillis, *The Disappearance of God: Five Nineteenth-Century Writers,* Cambridge, Harvard University Press, 1963.

Morley, F. V., *Dora Wordsworth: Her Book,* London, 1924.

Müller, F. Max, *Auld Lang Syne,* London, 1898.

Müller-Schwefe, Gerhard, *Das persönliche Menschenbild Matthew Arnolds in der dichterischen Gestaltung,* Tübingen, Max Niemeyer, 1955.

Parrish, Stephen Maxfield, ed., *A Concordance to the Poems of Matthew Arnold,* Ithaca, Cornell University Press, 1960.

Robbins, William, *The Ethical Idealism of Matthew Arnold,* Toronto, University of Toronto Press, 1959.

Sells, Iris Esther, *Matthew Arnold and France: The Poet,* Cambridge, 1935.

Stanley, Arthur P., *The Life and Correspondence of Thomas Arnold, D.D.,* 2 vols. London, 1845.

Tinker, C. B. and H. F. Lowry, *The Poetry of Matthew Arnold: A Commentary,* London and New York, Oxford University Press, 1950.

Trilling, Lionel, *Matthew Arnold,* New York, Columbia University Press, 1949.

Ward, Mrs. Humphry, *A Writer's Recollections,* London, 1918.

Warren, Alba H., Jr., *English Poetic Theory, 1825–1865,* Princeton, Princeton University Press, 1950.

Whitridge, Arnold, *Dr. Arnold of Rugby,* New York, 1928.

Wilkins, Charles T., "The English Reputation of Matthew Arnold, 1840–77," Ph.D. dissertation, University of Illinois, 1959, University Microfilms, Inc., Ann Arbor, Mich.

Woodward, Francis J., *The Doctor's Disciples: A Study of Four Pupils of Arnold of Rugby: Stanley, Gell, Clough, William Arnold,* Oxford, 1954.

Wymer, Norman, *Dr. Arnold of Rugby,* London, 1953.

III. ARTICLES

Allott, Kenneth, "A Birthday Exercise by Matthew Arnold," *N&Q,* 203 (1958), 225.

———, "An Arnold-Clough Letter: References to Carlyle and Tennyson," *N&Q,* 201 (1956), 267.

———, "Matthew Arnold's Original Version of 'The River'," *TLS*, 57 (1958), 172.

———, "Matthew Arnold's Reading-Lists in Three Early Diaries," *Victorian Studies*, 2 (1959), 254–66.

———, "Matthew Arnold's 'Stagirius' and Saint-Marc Girardin," *RES*, n.s. 9 (1958), 286–92.

———, "Thomas Arnold the Younger, New Zealand, and the 'Old Democratic Fervour'," *Landfall*, 15 (1961), 208–25.

Arnold, T[homas, Jr.], "Arthur Hugh Clough: a 'Sketch'," *The Nineteenth Century*, 43 (1898), 105–16.

———, "Matthew Arnold," *Manchester Guardian* (May 18, 1888), p. 8.

Arnold, W. T., "Thomas Arnold the Younger," *The Century Magazine*, 66 (1903), 115–28.

Bonnerot, Louis, "La jeunesse de Matthew Arnold," *Revue anglo-américaine*, 7 (1930), 520–37.

Brick, Allan, "Equilibrium in the Poetry of Matthew Arnold," *University of Toronto Quarterly*, 30 (1960), 45–56.

Broadbent, J. B., "Milton and Arnold," *Essays in Criticism*, 6 (1956), 404–17.

Brooks, Roger L., "The Genesis of Matthew Arnold's 'Thyrsis'," *RES*, n.s. 14 (1963), 172–74.

Brown, E. K., "The Scholar-Gipsy: An Interpretation," *Revue anglo-américaine*, 12 (1935), 219–25.

Buckler, William E., "An American Edition of Matthew Arnold's Poems," *PMLA*, 69 (1954), 678–80.

Butler, Elsie M., "Heine in England and Matthew Arnold," *German Life and Letters*, n.s. 9 (1956), 157–65.

C., T. C., "Matthew Arnold and Sophocles," *N&Q*, 174 (1938), 57–58.

Cairncross, Andrew S., "Arnold's 'Faded Leaves' and 'Switzerland'," *TLS*, 34 (1935), 210.

Cestre, Charles, " 'The Church of Brou' de Matthew Arnold," *Revue germanique*, 4 (1908), 527–38.

Curgenven, J. P., "Matthew Arnold in Two Scholarship Examinations," *RES*, 22 (1946), 54–56.

———, "The Scholar Gipsy: A Study of the Growth, Meaning, and Integration of a Poem," *Litera* (Istanbul), 2 (1955), 41–58; 3 (1956), 1–13.

———, "Theodore Walrond: Friend of Arnold and Clough," *Durham University Journal*, 44 (1952), 56–61.

——, " 'Thyrsis' IV. Models, Sources, Influences. The Landscape Hellenized," *Litera* (Istanbul), 4 (1957), 27–39; 5 (1958), 7–16; 6 (1959), 1–8.

Dahl, Curtis, "The Victorian Wasteland," *College English*, 16 (1955), 341–47.

Donovan, Robert A., "Philomela: A Major Theme in Arnold's Poetry," *Victorian Newsletter*, No. 12 (1957), 1–6.

Dyson, A. E., "The Last Enchantments," *RES*, n.s. 8 (1957), 257–65.

Elliot, G. R., "The Arnoldian Lyric Melancholy," *PMLA, 38* (1923), 929–32.

Fitzgerald, Penelope, "Matthew Arnold's Summer Holiday (Notes on the Origin of 'The Forsaken Merman')," *English*, 6 (1946), 77–81.

Garrod, H. W., "Matthew Arnold's 1853 Preface," *RES, 17* (1941), 310–21.

Gosse, Edmund, "Matthew Arnold and Swinburne," *TLS, 19* (1920), 517.

Gottfried, Leon A., "Matthew Arnold's 'The Strayed Reveller'," *RES*, n.s. 11 (1960), 403–09.

Halliday, E. M., "Shakespeare," *Explicator, 6* (1947), 4; see also 4 (1946), 57; 5 (1946), 24.

Harris, Alan, "Matthew Arnold, the 'Unknown Years'," *The Nineteenth Century, 113* (1933), 498–509.

Hicks, John, "The Stoicism of Matthew Arnold," in *Critical Studies in Arnold, Emerson, and Newman*, intro. Joseph E. Baker, University of Iowa Humanistic Studies, 6, No. 1, Iowa City, 1942.

Hornstein, Lilliam H., " 'Rugby Chapel' and Exodus," *MLR, 47* (1952), 208–09.

Houghton, R. E. C., "Letter of Matthew Arnold," *TLS, 31* (1932), 368.

Houghton, Walter E., "Arnold's 'Empedocles on Etna'," *Victorian Studies, 1* (1958), 311–36.

Hussey, R. et al., "Arnold on Shakespeare," *N&Q, 182* (January–June, 1942) 221, 276, 348; *183* (July–December, 1942), 52, 264.

Hutton, R. H., "Matthew Arnold," in *Essays on Some of the Modern Guides to English Thought in Matters of Faith*, London, 1900.

Hyder, Clyde K., "Arnold's 'The Scholar-Gipsy'," *Explicator, 9* (1950), 23; see also *8* (1949), 51.

Johnson, W. Stacy, "Arnold's 'In Utrumque Paratus'," *Explicator, 10* (1952), 46.

——, "Matthew Arnold's Sea of Life," *PQ, 31* (1952), 195–207.

——, "Parallel Imagery in Arnold-Clough," *English Studies* (Amsterdam), *37* (1956), 1–11.

Ker, W. P., "Matthew Arnold," in *The Art of Poetry*, Oxford, 1923.

Knickerbocker, William S., "Matthew Arnold at Oxford: The Natural History of a Father and Son," *Sewanee Review*, *35* (1927), 399–418.

——, "Semaphore: Arnold and Clough," *Sewanee Review*, 41 (1933), 152–74.

——, "Thunder in the Index," *Sewanee Review*, 47 (1939), 431–45.

Knight, G. Wilson, "*The Scholar Gipsy*: An Interpretation," *RES*, n.s. *6* (1955), 53–62.

Knoepflmacher, U. C., "Dover Revisited: The Wordsworthian Matrix in the Poetry of Matthew Arnold," *Victorian Poetry*, *1* (1963), 17–26.

Lake, W. C., "More Oxford Memories," *Good Words*, *36* (1895), 828–32.

——, "Rugby and Oxford: 1830–1850," *Good Words*, *36* (1895), 666–70.

Lamborn, E. A. Greening, "Matthew Arnold's Tree," *N&Q*, *188* (1945), 71–74.

Legard, A. G., "Matthew Arnold: The Man and His Work," *Cornhill Magazine*, *120* (1919), 252–61.

Leonard, Chilson H., "Two Notes on Arnold," *MLN*, *46* (1931), 119.

Nagarajan, S., "Arnold and the *Bhagavad Gita*: A Reinterpretation of *Empedocles on Etna*," *Comparative Literature*, *12* (1960), 335–47.

Neiman, Fraser, "Plotinus and Arnold's 'Quiet Work'," *MLN*, *65* (1950), 52–55.

Orrick, James Bentley, *Matthew Arnold and Goethe*, Publications of the English Goethe Society, n.s. 4, London, 1928.

Pollard, A. F., et al., "Matthew Arnold's Elm," *TLS*, *38* (1939), 163, 175, 189–90, 203, 217–18, 233–34.

Robertson, David Allan, Jr., " 'Dover Beach' and 'Say Not the Struggle Nought Availeth'," *PMLA*, *66* (1951), 919–26.

Romer, V. L., "Matthew Arnold and Some French Poets," *The Nineteenth Century*, *99* (1926), 869–80.

Roper, Alan H., "The Moral Landscape of Arnold's Poetry," *PMLA*, *77* (1962), 289–96.

Rudman, Harry W., "Clough: 'Say Not the Struggle'," *N&Q*, *198* (1953), 261.

Sells, Iris E., "Marguerite," *MLR*, *38* (1943), 289–97.

Shairp, J. C., "Balliol Scholars, 1840–43. A Remembrance," *Macmillan's Magazine*, *27* (1873), 376–82.

Sundell, M. G., "The Intellectual Background and Structure of Arnold's *Tristram and Iseult*," *Victorian Poetry, 1* (1963), 272–83.

Super, R. H., "Arnold's 'Tyrian Trader' in Thucydides," *N&Q, 201* (1956), 397.

——, "Emerson and Arnold's Poetry," *PQ, 33* (1954), 396–403.

——, "The First Publication of 'Thyrsis'," *N&Q, 206* (1961), 229.

——, "Matthew Arnold and Tennyson," *TLS, 59* (1960), 693.

Tillotson, Kathleen, "Arnold and Johnson," *RES*, n.s. *1* (1950), 145–47.

——, "Dr. Arnold's Death and a Broken Engagement," *N&Q, 197* (1952), 409–11; see also pp. 503–04.

——, "Matthew Arnold and Carlyle," *Proceedings of the British Academy, 42* (1956), 133–53.

——, "Rugby 1850: Arnold, Clough, Walrond, and *In Memoriam*," *RES*, n.s. *4* (1953), 122–40.

——," 'Yes: in the Sea of Life'," *RES*, n.s. *3* (1952), 346–64.

White, Helen C., "Matthew Arnold and Goethe," *PMLA, 36* (1921), 436–53.

Wickelgren, Florence R., "Matthew Arnold's Literary Relations with France," *MLR, 33* (1938), 200–14.

Woods, Margaret, "Matthew Arnold," in *Essays and Studies by Members of the English Association, 15*, Oxford, 1929.

INDEX